Praise for *Great Cloud of Witnesses*

"A quiet revolution is underway in Christian theology. East and West, Protestant and Catholic, theologians are working to renew Christianity by retrieving long-neglected beliefs and practices. In *Great Cloud of Witnesses*, Jackson Lashier adds his voice to the chorus by challenging Protestants in particular to recover the role of the saints in discipleship, formation, and biblical interpretation. This is a tall order—on par with recovering the practices of penance and demon exorcism. Lashier makes a case for the saints that is both convincing and inspiring."

—Jason E. Vickers, William J. Abraham Professor of
Theology and Wesleyan Studies, Baylor University

"Is there a biblical case for living out our Christian life in communion with the holy dead? The traditional Protestant answer is a resounding 'No.' Lashier helpfully shows us that this answer needs deeper reflection, and enlists a great cloud of witnesses to help us see why this is so. What emerges is a fecund vision of the church and her sacred book, and of the many companions who join us along our way to Christ, whether we realize it or not."

—Justus H. Hunter, associate professor of church
history, United Theological Seminary

"Protestants typically have an uneasy relationship with the tradition of the saints. As a result, we miss the many benefits—dare I say, blessings—that come from a deeper appreciation of the 'great cloud of witnesses' who have preceded us. In this wonderful book, Jackson Lashier addresses concerns that deter Protestants from revering the saints of old, challenges us to rethink our often-misinformed conceptions about them, and highlights lessons from their lives so that we too may run well the race marked out for us."

—Anthony Briggman, associate professor of Early Christianity,
Candler School of Theology, Emory University

Great Cloud of Witnesses

GREAT CLOUD OF
WITNESSES

HOW THE DEAD MAKE A LIVING CHURCH

JACKSON LASHIER

FORTRESS PRESS
MINNEAPOLIS

Library of Congress Control Number 2023007385 (print)

Cover design: John Lucas
Cover image: Predella of the San Domenico Altarpiece (detail), Fra Angelico, tempera
and gold on panel, between 1423 and 1424

Print ISBN: 978-1-5064-8965-0
eBook ISBN: 978-1-5064-8966-7

Contents

And so, with your people on earth and all the company of heaven
we praise your name and join their unending hymn:
Holy, holy, holy Lord, God of power and might,
heaven and earth are full of your glory. Hosanna in the highest.
Blessed is he who comes in the name of the Lord. Hosanna in the highest.

—"The Great Thanksgiving," United Methodist Book of Worship

Introduction

Protestants are often skeptical of the saints. Don't get me wrong: we desire holiness and are drawn to holy people as much as anyone, but the term *saint* strikes most Protestants as implausible and the spiritual practice of engaging the saints idolatrous. Anecdotal experiences of Catholic friends who pray to St. Anthony when they can't find their keys or who bury a statue of St. Joseph in their yard when they want to sell their houses don't help matters. While notoriously disagreeing about every possible belief or practice, Protestants of all different denominations, progressive and conservative, seem to unite around a rejection of the spiritual discipline of communing with and praying to dead Christians from past eras as commonly practiced by Catholic and Orthodox Christians. Consequently, a book about the saints and the spiritual discipline of communing with the saints addressed to Protestants risks falling on deaf ears, and prayers to St. Cornelius, the patron saint of ear problems, are not likely going to help.

The most common Protestant argument against the practice of communing with the saints is its lack of scriptural pedigree. The sixteenth-century Reformers, whose writings sparked the various Protestant denominations, believed that Scripture was the only divinely revealed authority and, therefore, the only source of all doctrine and practice. Devotion to the saints and their writings, by contrast, seems to be a development of Church tradition and thus to be rejected along with other so-called Catholic innovations, such as purgatory and papal infallibility, that have not found a home in Protestant spirituality. What is more, this lack of scriptural foundation explains for Protestants the perceived abuses involved with the practice of communing with the saints, notably the notion that they are mediators to Christ or even that they somehow play a role in our salvation.[1] One can hear in these arguments the Reformation *solas* (Faith alone! Christ alone! Scripture alone!) that remain very much a part of the Protestant DNA. As a lifelong Protestant, I appreciate this argument and agree that aspects of the spirituality that have developed around the saints in modern Catholicism are more attributable to medieval Christianity than to Scripture. Nevertheless, I would argue that if one goes beyond a facile search for proof texts to the logic and nature of the story of Scripture, communing with the saints emerges not only as a deeply scriptural practice but also as a grace given by God to strengthen our lives of discipleship.[2]

WHY THE SAINTS? A SCRIPTURAL ACCOUNT

One of the peculiar realities of the God revealed by Israel and Jesus, and testified to in the Old and New Testaments of Christian Scripture, is that this God involves human beings in his acts of salvation, or what are often called salvific acts. This is true not only in the required human response of faith but also in the proclamation of the acts themselves. "For, 'Everyone who calls on the name of the Lord shall be saved,'" wrote the apostle Paul. "But how are they to call on one in whom they have not believed? And how are they to believe in one of whom they have never heard? And how are they to hear without someone to proclaim him?" (Rom 10:13–14). This means the gospel necessarily includes the story of human activity as well.

---

1 The official confessions of the Reformation period regularly cite such abuses and counter with Scriptures such as 1 Timothy 2:5, "For there is one God; there is also one mediator between God and humankind, Christ Jesus, himself human" or 1 John 2:1, "But if anybody does sin, we have an advocate with the Father, Jesus Christ, the righteous."

2 I am by no means the first Protestant to consider the importance of the saints. In particular, I was influenced by the canonical theism movement in my own Methodist/ Wesleyan context, sparked by William J. Abraham's work *Canon and Criterion in Christian Theology: From the Fathers to Feminism* (Oxford: Oxford University Press, 1998). This movement argued for a recovery of all of the canonical resources gifted to the Church by the Spirit, the canon of saints among them, for growing in holiness. Most Protestants who write on the saints, however, continue to reject an adoption of the spiritual practice of communing with the saints and so consider them as historical figures to learn from but not living figures to engage in prayer and devotion. See, for example, Bryan M. Liftin, *Getting to Know the Church Fathers: An Evangelical Introduction* (Grand Rapids, MI: Baker Academic, 2016) and Karen Wright Marsh, *Vintage Saints and Sinners: 25 Christians Who Transformed My Faith* (Downers Grove, IL: InterVarsity Press, 2017).

The New Testament enshrines this somewhat shocking reality by following the four accounts of Jesus's life with the book of Acts, the story of the human proclamation of the gospel by the power of the Holy Spirit. Through the lives and witness of people like Peter and John, Stephen, Philip and Tabitha, Paul, Priscilla, and Aquila, we see the gospel traveling out from Jerusalem, into Judea and Samaria, and to the ends of the earth (see Acts 1:8). The narrative of Acts ends with Paul in Rome under house arrest, preaching the gospel to his captors as he awaits his trial.

The intriguing thing about Acts, though, is that it lacks a conclusion. We never read about Paul's trial. We never know if he converts his captors. We never know, at least from Acts, if he lives or dies. For the modern reader, this lack of an ending is quite unsatisfying. Likely for this reason, some scholars have suggested that Luke, the writer of both the third Gospel and Acts, intended to write another volume that would have included the account of Paul's trial and martyrdom and thus provided a more suitable ending to his whole story.

But perhaps Luke's open-ended narrative was intentional. Perhaps he was communicating the theological truth that the proclamation of God's salvific acts does not end with Paul but continues through witnesses unknown to Luke. The implication of this manner of reading Acts is that the lives and proclamation of those humans who carry on the message of God's salvific acts through history continue to be a living part of that very same gospel enshrined in the pages of the New Testament. This insight further suggests that the lives of those humans would be worthy of study for their potential both to deepen our understanding of the gospel they proclaimed and to strengthen our own lives of discipleship. Luke's unknown witnesses, in other words, should be known.

The traditional word for these unknown witnesses is *saints*. They are saints not because they are divine or because they are perfect (as anyone who has read the Gospel accounts of Jesus's disciples can attest). They are saints because they have devoted themselves so completely to following Christ, and the result is lives that embody the gospel. They are those who have been crucified with Christ, to paraphrase Paul, and it is no longer they who live but Christ who lives in them (Gal 2:20). Their stories are readily available if we would just, to borrow a famous phrase from Church history, "take up and read."

Of course, the life of any historical figure can be an example for lives lived in the present. Nevertheless, with the Church's saints, a deeper and more mysterious reality is at play, one rooted in the central Christian hope of resurrection, namely, the Christian belief that these past saints are not dead but alive. "But if we died with Christ," Paul writes, "we believe that we will also live with him" (Rom 6:8). Though they, too, are waiting for final resurrection, the saints are living with Christ now. According to the New Testament, in this triumphant state, they offer continual praises to God *and* watch over us, cheer us on, and intercede for us.[3] The writer of Hebrews, for example, speaks of them as a great "cloud of witnesses" who are watching those of us still on earth as we "run with perseverance the race that is set before us" (Heb 12:1). Likewise, Jesus talked about the rejoicing that occurs in heaven over a repentant sinner (Luke 15:7). And John of Patmos describes a vision of heaven in which the prayers of the saints are being offered by an angel to God (Rev 8:3–4). As such, the dead in Christ are part of our communities. To again use more traditional language, God's Church includes both the Church militant and the Church triumphant, both living saints and dead ones.[4] To commune with the saints, then, is to embody the Christian hope in resurrection.

While *sola scriptura* (Scripture alone) may be in the Protestant DNA, so, too, is a bent toward practicality. So if I have gained the ears of my Scripture-loving Protestant brothers and sisters thus far, let me offer some practical ways that communing with the saints helps us to become more faithful disciples. Though the reader may encounter numerous reasons in the course of this book, I will list three primary reasons here. First, the saints help us to interpret and rightly understand Scripture, often in creative ways that make it speak anew in our time. Second, the saints help us to understand the scriptural rootedness of our Christian beliefs, practices, and polity. Third, the saints demonstrate what lives conformed to Christ look like and inspire us to follow that same way.

---

3 The question of prayers to the saints and the prayers of the saints, a hard one for Protestants, will be addressed in chapter 1.

4 Catholics have a third dimension of the Church called the Church suffering, which refers to those who have died and gone to purgatory, a holding place of sorts where the dead are further refined for heaven. Protestants rejected the belief in purgatory in the sixteenth century, the reasons for which I will address in chapter 9. Belief in purgatory is by no means necessary to a recovery of the spiritual practice of communing with the saints.

THE SAINTS AS INTERPRETERS OF SCRIPTURE

In the book of Acts, an early Christian by the name of Philip is led by the Spirit to encounter an Ethiopian eunuch who is reading in the prophet Isaiah about the suffering servant, which early Christians took as a prophecy of Jesus. As the eunuch is reading, Philip asks him, "Do you understand what you are reading?" The eunuch humbly replies, "How can I, unless someone guides me?" (Acts 8:30–31).

Anyone who has read Scripture has probably felt like the eunuch in this moment of honesty; the words of Scripture are not as clear as they are often assumed to be.[5] This should not surprise us. The Bible, after all, is an ancient document, written in contexts completely different from ours by a number of different authors in three different languages. We would expect any document with this description to be difficult to read. No one thinks, in other words, that the words of Homer, Plato, or Aristotle will be fully grasped by a casual reading over coffee. The only reason we assume the Bible should be more understandable than any of these texts is because of our theological belief that it is inspired and that through these words, God is speaking not just to the ancient audiences but to us. True though these convictions may be, the inspired nature of Scripture does not negate all the realities of its human composition. Therefore, despite its inspired content, Scripture is difficult to read and understand, as attested to by all of the varying versions that exist today. Like the Ethiopian eunuch, therefore, we need a guide.

Thankfully, the Church has a wealth of such guides, namely, the great cloud of witnesses who have traveled before us. As such, they are not only our audience as we run the race set before us, but more importantly, they are the ones who make clearer the path on which we run. Like early explorers in a new land, they marked the path for us better to follow. They cut away the brush and removed the fallen logs that once hindered the path. They set up roadblocks along the way to side trails that lead to potential danger. They did these things not by inventing a new faith or system of belief but by interpreting the revelation entrusted to them, as Philip did by pointing out to the eunuch the connection between Isaiah's suffering servant and Jesus Christ. They did these things, in other words, through their interpretations of Scripture.

---

5 Scripture was never assumed to be clear or easy to read until the Protestant Reformation, a topic I will again address further in chapter 9.

When we open the Bible, therefore, we never read in isolation. We read in a community of living and dead, and we benefit from the wisdom of the living and the dead. This community is a gift of the Spirit; Paul writes, "The gifts he gave were that some would be apostles, some prophets, some evangelists, some pastors and teachers, to equip the saints for the work of ministry, for building up the body of Christ, until all of us come to the unity of the faith and of the knowledge of the Son of God, to maturity, to the measure of the full stature of Christ" (Eph 4:11–13). Through their interpretations of Scripture, the saints in the cloud of witnesses teach us how to rightly read and apply Scripture in our own time so that we may be unified in the faith and develop into mature Christians.

Protestants may initially balk at such a suggestion. We have this idea, more modern than Christian, that we can understand the Bible with only the help of the Spirit. If I have direct access to the Spirit, as the Scriptures tell me I do, then I must have direct access to the right interpretation. Put differently, we not only believe that our authority is Scripture alone; we think we should read and interpret Scripture *alone*. And so many a Protestant Bible study ends with contradictory interpretations lingering in the air because "what it means to me" is equivalent to "what it means." Likewise, many a Protestant church has split not because one side is following the Bible and the other is not but rather because both sides are following their own interpretations of the Bible. Nevertheless, our practices suggest that we implicitly know we need this guidance. Our small group Bible studies, for example, rarely consist of simply studying the Bible but more often include a guidebook with text and questions that help us understand. Our Study Bibles come with copious footnotes for nearly every verse, and we rarely read the biblical text without reference to them. My claim is not that these are bad ways of reading Scripture; in fact, I would argue they are deeply Christian ways of reading Scripture. We just have to get, as it were, the *right* set of footnotes.

The interpretations of the saints should be those footnotes, the running commentary that we consult while reading Scripture to help us better grasp its meaning. Importantly, because the saints exist in a community, we are not relying on one person's opinion or one person's idiosyncratic interpretation. Rather, we are guided by the readings of Christians from vastly different times and far-away cultures; readings from women and men; readings from clergy, lay, and monastic figures; readings from missionaries and masons; readings from Catholic, Orthodox, and Protestant communities. This diversity of cultures and times in which the Church exists is precisely what makes the Church catholic.[6] And the different experiences of these saints through time and space result in a treasure trove of scriptural interpretations that are embraced as one and goes by the name *tradition*.[7]

This does not mean, however, that the interpretations of the saints are simply repetitions of one another, all toeing the party line. Indeed, on many Scriptures, the saints do not agree but exhibit a diversity of interpretations that when taken together produce a pleasing harmony of the multiple senses of Scripture. Contrary to common claims, therefore, the meaning of Scripture is not suppressed by the saints, nor is the creativity of the modern interpreter who considers them. Rather, the saints themselves show us that Scripture can mean different things based on different reading contexts. Moreover, the saints are far more creative in their readings than modern Christians. For example, the saints frequently read the Scriptures allegorically, a practice modern Christians have long since forgotten or consciously suppressed.[8] And because the saints believed the Bible was one document ultimately written by one author (God), they had the freedom to read all the works as different parts of one story and therefore to pair verses from different books together to unlock new meanings. Paradoxically, then, the more we read the saints' interpretations, the more creative we will become as interpreters because we will be formed to read as they did.

Nevertheless, in certain interpretations, the saints of diverse times and places speak with one resounding voice. For example, the saints' interpretations of Scripture in reference to the triune nature of God, the divinity and humanity of Christ, the centrality and reality of the resurrection, and other beliefs that the Church has formed into creeds diverge little. Indeed, the Church has recognized such interpretations as foundational beliefs precisely because there is such widespread agreement among Christians through the ages. In these areas, my reading in communion with the saints helps me to

---

6 The Latin word *catholic* as originally applied to the Church meant "universal" in the sense noted above. Although it comes to refer to the specific Roman Catholic Church to distinguish it from Protestant denominations, *catholic* is still an appropriate descriptor of the nature of God's Church all over the world and through time.

7 All Christians recognize the authoritative role that tradition plays in helping us understand and interpret Scripture. However, the question of what equates to authoritative tradition stands at the heart of many doctrinal differences among Catholic, Orthodox, and Protestant Christians. After the various divisions, which I will discuss in the course of this book, each form of Christianity developed distinct traditions, though they hold as a core a common tradition expressed, most succinctly, in the creeds.

8 Allegorical interpretation will be one of the topics covered in chapter 4.

stay on the path, to not wander from consensus and thus find myself on the outside of the Church.

I suppose at this point one could counter with the objection that a twenty-first-century Christian's interpretation should have just as much authority and validity as those of Christians from earlier centuries and that widespread agreement does not necessarily ensure accuracy. These objections may be valid in the logic of the world. But the Church has always operated according to a different logic, one that is neither recognized by nor consonant with the logic of the world. As Paul wrote, "For the message about the cross is foolishness to those who are perishing, but to those who are being saved it is the power of God . . . it is not a wisdom of this age or of the rulers of this age, who are doomed to perish. But we speak God's wisdom, secret and hidden, which God decreed before the ages for our glory. None of the rulers of this age understood this; for if they had, they would not have crucified the Lord of glory" (1 Cor 1:18, 2:6–8). The Church does not value above all human ingenuity but looks to the Holy Spirit as the guide, the Holy Spirit who has lived in the hearts of all Christians through the years. Therefore, widespread agreement over the ages and spaces, what is called in some theological traditions the *sensus fidelium,* or the sense of the faithful, is precisely the indicator of accuracy. As the saints in Jerusalem who sought the Spirit's guidance on the question of the full inclusion of non-Jewish people, called Gentiles, put it so long ago, "It has seemed good to the Holy Spirit and to us" (Acts 15:28). Given this logic, therefore, an interpretation that is at odds with the great tradition ought to be rejected as false. We cannot know, however, whether our interpretations are in line with the voice of the cloud of witnesses unless we are reading in communion with them.

THE SAINTS AS BEARERS OF HISTORY

Some time ago, I attended a church whose motto for every question, whether it was a question of belief, practice, or polity, was "Where stands it written?" The conviction implied in this motto is that everything we believe and do should be supported in Scripture. This is an admirable and, more importantly, thoroughly Christian way of approaching organized life in the Church, one that reaches back to the very roots of Christianity as it developed from Judaism. Nevertheless, it was my experience that many of the people in this particular church were not always clear on *how* their beliefs, practices, and polity were rooted in what was written, primarily when there was not a direct verse to support them. This lack of clarity led to some interesting debates, which I witnessed firsthand. Some of these were funny; I saw, for example, a somewhat tense discussion between two Christians of different generations where the younger one actually said, in what may have been a brilliant piece of rhetoric, "Where stands it written that we should not worship in a gym with guitars and drums?" Some of these, however, were more concerning. I heard of a Sunday school teacher who, when pressed, was unable to express any biblical support for the doctrine of the Trinity and an elder who was puzzled at how to answer a parishioner who questioned why we continued to place such an emphasis on the practice of communion, traditionally called the Eucharist. The parishioner did not say it, but she could have: "Where stands it written that we should celebrate the Eucharist so often?"

The example of this little church, likely not dissimilar from countless churches in communities all over this country, demonstrates a big problem facing *sola scriptura* Christians with little to no knowledge of the writings of the saints in the cloud of witnesses. Namely, the twenty-first-century Church has inherited beliefs, practices, and polity that are not always clearly prescribed or reflected in Scripture. Why do we baptize infants? Why do we sing worship songs? Why do we meet in small groups? Why are we Trinitarian? Why do we read the Bible regularly? Why do we require our pastors to be ordained? (The converse to each of these questions could be articulated, and the underlying point would remain.) We who hold to such deeply ingrained Christian beliefs and practices say we follow Scripture, but most of us have little idea how the things we believe and practice developed from Scripture. We are, in other words, missing an important bridge from the content of Scripture to the shape of the Church in the twenty-first century.

Thankfully, we are not without resources in this area. The cloud of witnesses is precisely the bridge we need to understand better the lineage of the beliefs, practices, and polity we hold so dear. Indeed, the reason we believe and practice these things is because we have inherited not only the Scriptures but the Scriptures *as interpreted by the saints*. Their writings, therefore, reveal, often in a scrupulous manner, the scriptural rootedness of the beliefs, practices, and polity they have passed on to us.

But if these things are rooted in Scripture, one might respond, why can't we just go the Scriptures and find them there? The answer to this logical question comes in the previous section: Scripture is difficult to read. It is neither a list of doctrines nor a manual of Christian practice. It is a story about God and his people and the work of redemption brought through Christ. The beliefs, practices, and polity that we embrace as Christians, therefore, largely come from the centuries of reflection made by faithful men and women in working out what it means to embrace this redemptive story as true. What should we believe about the God who is revealed in this story? How should we live in light of this story? How should we organize ourselves as the community that is formed by this story? The answers to these questions give us our beliefs, practices, and polity.

These answers, moreover, were worked out by the saints in the course of rejecting bad interpretations of Scripture. Precisely because Scripture is so difficult to read, there has been no shortage of misguided interpretations in the course of Christian history. The Church has come to label such readings and the beliefs that result from them as *heresy*. The problem is, however, that the Church cannot recognize heresy until it is articulated. As theologian Roger Olson has aptly put it, "Heresy is the mother of orthodoxy." He means not that wrong belief is older than right belief but rather that, historically, the Church typically does not define a doctrine, and its scriptural pedigree, until someone articulates what is implicitly recognized as a wrong belief.

The logic of this development can be discerned within the pages of the New Testament itself. Some Christians in Corinth in the mid-first century, for example, believed and taught that the promise of resurrection at the end of the age for those who follow Christ was metaphoric, that is, resurrection simply meant the new life that comes with becoming a Christian. While certainly the reality of new life is an immediate experience for Christians, and many places in the New Testament affirm this truth, the reduction of resurrection to a metaphor was problematic for salvation, for it necessarily called into question the reality of Christ's *real* resurrection. The apostle Paul discerned this unintended implication of the Corinthian teaching and, as a result, penned the most robust defense of the physical resurrection of Christ, and that of his followers by consequence, in the whole of the New Testament: "Now if Christ is proclaimed as raised from the dead, how can some of you say there is no resurrection of the dead? If there is no resurrection of the dead, then Christ has not been raised; and if Christ has not been raised, then our proclamation has been in vain and your faith has been in vain" (1 Cor 15:12–14). Apart from this defense, which Paul would not have written without a faction of the Corinthians expressing belief in something different, the New Testament's teaching on resurrection may have been unclear. But the existence of the false belief forced Paul to be absolutely clear on his belief in the physical resurrection of Christ and the future resurrection of believers.

This same pattern holds for numerous other beliefs and practices whose clear defense was not yet articulated in the New Testament, though necessitated in the following centuries. When we are questioned why we worship and pray to three divine persons with different names but still insist that we believe in only one God (the doctrine of the Trinity), we can go to saints like Athanasius, Gregory of Nyssa, or Augustine, who all clearly articulated the reasons for this manner of understanding Scripture. When we wonder what the purpose of prayer is if we cannot see immediate results, we can read Teresa of Ávila or Teresa of Calcutta to grasp the manner in which it forms us. When we wonder why we meet together in small groups, we can read the sermons of John Wesley to understand the indispensable nature of this practice for our discipleship. And the remarkable truth of the writings of the saints is that they turn us not away from Scripture but always lead us back to Scripture, where all of the answers to these questions and dilemmas are located.

THE SAINTS AS MANIFESTATIONS OF CHRIST

While Christians rightly emphasize the cross and resurrection as central to our salvation, we often forget, or perhaps underemphasize, the importance of Jesus's *life* to our salvation. For if the tragic result of human sin is to separate us from the God who created us for fellowship with him, then the incarnation (God becoming human in Jesus Christ) has already healed this division. "And the Word became flesh and lived among us," John testifies, "and we have seen his glory, the glory as of a father's only son, full of grace and truth . . . No one has ever seen God. It is God the only Son, who is close to the Father's heart, who has made him known" (John 1:14, 18). Moreover, Jesus's life is central to our salvation not just in this theoretical sense but on a much more practical level. If Jesus reveals the full character of God, then the very form of his life demonstrates God's desire for each one of us. His teachings reveal God's will; his actions reveal God's heart. "When you have lifted up the Son of Man," Jesus told the Pharisees, "then you will realize that I am he, and that I do nothing on my own, but I speak these things as the Father instructed me. And the one who sent me is with me; he has not left me alone, for I always do what is pleasing to him" (John 8:28–29). This means, then, that conforming our lives to Jesus's life is the goal of discipleship. In this way, the life of Jesus does for Christians what the Law did for Israel—it shows us how to live a life that is glorifying to God; it shows us how to "be perfect, as [our] heavenly Father is perfect" (Matt 5:48).

The difficulty that confronts twenty-first-century Christians, and really every Christian since Pentecost, is that Jesus, the one in whom we see God and the one whose life shows us how God wants us to live, is no longer seen. Jesus's presence on earth, as recorded in the Gospel of Luke, ends with his ascension to the place of the Father and results in his apparent invisibility, just as the Father has been invisible since the beginning. Of course, the Trinitarian mystery convinces us that Christ remains in some way present through the Spirit, who dwells in our hearts (by which we should understand passages such as Matthew 18:20 and 28:20). But however we conceive of the Son's Trinitarian presence in the Spirit, it remains an invisible presence as we empirically know, and as Acts's account of the ascension emphasizes, "When he had said this, as they were watching, he was lifted up, and *a cloud took him out of their sight*" (Acts 1:9, italics added). Thus, regardless of Trinitarian affirmations of Christ's presence, the question remains: If we understand the form of our discipleship through observing the life of Jesus, what are we to do now that he is not visibly present?

Here again, Protestants have resources that we have been reluctant to engage, namely, the cloud of witnesses. The Christians who have gone before us, and particularly those whom the Church has officially designated "saints,"[9] have so conformed their lives to Christ that when we look at them and read their stories, we see not them but Christ who lives in them and shines from them. Just as their writings serve as a bridge between Scripture and our beliefs, so their lives serve as a bridge between Christ and us. In other words, the holy lives of the saints encourage us not simply because of their own holiness but because through their conformity to Christ, they manifest Christ anew in every age.

This truth is nowhere better demonstrated than in a little-known account of a group of Gallican martyrs from the late second century. Among the martyrs mentioned by an eyewitness account of the event is a young woman named Blandina. Not much is known of this woman except that she had a frail body and that she was regarded by the Roman soldiers who tortured her as "worthless, ugly, and contemptible," which made their inability to either

---

9 I will address the process of how the Church officially recognizes saints in chapter 4.

extract a denial of Christ from her or kill her by their constant tortures all the more infuriating.[10] In the course of events described, the Christians, Blandina among them, were led to the amphitheater and attacked by wild animals, but the soldiers, perhaps feeling humiliated, hung the young Blandina on a pole so as to make her easy prey. The eyewitness describes the unintended effect: "The sight of Blandina hanging there in the posture of a crucified person, and the intense way she was praying, caused utmost devotion to well up in the other martyrs suffering the ordeal. Gazing at Blandina in the midst of their own agony, their outward eyes saw, through their sister, the one who was crucified for them." Blandina, a woman of whom the world took no account, likely because she was a woman, was so conformed to Christ in her life and her death that when other Christians looked at her, they saw not her but Christ in her. As a result, they were encouraged in their struggles and fulfilled the high calling of martyrdom in their own lives.

Protestants, once again, are likely to be skeptical of such claims, perhaps worried that this emphasis on the lives of saints diminishes the life of Christ as the supreme model for discipleship. But here again, a reading of the lives and writings of the saints easily dispels this worry. For the whole point of lifting up the saints in this manner is not to praise and honor their lives but rather through their lives to be pointed back to Christ. His life becomes clearer, not more opaque, in the lives of the saints. Like John the Baptist, the saints are constantly saying, "He must increase, but I must decrease" (John 3:30). Moreover, the Scriptures themselves point to this function of the saints. The occasion of the writer of Hebrews coining the phrase "cloud of witnesses" was a chapter-long discussion of the lives of faithful Old Testament figures used to encourage Christians in their struggles. Paul, after urging the Philippians to have the same mind that was in Christ Jesus (Phil 2:5), lifts himself up as another example to follow: "Keep on doing the things that you have learned and received and heard and seen in me" (Phil 4:9). Similarly, to the Corinthian Church, he writes, "Be imitators of me, as I am of Christ" (1 Cor 11:1). Finally, John, the same figure who wrote in the Gospel that the Son reveals the God

---

10 The eyewitness account, written as a letter, is preserved by the fourth-century Christian historian and bishop of Caesarea, Eusebius. *Church History*, trans. Paul L. Maier, *Eusebius: The Church History* (Grand Rapids, MI: Kregel Publications, 1999), 5.1.3–63. As the first church historian, and a preserver of ancient writings that have otherwise been lost, Eusebius provides a wealth of information on these early centuries, and we will return to him often in the first few chapters.

that no one has ever seen, says the following in his first letter: "No one has ever seen God; if we love one another, God lives in us, and his love is perfected in us" (1 John 4:12). After Christ's ascension, God is now seen in the body of Christ, his Church on earth. Therefore, we can look to the saints and imitate them because they have imitated Christ, and Christ shines through them.

Ultimately, then, communing with these saints helps us to be better disciples. By helping us to be better readers of Scripture, giving us the biblical foundation of our beliefs and practices, and showing us lives that are attuned to the life of Christ, the saints can form us into disciples better prepared to tread the sacrificial path forged by Christ, the path on which they have walked before us. Put differently, the dead help us find our life in Christ.[11]

THE STORIES

What follows are biographical accounts of twelve extraordinary saints who represent the incredible richness and demographic diversity of the kingdom of God. Six are men, and six are women. Six come from Western countries, three from Eastern and Far Eastern countries, and three from Africa, variously representing Roman Catholicism, Eastern Orthodoxy, and different denominations within Protestantism. Roughly speaking, five come from the ancient period, three from the medieval period, and four from the modern period. Some are bishops and pastors, others are monastics, and still others are laypersons. Each chapter will include an account of the saint's life in historical context and will focus on one of the three functions outlined above, though there will be some overlap. Irenaeus, Origen, and Julian, for example, will form us in ways of reading Scripture, whereas John, Martin,

---

11 This third area is the place where most other Protestant books on the saints focus. This makes sense as there is nothing particularly objectionable (or mystical or theological) about looking to another as an example of faithfulness. Nevertheless, what I will argue in the course of this book is not simply that the saints are examples of faith but that their faithfulness can act as a means of grace in our own lives, mysteriously mediating their faithfulness to us through our prayers. As such, this function of the saints corresponds to the Eucharist, the other means of grace where Christ's presence is manifested after his ascension. Here again, I am in line with the canonical theism project. See, in particular, Horace Six-Means, "Saints and Teachers: Canons of Persons," in *Canonical Theism: A Proposal for Theology and the Church*, ed. William J. Abraham, Jason E. Vickers, and Natalie E. Van Kirk (Grand Rapids, MI: Eerdmans, 2008), 97–118.

and Phoebe will show us the scriptural origins of certain Christian practices and beliefs. From the remaining six, we will find lives conformed to Jesus, but the different contexts and different challenges faced in this process will be most instructive. The chapters are ordered chronologically to give the reader a sense of the developing historical context in which these saints lived. Although this approach disperses the three organizing themes somewhat haphazardly among the twelve chapters, it turns out to be an effective way of narrating Church history. This should not really surprise us; the Church has always been the gathered people.

The result, I am hopeful, will be a compelling portrait of the great cloud of witnesses that will find a connection, through at least one of the stories, to every reader. These twelve saints are by no means the only saints, or even the best-known saints, in Christian history, and I could have easily written numerous other chapters with completely different selections. But I hope that through this short introduction, my readers are encouraged to not stop here but to continue exploring the living and breathing world of the dead in Christ.

CHAPTER ONE

Mary's Yes

Here am I, the servant of the Lord;
let it be with me according to your word.

—Mary of Nazareth, Luke 1:38

We start with Mary of Nazareth, who stands as the first among all the saints, both chronologically and theologically. Chronologically because, as the mother of Jesus, she is the first to meet him and be forever transformed by the encounter. Theologically because, as the mother of Jesus, she is the one who births him to the world. If, as I have argued thus far, the primary role of the saints is to point us to Jesus, then Mary is the saint *par excellence*. For just this reason, however, Mary has come to embody all of the criticisms Protestants have with the practice of engaging the saints in general. As such, beginning with Mary offers a means of clearing the deck with respect to these criticisms, two of which are most prominent. Stated as questions, they are as follows: (1) What is the relationship between Mary and Jesus? and (2) How should we think about praying to Mary, if we should at all? The answers to these questions, provided by an examination of Mary's life and the Marian piety that developed in her wake, will be instructive for our understanding of the rest of the saints and the function they may play in our discipleship.

The earliest sources of Mary's life, and likely the only ones that bear any kind of historical reliability, come from the New Testament.[1] But despite her

---

1 Later sources such as the mid to late second-century text *Protoevangelium of James* offer details about Mary herself but are more useful for understanding the development

later popularity, these sources tell us very little about her. As New Testament scholar Beverly Roberts Gaventa has aptly noted, "The New Testament exhibits no interest in Mary as such, but in Mary as a character in the story of Jesus."[2] She was born into a Jewish family near the end of the Second Temple period in Nazareth,[3] a small village in Galilee of north Palestine (Luke 1:26).[4] Nazareth was a rather insignificant place, which, unlike Bethlehem or Jerusalem, had no history in Israel's story and was somewhat suspect among the Jewish aristocracy for its proximity to non-Jewish territory where Gentiles lived. Most Second Temple Jews did not consort with Gentiles because of an emphasis on keeping the Jewish bloodline pure so as not to fall into the idolatry that they felt had caused their original exile.[5] Nazareth, then, was the ancient equivalent of a border town little respected among xenophobic elites who were interested in maintaining the national interest. Jesus's disciple Nathanael's reaction at hearing where the Messiah was from—"Can anything good come out of Nazareth?"—was likely representative of the majority opinion (John 1:46).

At the time of her appearance in the Gospel story,[6] Mary is of marrying age, which, in first-century Judaism, equated to the age when women could

---

of Marian piety than for constructing any kind of historical understanding of her life. In comparison to that text, the Gospels are quite understated in their descriptions of Mary.

2 Beverly Roberts Gaventa, *Mary: Glimpses of the Mother of Jesus* (Minneapolis: Fortress Press, 1999), 100.

3 The Second Temple period marks the time in Israel's history after the return from the Babylonian exile (539 BCE–70 CE), so named from the presence of a second temple built to replace Solomon's Temple, which had been destroyed when Israel was taken into exile.

4 The earliest known reference to Mary, made by Paul in a letter written in the early 50s, notes her Jewish heritage: "But when the fullness of time had come, God sent his Son, born of a woman, born under the law" (Gal 4:4). Later stories suggest she was a devout Jew as she and Joseph had Jesus circumcised on the eighth day and presented at the temple with sacrifices according to the law (Luke 2:21–22), and she traveled annually to Jerusalem to celebrate the Passover (Luke 2:41). It is unclear, however, from which tribe she descends. References to Jesus's Davidic descent (Matt 1:1, 16; Luke 3:23ff) are tied to his adoption by Joseph, a descendent of David. Luke's claim that she is a cousin of Elizabeth, a descendent of Aaron (Luke 1:5), suggests a priestly lineage.

5 This misguided ideal explains the emphasis on circumcision, Sabbath-keeping, and food laws, as well as the disdain for and avoidance of Samaritans (half-Jews), by many of the Jews with whom Jesus interacts in his ministry. Adherence to such laws was readily observable—one thinks of Jesus's criticism of the Pharisees as "white-washed tombs," pretty on the outside but dead on the inside (Matt 23:27).

6 The Gospels of Matthew and Luke both include stories of Jesus's birth, though Matthew's account is told through Joseph's perspective rendering Mary a much more passive figure than Luke's, which is the focus of this chapter. The Gospels of Mark and John do not include accounts of Jesus's birth, and Mary is even more remote, appearing only at

biologically bear children.[7] For this reason, she likely is between twelve and fourteen years old, a young woman in a culture centered on adult males (a patriarchal culture). Though the marginalized place of women in such cultures, and first-century Judaism in particular, is sometimes overstated, it is certainly the case that women were considered central neither to human affairs—there were no female governors or priests—nor to divine ones. The few exceptions in Israel's story—such as the female judge Deborah, who led her people in battle; Queen Esther, who saved her people from genocide; or Judith, who killed the leader of the enemy Assyrians—proved, as they say, the general rule that men were the normal actors in patriarchal cultures.[8] Indeed, a more prominent image of women in Judaism at that time came from the figure of Eve, who, far from being a positive agent in God's story, was widely interpreted as the cause of its ruin through her weakness to temptation.[9]

All this makes Mary of Nazareth the unlikeliest of actors in God's salvific story. Yet, according to Luke's Gospel, Mary is the lynchpin on which rests its climactic act, the coming of the Messiah to save his people. This act is first announced to Mary by the angel Gabriel: "In the sixth month the angel Gabriel was sent by God to a town in Galilee called Nazareth, to a virgin engaged to a man whose name was Joseph, of the house of David. The virgin's name was Mary. And he came to her and said, 'Greetings, favored one! The Lord is with you'" (Luke 1:26–28). The angel's salutation reveals much about Mary's character; unfortunately, many standard English translations—"Greetings,

---

different points during Jesus's ministry. Helpful comparisons of the Gospel material on Mary can be found in Tim Perry, *Mary for Evangelicals: Toward an Understanding of the Mother of Our Lord* (Downers Grove, IL: IVP Academic, 2006), part 1.

7 Raymond E. Brown, *The Birth of the Messiah: A Commentary on the Infancy Narratives in the Gospels of Matthew and Luke*, 2nd ed. (New York: Doubleday, 1993), 123–24.

8 These stories are told, respectively, in Judges 4, the book of Esther, and the book of Judith, an apocryphal book not included in Protestant Bibles but rather popular in early Christianity.

9 Such is a dominant interpretation among rabbinic literature, which, though dating to later centuries, reflects and includes first-century interpretations. See Leila Leah Bronner, *From Eve to Esther: Rabbinic Reconstructions of Biblical Women* (Louisville, KY: Westminster John Knox Press, 1994), ch. 2. Similar interpretations can be found in Philo, a first-century Jewish interpreter from Alexandria; Josephus, a first-century Jewish historian; and even some writings in the New Testament. For example, the writer of 1 Timothy makes this interpretation of Eve his basis for not allowing women as ministers (1 Tim 2:12–14). Worth noting, however, is that while Genesis 3 does describe Eve as the first to be tempted, it does not single her out but places equal blame on the man, the woman, and the serpent, to whom God gives the harshest curse.

favored one"—blunt its meaning. The initial word in Greek is *chaire*, a form of salutation less like a modern-day "Greetings" and more like an invitation to rejoice at the message about to be shared (as in the New King James Version's "Rejoice"). Likewise, the following words Gabriel uses of Mary do not simply mean "favored one" but the more theologically potent "graced one" as the Greek word *kecharitōmenē* derives from the word for "grace."[10] The significance of the statement, then, is that before Mary has done anything, she has received grace. Indeed, the whole expression—*chaire kecharitōmenē* ("Grace, graced one")—drives the point home. A better translation of this passage may be an older one: "Hail, full of grace. The Lord is with you."

Mary is, quite understandably, shocked and fearful at this apparition, causing the angel to reassure her with yet another reiteration of God's grace in her before describing the details of God's extraordinary plan: "You will conceive in your womb and bear a son, and you will name him Jesus. He will be great, and will be called the Son of the Most High, and the Lord God will give to him the throne of his ancestor David. He will reign over the house of Jacob forever, and of his kingdom there will be no end" (Luke 1:31–33). The angel's words here make clear that he is talking about the coming of the Messiah, whom Second Temple Jews had long awaited to deliver them. For while they were back in the land of Canaan, the land promised to Abraham, they were still an oppressed people dominated by foreign powers antithetical to the purposes of God.[11] At the time of this announcement, King Herod was on the throne. Besides the fact that his allegiance was not to God but to the Roman emperor, Herod was not a descendant of King David, meaning God's promise to David that he would always have a descendant on the throne of Israel was unfulfilled.[12] Thus, one of the clear indicators of the identity of the Messiah was his Davidic descent, out of which he would rightfully assume David's throne and defeat all of Israel's enemies.[13]

"How can this be," Mary asks in response, "since I am a virgin?" (Luke 1:34). Mary's question did not indicate surprise that she would birth the

---

10 Brown, *The Birth of the Messiah*, 288.

11 In Mary's day, the Romans were the foreign oppressor, Canaan having become a Roman province in 63 BCE.

12 2 Samuel 7:11–16.

13 For a helpful introduction on Second Temple Jewish hopes for the coming Messiah, see C. A. Evans, "Messianism," in *Dictionary of New Testament Background*, ed. Daniel G. Reid (Downers Grove, IL: InterVarsity Press, 2000), 698–707.

Messiah (for nothing in the prophecies indicated that the Messiah was to be divine) but rather at the pure biological fact that this was not possible given her virginity. And here is where the completely unexpected and miraculous nature of God's climactic saving act, and her place in it, is first revealed to her: "The angel said to her, 'The Holy Spirit will come upon you, and the power of the Most High will overshadow you; therefore the child to be born will be holy; he will be called Son of God'" (Luke 1:35). The Messiah, whom God was sending, was not going to be the human king the Jews expected. He was not even going to be some extraordinarily faithful human like a Moses or a David, who would have a special, adopted relationship with God. No, God intended to send his only begotten Son, the divine Word himself, to the world to be *born* as a human being. This Messiah was to be a fully divine and at the same time fully human person, a God-man, for whom Israel's story, not to mention world history, lacked an analogue.[14] And Mary's task in the plan was to birth him. Put differently, *the humanity of this completely unique God-man would come from her.*

Just as there is no analogue for Jesus, so, too, is there none for this call narrative, making it difficult to imagine what Mary felt in this moment. Was she scared? Certainly. Was she confused? Surely. Did she doubt that God could do such a miraculous thing through her? Perhaps. Gaventa has suggested that a close, though inexact, parallel to Mary's call narrative is found in those of the Old Testament prophets who, like Mary, were ordinary humans called to extraordinary tasks.[15] Isaiah, called into the heavenly throne room in the very presence of God, can only say, "Woe is me, for I am undone! Because I am a man of unclean lips" (Isa 6:5, NKJV). Ezekiel, on seeing the vision of God in the flaming chariot, falls flat on his face in silence (Ezek 1:28). Jeremiah, called to proclaim God's Word to an unfaithful people on the brink of exile, responds, "I do not know how to speak; I am only a boy" (Jer 1:6). Mary is every one of these figures, but her task is even more impossible. As any mother will testify, childbirth changes a woman physically, mentally, psychologically. Moreover, she knew the scandal that faced her as a pregnant, unmarried woman in her first-century Jewish culture, and she had no assurance that

---

14 How the humanity and divinity of Christ fit together is not at issue in this passage or anywhere else in Scripture. It would be left to the Church to work out the particulars in later centuries. I will address some of these issues in chapter 6.

15 Gaventa, *Mary*, 58–59.

the man to whom she was betrothed would be on board.[16] The Old Testament prophets were afraid of the scandalous nature of their words; Mary would wear the scandal on her body.

The parallel to the prophetic call narratives provides another insight into this passage, one we can easily miss in a quick read-through, namely, that Mary is given a choice. She could have said no. For, in keeping with the character of God as revealed throughout Scripture, God is not a God who forces himself on people or uses them against their will. Rather, God is a God in relationship with people and invites them to participate with him in that relationship.[17] Therefore, Scripture is full of examples of individuals who said no to God, which caused God to work his will by other means. The most notorious example is Eve herself, who, when told by God not to eat from the tree of the knowledge of good and evil, does so anyway, and the consequences are real and disastrous. Though she does not alone bear the blame for the fall of the world, it remains the case that, when given a choice to participate with God, Eve said no.

Mary says yes: "Here am I, the servant of the Lord; let it be with me according to your word" (Luke 1:38). What incredible faith! What profound hope in the plans of God! What indescribable love for God and for his people. Mary consents here to sacrifice her life fully to God and his will. Although Gabriel tells her God's plan, as every other clever tweeter points out to the Christmas anthem "Mary, Did You Know?," Mary couldn't possibly have known fully what she was saying yes to any more than we do when we say yes to our baptismal vows. This is precisely what makes her act one of extraordinary faith

---

16 This fear is borne out in Matthew's account, for when Joseph learns of Mary's pregnancy, he makes plans to end their engagement (Matt 1:18–19). To be sure, he plans to do so quietly so as not to bring shame on Mary (as opposed to dragging her before the authorities and demanding her public stoning, which was his right by law). Nevertheless, he still wanted to end the engagement, which would have left Mary destitute. Not until he receives his own angelic visitation and is brought into this somewhat crazy divine plan does Joseph change his mind (Matt 1:20–21).

17 This is a particularly important point to make in this context, where the conception of a child is at issue. Crucially, there are no sexual undertones in Gabriel's announcement of Mary's conception. Luke could have written it in such a way. There were stories in Greek mythology of the gods copulating with humans to produce demigods like Hercules. But Luke does not do this, which is instructive both for understanding the character of God vis-à-vis the gods of Greek mythology and for distinguishing Jesus from other Hercules-type characters. As the Scriptures testify, and the Church will later define with doctrinal clarity, Jesus is not a demigod but fully divine and fully human.

and a model for every other disciple. For the only thing she knows for sure when she says yes is that the God who has called her to this impossible task will be with her. Thus, in the moment of her consent, she is Isaiah, whose mouth was touched by the burning coal. She is Ezekiel, who is helped up from the floor. And she is Jeremiah, to whom God says, "I have put my words in your mouth" (Jer 1:9). Only in this case, God places not his words in Mary's mouth but the eternal Word in her womb.

In the story's next movement, Mary visits her cousin Elizabeth, who, being filled with the Holy Spirit, immediately perceives Mary's transformation resulting from her divine vocation. "Blessed are you among women and blessed is the fruit of your womb," she says (Luke 1:42, NJKV).[18] Elizabeth's address, the first such following Mary's virginal conception, is instructive for understanding the biblical view and, as we shall see momentarily, the traditional view of Mary. Elizabeth praises Mary to be sure, for she calls her, of all women, most blessed. But her second statement makes clear that the cause of Mary's exalted status has everything to do with the child she carries in her womb. Gaventa writes, "Mary's blessedness derives from God's gift rather than from some inherent goodness of her own."[19] Another way of looking at it is that Elizabeth's praise of Mary directs her ultimately to praise of Jesus.

Mary then speaks what is possibly the most beautiful song of praise in all of Scripture:

> My soul magnifies the Lord, and my spirit has rejoiced in God my Savior. For He has regarded the lowly state of His maidservant; for behold, henceforth all generations will call me blessed. For He who is mighty has done great things for me, and holy is His name. And His mercy is on those who fear Him from generation to generation. He has shown strength with His arm; He has scattered the proud in the imagination of their hearts. He has put down the mighty from their thrones, and exalted the lowly. He has filled the hungry with good things, and the rich He has sent away empty. He has helped His servant Israel, in remembrance of His mercy, as He spoke to our fathers, to Abraham and to his seed forever. (Luke 1:46–55 NKJV)

In this song, traditionally known as the *Magnificat*, from the Latin for Mary's first word, lie the great themes of Scripture now played out in Mary's own

---

18 Luke's Gospel, unique among the four, begins with the story of Zechariah and Elizabeth, who conceives the child who would grow to become John the Baptist, the one who heralds the coming of Jesus. This ministry of heralding begins in this moment through the prophecies of Elizabeth and the leaping of John in her womb at Mary's presence.

19 Gaventa, *Mary*, 57.

life. God is a merciful God who saves the world not through the standard human means of the rich and powerful but through those lowly and poor, not through Emperor Augustus or King Herod or even the high priest Caiaphas but through a young virgin from Nazareth. Additionally, in the same way that God had elected the little nation of Israel not for itself but that "all the families of the earth shall be blessed" through Israel, God likewise calls the Nazarene virgin and blesses her with Jesus, not for her own sake but for the sake of the world (Gen 12:3).[20] It is for this reason that all generations will call her blessed.

The earliest Christian theologians, referred to as the Church Fathers, drew great significance from Mary's yes and often juxtaposed it to Eve's original no in Eden. As a result, they interpreted Mary as the New Eve, just as Paul had interpreted Christ as the New or Second Adam (Rom 5:12–19). Her yes to God overturns Eve's no in the same way that Jesus's act of faithfulness overturns Adam's act of unfaithfulness, thereby taking humanity from a doomed path away from God toward death to a graced path leading to God and life. For example, the second-century saint Irenaeus of Lyons, whom we will meet in the next chapter, writes: "For just as Eve had Adam for a husband but was still a virgin . . . and by disobeying became the cause of death for herself and the whole human race, so also Mary, with a husband predestined for her but yet a virgin, was obedient and became the cause of salvation for herself and the whole human race."[21] Mary's yes to God, then, is a crucial moment in the history of salvation, for it is the moment that inaugurates the incarnation

---

20 Following an ancient trope, Lutheran theologian Robert W. Jenson connects Mary to Israel for her vocation to make space for God in his creation. "Mary is Israel concentrated," he writes. Robert W. Jenson, "A Space for God," in *Mary, Mother of God*, ed. Carl E. Braaten and Robert W. Jenson (Grand Rapids, MI: Eerdmans, 2004), 49–57. This insight leads to other connections in the tradition, such as Mary as Temple and Mary as Ark of the Covenant, which, again, are rooted in Scripture. For example, many scholars see in Gabriel's greeting to Mary, "*chaire*," an allusion to the Septuagint text of the prophet Zephaniah, "Sing aloud, O daughter Zion; shout, O Israel! Rejoice and exult with all your heart, O daughter Jerusalem! The Lord has taken away the judgments against you, he has turned away your enemies. The king of Israel, the Lord, is in your midst; you shall fear disaster no more" (Zeph 3:14–15). *Chaire* is here translated "sing." The prophetic promise that the Lord is "in your midst" literally means "in your womb." Benedict XVI, *Jesus of Nazareth, the Infancy Narratives*, trans. Philip J. Whitmore (New York: Image, 2012), 28.
21 Irenaeus, *Against Heresies* 3.22.4, trans. Robert M. Grant. *Irenaeus of Lyons*. The Early Church Fathers (London and New York: Routledge, 1997), 140.

that will be the means by which God saves the world. Without Mary's yes, the incarnation could not have happened.[22]

This interpretation, nevertheless, does not mean that Mary is in any way the savior or even that she is a co-savior, or co-redemptrix, with Christ, for this would necessarily mean that Mary herself is divine. Neither Scripture nor Church tradition, nor the Catholic or Orthodox Churches, who so venerate Mary, make any such argument.[23] Indeed, Christians of all stripes are united in their belief that God alone is divine and worthy of worship and that he alone saves the fallen world. By contrast, Mary, though most blessed as Elizabeth said, is a created human. As such, she was in need of salvation like the rest of us, for as Scripture says elsewhere, "*All* have sinned and fall short of the glory of God" (Rom 3:23; italics added). To return to the Christmas anthem "Mary, Did You Know?," the lyric "The child that you delivered will soon deliver you" makes this point beautifully.

As a human in need of salvation, Mary does not save us any more than any of the saints in this book save us. Her role, as I have said and the Gospel makes clear, is only to point us to Christ, the true means of our salvation, a function that is perhaps best dramatized in John's story of the wedding at Cana. There she appears briefly, without even a name, to say only to the wedding servants, "Do whatever he tells you," which leads to Christ's miracle of

---

22 Some Protestants immediately hedge at this point. If Mary said no, they say, God would have found a different way. This point is granted, but it misses the point of the story in some misguided attempt to downplay Mary's role. The crucial point is that Mary said yes, and this faithful act, made in cooperation with God, allows for the incarnation.

23 The Second Vatican Council, the latest authoritative council on belief and practice in the Catholic Church, makes this clear. The statement on Mary, for example, distinguishes the human Mary from the divine Christ: "Mary's function as mother of humankind in no way obscures or diminishes this unique mediation of Christ" and that "No creature could ever be counted along with the incarnate Word and Redeemer." *Lumen Gentium*, 8.3.60, 62 in Austin Flannery, ed., *Vatican Council II: The Basic Sixteen Documents* (Northport, NY: Costello Publishing Company, 1996), 85–86. Moreover, Perry's helpful discussion of the development of the Catholic Marian doctrines, which I discuss more below, demonstrates the careful lengths to which popes went to stay clear of the implication that Mary was divine. Perry, *Mary for Evangelicals*, 229–32, 239–45. The same goes for Orthodox Christians as, notes Orthodox theologian Kyriaki Karidoyanes Fitzgerald, "the Orthodox have always made it clear that there is an important distinction between our worship of God and the honor we give to Mary and the saints. Mary and the other saints are human persons. Worship belongs to God alone." Kyriaki Karidoyanes Fitzgerald, "Mary the Theotokos and the Call to Holiness," in *Mary, Mother of God*, ed. Carl E. Braaten and Robert W. Jenson (Grand Rapids, MI: Eerdmans, 2004), 80–99.

turning water into wine (John 2:5). In fact, this is one of the only stories that Mary appears in after the birth narratives, for after giving birth to Christ, she all but disappears from the story. Thus, the most common picture or icon of Mary through history is of her holding an infant Christ. In all of these pictures, regardless of the style or the period of the composition, Christ emerges as the focal point, while his mother, who holds him up to the viewer, fades into the background. Such is the role of all the saints.

This insight on Mary's person and role in relation to Christ, furthermore, is demonstrated in history by the development of the Marian title *Theotokos*, or "God-bearer," which translates to "Mother of God." In popular use for at least a generation prior, this title was officially adopted in 431 at the Council of Ephesus, the third ecumenical or universal council.[24] While the title may be jarring at first to Protestant readers, as it seems to accord a divine status to Mary that we have thus far rejected, the theological purpose for officially adopting the title actually had nothing to do with Mary and everything to do with Christ. According to a rather convoluted history, the technical details of which need not detain us,[25] a bishop named Nestorius in the years before the council denied that Mary was *Theotokos* and instead called her *Christotokos* ("Mother of Christ").[26] For Nestorius, that is, Mary was only the mother of the human but was not the Mother of God. Whatever he intended by this title, its clear implication was that Mary conceived and birthed not the God-man but a human who only later became God, an understanding of Christ inconsistent with Scripture's witness that the "Word became flesh" (John 1:14). Nestorius's understanding was rejected, therefore, *not* because his title failed to give Mary her due honor but because it called into question the reality of the incarnation, the basis of human salvation. As Perry puts it, "If Mary did not bear God in her womb—if she is not *Theotokos*—human beings are not saved."[27] By contrast,

---

24 The core doctrines of the Church, such as those appearing in the Apostles' Creed, were officially defined by Council in the earliest centuries in the Church. Seven such councils occurred prior to any major church divisions, namely the Council of Nicaea (325), the Council of Constantinople (381), the Council of Ephesus (431), the Council of Chalcedon (451), the Second Council of Constantinople (553), the Third Council of Constantinople (680–81), and the Second Council of Nicaea (787). In this book, I will have occasion to discuss several of these councils and the doctrines they officially defined.

25 For those interested, see Perry, *Mary for Evangelicals*, 168–71.

26 Elizabeth's statement of Mary as "the mother of my Lord" is sufficiently ambiguous to support either interpretation (Luke 1:43).

27 Perry, *Mary for Evangelicals*, 271. Jenson is even more terse: "If one balks at [*Theotokos*], one is simply a heretic." Jenson, "A Space for God," 50.

to call Mary *Theotokos* is to affirm the scriptural truth that she conceived and birthed the God-man, the Word become flesh.

Here, then, is the same pattern regarding Mary we saw in the Gospel. Mary is an exalted person, most blessed among women, but not because of anything inherent to her or anything that would necessitate that she has a divine status. Rather, she is exalted purely because of the fruit of her womb, Jesus. In this context, Mary is the same person whether we call her *Christotokos* or *Theotokos*, but only through the latter title do we form a right understanding of Christ. For this reason, Protestants should not only be unconcerned with Mary's title *Theotokos*, but we should use the title in our own practices. For, by doing so, we will not be honoring Mary in any way inconsistent with Scripture, and we will be honoring Christ in a way that is consistent with Scripture. Even in this most exalted of Marian titles, then, Mary fades into the background, where she longs to be.[28]

This brings us to the final topic of this chapter, namely, the question of praying to Mary. For Protestants, unused to praying to anyone but God, the act of any kind of prayer directed at a fellow human being not only seems to put the focus on them but, more problematically, risks according divine status to them. Yet a crucial part of Catholic piety, indeed arguably one of the most visible parts, is praying to Mary. Even people completely uninformed of

---

28 Three other Marian doctrines developed subsequent to the Council of Ephesus. They are Mary's perpetual virginity (she remained a virgin throughout her life), defined at the Second Council of Constantinople in 553; Mary's immaculate conception (she was conceived apart from original sin) by papal decree in 1854; and Mary's bodily assumption (at the end of her life, her soul and body are taken into heaven) by papal decree in 1950. The latter two apply only to Catholics, though Orthodox also affirm Mary's bodily assumption (which they call her dormition). Mary's perpetual virginity comes not from Scripture—indeed, a plain reading of certain Scriptures (e.g., Matt 1:25) suggests the opposite—but from the *Protoevangelium of James*. Despite this, it is the least problematic of the three, for it carries no doctrinal weight, and it was defined at an ecumenical council, which should be authoritative for Protestants. Indeed, many of the original Reformers, including Martin Luther, whom we will meet in chapter 9, believed in Mary's perpetual virginity. The other two developments, however, pose multiple issues for a Protestant view of Mary, for they suggest that she was immune from sin (Mary's bodily assumption is a corollary of her immaculate conception; if she was not conceived in original sin, then she does not experience sin's consequence of death). Additionally, they are the latest to be defined and not by church council but by papal decree. While these doctrines do not have the effect of making Mary divine, they do place her in a unique category, which I have argued is unnecessary to give her proper honor and certainly goes beyond a charitable reading of Scripture. For those interested in a lengthier discussion of these developments from a Protestant perspective, see Perry, *Mary for Evangelicals*, especially part 3.

Catholic faith and practice are probably familiar with the traditional "Hail Mary" prayer, prayed daily by millions of faithful Catholics around the globe. Since it is clear from Scripture and tradition that Mary is not divine, a Protestant rightfully may ask, "Why do Catholics pray to her?"

To answer this question, we must first look at the words of this famous prayer. In its traditional formula, it reads,

> Hail Mary, full of grace, the Lord is with thee.
> Blessed art thou among women, and blessed is the fruit of thy womb, Jesus.
> Holy Mary, Mother of God,
> pray for us sinners now and at the hour of our death.

What immediately strikes us are the scriptural origins of many of the words. "Hail Mary, full of grace, the Lord is with thee" is the greeting Gabriel offers her in Luke 1:28. The word *hail* in the Lukan context carries the connotation of a simple greeting, but divorced from that context, it can take on the additional meaning of honor, which is undoubtedly what Catholics intend in the prayer. Nevertheless, this word does not equate to worship, as indicated by the second line, "Blessed art thou among women, and blessed is the fruit of thy womb, Jesus," the greeting that Elizabeth offers Mary in Luke 1:42. As we saw above, this is an appropriate means of honoring Mary, for it places her with humans ("among women") and identifies the source of her blessedness as the Christ that she bears, which, in turn, further qualifies the opening "hail." Mary is honored and blessed because of the fruit of her womb, Jesus, whose name stands at the very center of this prayer. The prayer continues in the second part to address Mary by her traditional title *Theotokos* before closing with a simple request for her prayers on our behalf.

"Hail Mary," then, follows the Gospel pattern where Mary serves only to point us to Christ. As Pope John Paul II wrote, "Although the repeated Hail Mary is addressed directly to Mary, it is to Jesus that the act of love is ultimately directed, with her and through her."[29] This admittedly abstract claim finds powerful form in the Catholic prayer practice with which the

---

29 John Paul II, *Rosarium Virginis Mariae*, 26, http://www.vatican.va/content/john-paul-ii/en/apost_letters/2002/documents/hf_jp-ii_apl_20021016_rosarium-virginis-mariae.html.

"Hail Mary" is most often connected, namely, the Rosary.[30] The purpose of the Rosary is to meditate on the life of Christ, and the prayers uttered serve as a mantra of sorts that focuses one's mind on these mysteries. The "Hail Mary" is an appropriate prayer to lead the faithful into this contemplation not only because Mary birthed Christ to the world, as I said, but also because Mary herself was the first to meditate on these events, notably Christ's birth and the visitation of the shepherds. Luke ends that marvelous Christmas story by writing, "Mary treasured all these words and pondered them in her heart" (Luke 2:19).

This is all well and good, but it still does not fully answer the question of why prayer to Mary is necessary. If the point is ultimately Jesus, why not just pray to Jesus? I think for Protestants, the heart of this question lies in the meaning of the preposition to, as in praying to Mary. But what if we thought of this prayer not as directed to Mary but as praying with Mary to Christ? Or what if we thought of this prayer as a request for Mary to pray for us? These ways of thinking of the prayer are less foreign to Protestants, for we pray to Christ with other people all the time, and we frequently ask others to pray for us. Indeed, it has been my experience that corporate prayer and requests for prayer from others do not detract from individual prayer but enhance it. Put differently, I am more likely to pray alone if I am regularly praying with others. If this point is granted, then the only reason to frown on prayers to Mary, or any of the rest of the saints, is that they are not living among us. As I already noted in the introduction, however, the Christian belief in resurrection does not permit us to accept this as a viable reason, for the saints who form the cloud of witnesses are living. To not ask Mary and the rest of the saints to pray with us and for us is, at best, a missed opportunity for spiritual growth and companionship and, at worst, an implicit denial of the resurrection.

Thus, if Protestants decide to pray the "Hail Mary," or to pray to any of the saints, we are praying not to them because they are divine or because they

---

30 The Rosary refers to a set of prayers prayed with a necklace with a specified number of beads, corresponding to the prayers, from which a crucifix hangs. The practice goes back to the fifteenth century, well before the Reformation and so, as Gary Wills points out, is a part of the Protestant heritage as well as the Catholic heritage. Its rejection by Protestants has less to do with the practice itself and more to do with its unfortunate connection in the Reformers' mind to the corrupt practice of indulgences, which I will address in chapter 9. For those interested in the history of the Rosary, see Gary Wills, *The Rosary: Prayer Comes Round* (New York: Penguin Books, 2005), 3–11.

will give us some gift or blessing on their own merit. Nor are we praying to them as a substitute for prayers directly to God. Rather, we pray with Mary and the saints *to* God, asking them for their prayers on our behalf, just as we would ask any of our Christian brothers and sisters. The last lines of the "Hail Mary" clearly demonstrate this truth: "Holy Mary, Mother of God, *pray for us* sinners now and at the hour of our death." Though praying with the saints in this manner is not a necessary practice to a fruitful life of discipleship, or even to a robust appreciation of the saints, it can be an effective one. And it is certainly a faithful one.

With many of the saints in this book, we will read of their whole lives, including their often faithful and profound deaths. Not so with Mary. As mentioned, after she births Christ to the world, she all but disappears. In fact, the last time we see her in the scriptural story is a brief mention in Acts 1:14. There she sits among a small band of disciples after the ascension of Jesus, praying constantly and waiting faithfully for the gift of the Holy Spirit that would mark the coming of the Church in power. So she remains amid the much larger band of faithful witnesses. She still prays constantly, but her prayers are now on our behalf and on behalf of the world. May we feel the freedom to ask for her prayers, and may we follow her faithful example of saying yes to God so that Christ the Word might be born anew in us.

CHAPTER TWO

Irenaeus's Story

*For the glory of God is the living man, and the life of man
is the vision of God.*

—Irenaeus of Lyons, *Against Heresies* 4.20.7

As with Mary of Nazareth, we know very little about the life of our second saint, Irenaeus, a bishop who lived and wrote near the end of the second century. We catch only glimpses of him in short autobiographical passages from his own work or in ancient traditions preserved in the work of early Church historians. Nevertheless, what he leaves us with, and why his presence in the cloud of witnesses is worthy of remembrance, is a written record of biblical interpretation that helps us see how the earliest Christians understood Scripture's redemptive story and the God revealed in that story. And while Irenaeus wrote during a time in which the Church had become almost exclusively Gentile, the story, as we shall see, remains a fundamentally Jewish one. It's about a good God who creates the world as the dwelling place for his glory, calls Israel in order to bring humans back from the bondage to death they chose in their unrighteousness, and sends his Son Jesus, the faithful Jew who destroys the barrier of death through the cross and redeems the creation through his resurrection. It has rightly been called the greatest story ever told, yet were it not for the faithful work of Irenaeus, twenty-first-century Christians might not have read it this way.

In just the second generation of Christianity, two alternative interpretations of the scope and meaning of this story became popular among Gentile Christian communities. First was that of the dynamic teacher Marcion, who argued from a literal reading of Scripture that the God revealed in Jesus was completely different from the god who created the world and was known to Israel. Thus, the good news of Jesus did not continue the story started at creation but supplanted it with an entirely new one. Marcion's evidence for his interpretation were the apparent contradictions between the ancient Jewish Scriptures and the newer Christian writings, particularly those of Paul and Luke's Gospel.[1] That he apparently had to edit Jewish content out of these writings did not blunt the force of his argument: how could the god who commanded the destruction of the Canaanite people be the same God revealed in Jesus's death for all people? How could the god whose law required an eye for an eye and a tooth for a tooth be the same God who, through Jesus, taught his followers to turn the other cheek? How could the god known by Israel be the same God whom Jesus said no one knew but him (Luke 10:22)?

The second alternative was the story told by various communities spread through the Roman Empire known to history as Gnostics. If Marcion's interpretation of Scripture was overly literalistic, the Gnostics were on the opposite end of the spectrum, taking everything in Scripture as allegory.[2] Accordingly, they did not believe that God was one but rather that the divine nature was made up of a host of spiritual beings of varying degrees of divinity and called scriptural names such as Mind, Word, Wisdom, and the like.[3] Moreover, they did not believe the world to be the good creation of one God, but rather an

---

1 The common titles of "Old Testament" and "New Testament" are not widely used until the third century. For the New Testament writers and all first- and second-century Christians, the "Scriptures" refer to what we now call the Old Testament. The process by which the early Christian writings are recognized as Scripture alongside the Jewish Scriptures (and so form a "New" Testament) is fluid and lasts until around the mid-fourth century. In this chapter, I will use the distinction of "Jewish Scriptures" and "Christian Scriptures" to refer to the Old and New Testaments since the traditional titles would be inaccurate at this early date.

2 Allegory refers to a type of reading that finds little direct connection to the text but rather imposes different meaning not found in its actual words. To cite one example from Gnostic interpretation, Luke's statement that Jesus was thirty years old when he began his ministry (Luke 3:23) was for Gnostics actually a reference to the thirty spiritual beings whom they believed made up the divine realm. In chapter 4, we will return to this method of reading Scripture in the context of the Christian tradition.

3 The closest familiar analogue would be to the various gods and goddesses of Greek mythology. The Gnostic spiritual beings, called "Aeons," existed in a hierarchical chain, with the most divine being as the oldest and the least divine being as the youngest and most ignorant.

unintended mistake caused by the ignorant actions of the youngest spiritual being.[4] Humans, likewise, are not the good divine image-bearers in body and soul but are themselves spiritual beings imprisoned in evil and decaying flesh that is part of this ignorant mistake of a creation. Consequently, Jesus did not come to redeem God's creation, nor, as a spiritual being himself, did he become human to redeem humans. Rather, Jesus came to release spiritual humans from their imprisonment in flesh. While the Gnostics claimed that this knowledge came from secret teachings Jesus only gave certain disciples, their real evidence was empirical in nature: Does this creation really seem good? Do our bodies seem to be redeemable? Aren't our minds and souls by nature higher than our base, material bodies?[5]

While both of these alternative stories may sound foreign to us, they were quite persuasive to many Christians in the young movement. To get a sense of why this is the case, consider how many times Christians wonder why the God of the Old Testament seems so different from Jesus. Or how little the Jewish roots of the Christian faith are ever considered. Or how the common view of heaven is a disembodied paradise where our souls exist apart from the evils of this creation and our sinful, physical bodies. These are the very considerations that persuaded many second-century Christians to join these groups and embrace these alternative stories of redemption, ones with no relation to Israel and ones that pitted the work of salvation against the work of creation.

Irenaeus was a contemporary of these persuasive teachers. Born in Smyrna of Asia Minor (modern-day Izmir, Turkey) sometime in the 130s,[6] he was a Gentile but, at an early age, was influenced by Jewish and Jewish Christian thinkers, among them the revered Bishop of Smyrna and eventual martyr Polycarp, who is said to have been a disciple of the apostle John.[7] This encounter connects Irenaeus to the earliest apostles, and it may have been

---

4 The story is a technical and confusing one, but essentially the least divine spiritual being mistakenly tried to contemplate the knowledge of the whole divine being and the result was the mess (literally called an *abortion*) that becomes material creation.

5 For a scholarly introduction to these two alternate traditions, see Petri Luomanen and Antti Marjanen, eds., *A Companion to Second-Century Christian "Heretics"* (Leiden: Brill, 2005), especially chapters 1–4.

6 The Church in Smyrna is of ancient origin, being one of seven churches to which the book of Revelation is addressed. See Revelation 2:8–11.

7 Irenaeus mentions their encounter in detail in a letter preserved by Eusebius. *Church History*, 5.20.5–7. Irenaeus also refers to the encounter in one of his two works still in existence, *Against Heresies*, 3.3–4.

what inspired Irenaeus to devote his life to God and service to his Church. At some point, Irenaeus left Smyrna and made his way to Rome, where he likely met and learned from the famed Christian teacher Justin Martyr.[8] It was also in Rome where Irenaeus first encountered the teachings of the Gnostics, and perhaps those of Marcion, through reading their commentaries on Scripture.

By the 170s, sometime in his forties, he has settled in Lugdunum of Gaul (modern-day Lyons, France), where he became a presbyter, a pastoral office equivalent to a contemporary priest or minister.[9] In 177, the Christians in Gaul became the targets of persecution at the hands of the Roman Empire, and many prominent Christians, including Bishop Pothinus, were arrested and eventually martyred.[10] Irenaeus would have certainly been one of these, but in his role as presbyter and possibly because of his familiarity with Rome from his earlier travels, he had gone to Rome to deliver letters from the imprisoned Christians to the Roman bishop. By the time he returned to Gaul, the persecutions had stopped, though the damage was extensive. In the vacuum of leadership, this trusted presbyter ascended to the role of bishop. He remained in this important leadership role, working to restore and strengthen the churches torn by persecution, until his death from old age around the year 200. In this capacity, he wrote the first and definitive defense of Christianity's redemptive story, and the God who authored it, against the alternative versions preached by Marcion and the Gnostics.[11]

---

8 Justin wrote several important defenses (apologies) of the Christian faith in order to highlight the injustice of the Roman Empire's practice of persecuting Christians (*First* and *Second Apologies*). I will address the Christian experience of persecution and martyrdom in the first few centuries in more detail in chapter 3.

9 In the second century, church leadership structures were coalescing around three offices, namely, bishops over large areas, presbyters over churches within the area, and deacons assisting presbyters. For a readable account of this development, see Robert Louis Wilken, *The First Thousand Years: A Global History of Christianity* (New Haven, CT: Yale University Press, 2012), chapter 3.

10 This is the same episode that claimed the life of Blandina, mentioned in the introduction.

11 Although Irenaeus wrote many works, only two have survived, namely, the rather long and technical *Against Heresies* and the much shorter and more accessible *Demonstration of the Apostolic Faith*. Though Irenaeus originally wrote in Greek, these works survive only in Latin and Armenian, respectively. Unless otherwise noted, I will use the highly readable translations of Grant, *Irenaeus of Lyons* for *Against Heresies* and John Behr, *St. Irenaeus of Lyons, On the Apostolic Preaching* (Crestwood, NY: St. Vladimir's Seminary Press, 1997) for *Demonstration of the Apostolic Faith*. References to these works will be marked in the text as *AH* and *Dem*, respectively.

Irenaeus argues that the problem with his opponents is not that they are reading the wrong Scriptures (though Marcion's Bible was certainly incomplete, and certain Gnostic gospels, such as the Gospel of Judas or the Gospel of Phillip, were later fabrications). Rather, the problem is that they are reading the right Scriptures *wrongly*, and the reason for this is that they read them apart from the right hypothesis. A concept drawn from ancient rhetoric, the hypothesis of a work is a short summation of its plot, which is essential for right interpretation. A hypothesis is like the box score of a baseball game, which gives fans the very basics of the game (hits, runs, stolen bases, etc.). However, if we watched a replay of a baseball game with reference to the wrong box score, we may believe throughout the whole game that our team has won only to discover in the ninth inning that they lost.[12] Similarly, if we read the Scriptures according to the wrong hypothesis, like Marcion's identification of two gods or the Gnostics' identification of a mistaken and evil creation, we will interpret those Scriptures incorrectly. We will conclude, like Marcion, that the battles of Joshua reveal a God who is violent or, like the Gnostics, that Jesus only *appeared* human and was never really crucified. To cite Irenaeus's famous analogy, we will be like a person who "destroyed the figure of a man in the authentic portrait of a king, carefully created by a skillful artist out of precious stones, and rearranged the stones to make the image of a dog or fox, declaring that this badly composed image is that good image of the king" (*AH* 1.8.1).

Irenaeus argues that Scripture's true hypothesis, or "rule of faith" as it came to be known, is the well-known summary I related at the beginning of this chapter, organized under the three articles of faith in the Father, the Son, and the Spirit. To cite but one of Irenaeus's many renditions of this largely consistent summary,

God the Father, uncreated, uncontainable, invisible, one God, the Creator of all: this is the first article of our faith. And this is the second article: the Word of

---

12 This analogy breaks down, however, because with Scripture, unlike baseball, there is no definitive way to know we have the wrong hypothesis. A more accurate analogy, though somewhat less universally known (hence its place in a footnote), is the popular YouTube video "The Karate Kid: Daniel is the REAL bully." This video purports to summarize the '80s movie *The Karate Kid*, but through clever editing and splicing together scenes in a different order, it makes the movie's actual protagonist, Daniel, look like the villain and the movie's clear antagonist, Johnny, the victim. Although it is a really bad interpretation of the movie, its plausibility, like the scriptural interpretations of Marcion and the Gnostics, has made it enormously popular. For those who are interested, it can be viewed here: https://www.youtube.com/watch?v=C_Gz_iTuRMM.

God, the Son of God, Christ Jesus our Lord, who was revealed by the prophets, according to the character of their prophecy and according to the nature of the economies of the Father, by whom all things were made, and who, in the last times, to recapitulate all things, became a man amongst men, visible and palpable, in order to abolish death, to demonstrate life, and to effect communion between God and man. And the third article: the Holy Spirit, through whom the prophets prophesied and the patriarchs learnt the things of God and the righteous were led in the path of righteousness, and who, in the last times, was poured out in a new fashion upon the human race renewing man, throughout the world, to God. (*Dem* 6)[13]

While this threefold organization of the story predates Irenaeus,[14] he is the first to draw out the deep scriptural logic of how Father, Son, and Spirit are united as one God. Indeed, the simultaneous unity and diversity within the Godhead is crucial to his argument, for it shows, in opposition to Marcion, the existence of only one God working consistently throughout the Jewish and Christian Scriptures (a unity or arrangement of God's work that Irenaeus refers to as the "economy"). Yet, in opposition to the Gnostics, it shows that Son and Spirit are not lesser gods, like the Gnostic spiritual beings, but one in divine nature with the Father, making the work of Jesus on earth a continuation of the work God began with creation and Israel. These scriptural arguments form the core of what will eventually become the defining Christian doctrine, namely, the Trinity.[15]

Using the rule of faith as his hypothesis for interpreting Scripture, Irenaeus begins his reading of Scripture by noting that the God who creates all things in the beginning does so through the Son and the Spirit:

---

13 Similar renditions of the rule of faith exist in numerous other writers to suggest that this was a widely known and accepted oral tradition in the second and third centuries. As such, it anticipates the official creeds of the Church, such as the Apostles' Creed, to which it is similar in both form and content. I will define the terms that are original to Irenaeus, and likely foreign to readers (*economies* and *recapitulate*), in the course of this chapter.

14 This manner of summarizing the faith likely developed early out of the baptismal creed that goes back to Jesus's words in Matthew 28:19: "Therefore go and make disciples of all nations, baptizing them in the name of the Father and of the Son and of the Holy Spirit."

15 Since the doctrine of the Trinity is not officially defined by Church councils until the fourth century (the Council of Nicaea in 325 and the Council of Constantinople in 381), critics sometimes claim that the doctrine was invented by the Church and has little connection to Scripture. Writing almost two centuries before these councils, Irenaeus shows otherwise. For a scholarly and more in-depth account of Irenaeus's Trinitarian thought and its place in the development of Trinitarian thought, see my *Irenaeus on the Trinity*, Supplements to *Vigiliae Christianae 127* (Leiden: Brill, 2014).

Angels did not make or form us, for angels could not have made an image of God, nor any other but the true God, nor any power far distant from the Father of all things. God needed none of these to make whatever he foreordained to make, as if he did not have hands of his own. For always with him are his Word and Wisdom, the Son and the Spirit, through whom and in whom he made everything freely and independently, to whom he also speaks when he says, "Let us make man after our image and likeness" (Gen. 1:26), taking the substance of the creatures from himself as well as the pattern of the things he adorned. (*AH* 4.20.1)

For Irenaeus, this interpretation of Genesis is confirmed by the Christian Scriptures, which say specifically that everything was created through the Word (John 1:3). Thus, God *speaks* everything into existence (Gen 1:3), while the Spirit hovers over the waters (Gen 1:2). As participants in the act of creation, which by definition is something only God can do, the Son and Spirit are necessarily divine with the Father over and against all other things that have their source in God. Put differently, only Father, Son, and Spirit are uncreated, and thus eternal, while everything else in the world is created and has a starting point. Furthermore, each of the divine beings (later called "persons") has a specific and necessary function to play in the one divine work of creation. He writes, "He who made and formed and breathed in them the breath of life, and nourishes us by creation, establishing all things by his Word, and binding them together by his Wisdom—this is he who is the only true God" (*AH* 3.24.2).[16] In the act of creation, in other words, the Father wills, the Son establishes or forms, and the Spirit completes or perfects.[17] Like an assembly line that creates a car, all actions are necessary for the result of the good creation. This makes Father, Son, and Spirit real entities as opposed to different modes or ways that one God works. Conversely, the cooperation of Father, Son, and Spirit in the one act of creation reveals their eternal oneness. So the writer of Genesis can rightly say, "In the beginning, *God* created the heavens and the earth." The rule of faith reveals that the meaning of "God" is Father, Son, and Spirit working in unison.

Precisely because creation is the intentional and free act of the good God, it is by nature a good creation in contrast to Gnostic claims. "God saw everything that He had made, and indeed, it was very good," concludes the original creation story (Gen 1:31). Thus, the sin and decay and death that currently mark creation are due neither to its nature nor to the nature of its creator

---

16 My translation.

17 Irenaeus uses the titles *Word* and *Wisdom* interchangeably with the more traditional titles *Son* and *Spirit*, respectively.

but to the humans who, being innocent but not yet perfect, disobey God like rebellious children (Gen 3).[18] Necessarily, then, salvation is not creation's destruction but its redemption or restoration. Moreover, this redemption happens not in a moment (Jesus's birth, death, or resurrection, for example) but is rather a process that begins immediately following Adam and Eve's sin. Indeed, God (defined as Father, Son, and Spirit) continues to be present throughout the first part of the economy. The Father calls the people back to himself, first through Noah and then through Abraham, the father of Israel. The Son acts as the agent of the Father's revelation—God's Word—seen most clearly when God is manifested to the people. Thus, the Word of God walked with Adam and Eve in the garden, "appeared to Abraham, revealing Himself through the Word, as through a ray of light" and to Moses on Mt. Sinai, among other examples (*Dem* 12, 24, *AH* 4.20.9).[19] The Spirit acts as the agent of prophecy—God's Wisdom—seen most clearly when God's message is proclaimed to the people. Thus, the law is "written with the 'finger of God' (Exodus 31:18) and the 'finger of God' is the Holy Spirit," and the Holy Spirit continues to speak, first through the prophets and then in the writing of the Scriptures (*Dem* 26, 7, *AH* 4.33.7). The same cooperative work of Father, Son, and Spirit witnessed in creating continues throughout all divine acts of the economy. "Thus, then, God was manifested," Irenaeus writes, "for through all these things God the Father is shown forth, as the Spirit works and the Son administers and the Father approves, and man is made perfect for his salvation" (*AH* 4.20.6).

This means, of course, that God—Father, Son, and Spirit—works in the same way today, and if we think about the God we commune with through this theological lens, we can sense this Triune manner of working. Take the common Christian practice of the Eucharist, which most Christians partake in regularly. The gifts of bread and wine that come from the Father are changed (spiritually or literally depending on one's tradition) into the body

---

18 The commonly held notion that Adam and Eve were perfect comes in the fourth century with the enormously influential writer Augustine. Irenaeus's view of Adam and Eve as innocent (that is, without sin) but not perfect makes more sense of their succumbing so easily to the serpent's temptation.

19 Anyone familiar with the writings of Luke or Peter or Paul ought to recognize this approach. For Luke, Jesus was Isaiah's suffering servant (Acts 8:30–35); for Peter, the Psalmist's rejected cornerstone (1 Pet 2:4–7); and for Paul, perhaps most boldly, the rock in the desert that provided the Israelites water (1 Cor 10:4).

and blood of the Son by the power of the Holy Spirit. When we consume the Son's flesh and blood (again, spiritually or literally), we are thereby connected to and transformed by all three persons. Or consider the discipline of prayer. Our prayers can be addressed to God or to any of the divine persons. Many in my tradition, for example, pray to Jesus. Yet because of the cooperative work of Father, Son, and Spirit, in praying to one person, we are connected to and communing with all three. We are praying, in other words, to God. In one traditional formulation, the answers to our prayers find their source in the Father, carried through the revelation and mediation of the Son, in the power of the Spirit. It is a beautiful mystery that we will never fully grasp; however, the Scriptures, when read through the rule of faith, can bring us more deeply into its reality.

For Irenaeus, then, the work of God as revealed in Jesus in the Christian Scriptures is, contrary to Marcion's claims, not a new beginning but a continuation of the same divine work begun at creation and worked in Israel. "The Word [who] became flesh," John's Gospel tells us, was "in the beginning with God" (John 1:14, 2). Or in the words of the book of Hebrews, "In the past God spoke to our ancestors through the prophets at many times and in various ways, but in these last days he has spoken to us by his Son, whom he appointed heir of all things, and through whom also he made the universe" (Heb 1:1–2 NIV). The new covenant Jesus brings, in other words, is not "new" in the sense of being completely unknown but is rather the culmination of the covenants God had already made with the people. He writes, "One and the same householder produced both covenants, the Word of God, our Lord Jesus Christ, who spoke with both Abraham and Moses, and who has restored us anew to liberty, and has multiplied that grace which is from himself" (*AH* 4.9.1). As Jesus himself once said, "Do not think that I have come to abolish the law or the prophets; I have not come to abolish but to fulfill" (Matt 5:17).

While the Son as God is present in every act of the economy, the Son as human enters the economy at a specific point in time. As Irenaeus says in his long rendition of the rule of faith quoted above, "The Word of God . . . *became* a man amongst men, visible and palpable" (*Dem* 6, italics added). This passage echoes the Gospel of John's teaching that the Word, who "was in the beginning with God . . . *became* flesh and dwelt among us" (John 1:2, 14, italics added). This means that, though God begins the work of salvation immediately after humanity turns from him in the garden, the Word made flesh is the new and decisive act in the process. Put differently, the newness of the new covenant is found in the incarnation:[20] "No one has ever seen God. It is God the only Son, who is close to the Father's heart, who has made him known" (John 1:18). Or in the words of Paul, "For it is the God who said, 'Let light shine out of darkness,' who has shone in our hearts to give the light of the knowledge of the glory of God in the face of Jesus Christ" (2 Cor 4:6). So it was, Irenaeus notes, that Moses, who was only permitted to see the back of God's glory on Mt. Sinai (Exod 33:8–10), gazed upon the glory in the face of Jesus on the mountain of transfiguration (Matt 17:1–8).

Irenaeus's insistence that creation is originally good as the purposeful product of the good God means the incarnation is not a fiction. God does not need to be kept from comingling with flesh, as the Gnostics believed, because flesh (along with all material creation) is not inherently evil. Fallen, yes, but not inherently evil and therefore not irredeemable. Indeed, in this decisive act of salvation, God uses material creation in its original created goodness (the incarnate Word) to restore material creation in its fallen state back to its original goodness. Fans of C. S. Lewis's *The Chronicles of Narnia* might think here of how the God figure Aslan the lion sends the boy Digory on a quest to save Narnia from the evil witch he brought there. He says, "And as Adam's race has done the harm, Adam's race shall help to heal it."[21] Irenaeus explains this same surprising reality more technically through the theory for which he is best known, recapitulation (a fancy word meaning "to sum up").

To say that Jesus sums up the story of Scripture means not only that this story points to and finds its conclusion in him (as we have seen from the rule of faith) but more specifically that, in his human life, Jesus *lives again* this same story, even down to certain similar plot points. Thus, when the Word becomes flesh, his birth mirrors that of the first man's: "And as the first-fashioned Adam received his substance from earth uncultivated and still virgin . . . thus the Word, recapitulating Adam in himself, from Mary still virgin rightly received the generation that is the recapitulation of Adam" (*AH* 3.21.10).[22] Like Adam, and all other humans, Jesus lives a full human life differing from Adam's in only one way: He never sins (see Heb 4:15). Indeed,

---

20 Irenaeus is elsewhere clear that the appearances of the Son in the Jewish Scriptures (to Adam and Abraham and Moses, etc.) are not incarnate appearances.

21 C. S. Lewis, *The Magician's Nephew*, Book Six of *The Chronicles of Narnia* (New York: Collier Books, 1955), 136.

22 This is one of the earliest and most comprehensive scriptural arguments in support of the centrality of Mary's virginity to the story of salvation (earlier writers like the author of the Gospel of Matthew and Justin had focused on it as a fulfillment of prophecy).

for Irenaeus, this is the theological payoff of the theory of recapitulation. It is a course correction, for, as Irenaeus writes, "What has been tied cannot be loosed unless one reverses the ties of the knot so that the first ties are undone by the second, and the second free the first" (*AH* 3.22.4). Accordingly, Jesus lives Adam's life again but remains faithful where Adam went astray and so allows humanity, who, following its first representative, Adam, had been moving away from God toward death, to follow its new representative, Jesus, toward God and the life for which they were created.

This crucial point is first made discursively by Paul, who writes, "Just as by the one man's disobedience the many were made sinners, so by the one man's obedience the many will be made righteous" (Rom 5:19). The Gospel writers likewise demonstrate the same course correction in narrative form. Thus, when Jesus is tempted in the wilderness by food, he resists and says to the tempter (as Adam *should* have said but did not), "One does not live by bread alone." When he is again tempted in the garden of Gethsemane to turn from the path God called him to, he remains faithful and says (as Adam *should* have said but did not), "Not my will but yours be done." Whereas Adam sought to be his own god, Jesus, in the words of the church's ancient hymn, "though [being] in the form of God, did not regard equality with God as something to be exploited, but emptied himself, taking the form of a slave, being born in human likeness. And being found in human form, he humbled himself and became obedient to the point of death—even death on a cross" (Phil 2:6–8).[23]

The cross, then, is not so much a sacrifice in his recapitulation theory as it is the necessary means by which Adam's unfaithful action is reversed. For the result of Adam's sin, the original knot as it were, is death.[24] To untie it, Jesus himself must experience it. Therefore, the narrative plot points between Adam's story and Jesus's story continue into Jesus's suffering and death. "And the transgression which occurred through the tree was undone by the obedience of the tree," Irenaeus writes, "so, by means of the obedience by which He obeyed unto death, hanging upon the tree, He undid the old disobedience occasioned by the tree" (*Dem* 33–34). This argument strikes

---

23 As we saw in the last chapter, Irenaeus also suggests that Mary recapitulated and so course-corrects Eve's poor decision by saying yes to the angel Gabriel to allow the Word of God to be born in her. Indeed, Irenaeus's elevation of Mary as central to salvation history is arguably the genesis of much of Marian piety and doctrine.

24 Although in certain contexts, Irenaeus also uses traditional sacrificial language to explain the cross. Like the Scripture writers, he is fond of piling up metaphors.

directly at the heart of Gnosticism by showing, from Scripture, the necessity of God's truly becoming human. Moreover, his argument destroys the Gnostic teaching on human bodies as inherently flawed. For it turns out it is Jesus in his perfection, not Adam in his sinful nature, who is the true image of God. This means that Jesus was not only fully human; he was in fact the only true human who ever existed.[25]

Jesus in his true humanity, therefore, is humanity's representative. In uniting his divinity to humanity in the person of Christ, Jesus reunites all humanity to God. He writes, "We could not receive imperishability and immortality unless we had been united with imperishability and immortality. And how could we have been united with imperishability and immortality unless imperishability and immortality had first been made what we are, so that what was perishable might be absorbed by imperishability and what was mortal by immortality" (AH 3.19.1). Likewise, Christ abolishes the barrier of death, not just for himself but also for all humanity, in his physical resurrection. Irenaeus writes that Christ raises "in Himself fallen man, raising [him] above to the highest heaven, to the right hand of the glory of the Father" (Dem 37). Jesus's resurrection, then, is the first fruits of a general resurrection wherein all who are found in him are raised to life in conjunction with the restoration of God's good creation: "Then [his disciples] will take back their bodies and rise perfect, that is, bodily, as also the Lord rose, and thus will come to the vision of God" (AH 5.33.3).

Thus, Irenaeus understood what the Gnostics, not to mention many twenty-first-century Christians, did not understood. Irenaeus understood that if creation was originally made good by God, then its salvation, and that of human beings along with it, cannot be its destruction or elevation to some ethereal, spiritual plain (the popular view of heaven).[26] Rather, salvation comes in resurrection and restoration of creation and humanity to the original, *material and bodily*, existence. The story comes full circle; as Irenaeus puts it, "The Word of God, Jesus Christ our Lord . . . because of his immeasurable love became what we are in order to make us what he is" (AH 5.Pref).

---

25 For a more detailed and scholarly account of recapitulation in Irenaeus's writings, see Eric Osborn, *Irenaeus of Lyons* (Cambridge: Cambridge University Press, 2001), chapters 5 and 6.

26 Christians who recite the creed profess this belief when they say, "I believe in the resurrection of the body and the life everlasting." Though I suspect that many Christians wrongly assume this line is referring to Jesus.

This sentence may be as good of a justification for the reality of living saints as would ever be penned. And Irenaeus's faithful reading of Scripture as a redemptive story, passed on to all other generations of Christians, provides one of the key means by which we can become like God.

Because of his forceful arguments against his opponents, however, Irenaeus might himself not seem saintly. Some have taken him more as an overzealous gatekeeper, anxious to point out other people's errors, a sort of patron saint for angry Christians who spend their days arguing on Twitter. The reality, however, is quite different. Indeed, he was much less interested in people agreeing with every minor point of doctrine than with people living in the harmony and love of the diverse body of Christ.[27] While aspects of his work indicate this generous perspective (he was critical of the elitism of the Gnostics, for example, and argued that the uneducated masses can grasp the rule of faith as well as any church leader or bishop), his heart in this matter shines through clearest in an incident recorded by the church historian Eusebius.

In the first several centuries, Christians did not celebrate Easter on the same date.[28] Churches in Asia Minor celebrated Easter on the traditional date of the Jewish Passover, regardless of when it occurred during the week, whereas churches in other parts of the Roman Empire always celebrated it on a Sunday. Around 195, the bishop of Rome, Victor, intended to make all churches celebrate Easter on a Sunday, in accordance with the practice of the Church in Rome. Although Irenaeus's churches in Gaul also celebrated Easter on Sunday, he was familiar with the alternate practice of Asia Minor churches because he grew up in Smyrna. Instead of arguing for uniformity with his practice, as one might assume from his arguments we have seen so far, Irenaeus disagreed with this move, recognizing the ancient provenance of the Asia Minor practice and fearing that it would cause unnecessary division. He wrote a letter to Victor urging him to allow the Asia Minor churches to follow their ancient custom even though it was at odds with *his own practice*.[29] As this episode clearly demonstrates, Irenaeus was not concerned with uniformity for its own sake, much less that everyone believe or practice the

---

27 The name *Irenaeus* means "peacemaker" (from which we get our word *irenic*). Eusebius, *Church History*, 5.24.18.

28 Today, Orthodox Christians often celebrate Easter on a different date from Christians in Catholic and Protestant traditions, though the reasons for this are different from those in Irenaeus's time.

29 Eusebius, *Church History*, 5.23.3–4, 24.11–18.

faith as he did out of some ecclesiastical power trip. Rather, he recognized that there were certain differences of practices and beliefs that could be sustained without breaking Christian unity.

One might ask why he did not take the same irenic approach with Marcion and the Gnostics. The answer is that the differences Irenaeus had with these communities struck at the very integrity of the scriptural story and the nature of God. Irenaeus rightly recognized that there could be no unity with such groups because they worshipped fundamentally different gods and preached fundamentally different gospels. Moreover, he worried that these groups' use of Scripture and claims to the name *Christian* were adulterating the true gospel for future generations, as evidenced by the numbers of Christians in his time who were joining their ranks. Therefore, as much as he valued Christian unity and peace, he was compelled to pick up his pen in these particular cases to patiently expose the errant beliefs of some and thoroughly expound the true nature of God, his saving purposes, and the scriptural story that reveals him.

Such keen discernment is desperately needed today. For ours is an age of great theological disagreement and division, particularly in Protestant Christianity. Some churches meet such disagreements by demanding total uniformity of belief and practice and, as a result, become so narrow as to not reach anyone or to never enjoy the gift that is universal Christian unity. Other churches issue empty calls of unity no matter the nature of the disagreement and, as a result, become so broad as to be unclear of what, if anything, they actually believe. Irenaeus shows a better, more nuanced approach, one that can produce a more unified and faithful Christian communion. May we, like him, seek peace and unity among our churches when the nature of our differences can be respected. But may we also, like him, have the courage and patience and faith to speak up and make an argument when the core beliefs of the faith—Trinity, incarnation, resurrection—are challenged. And may Irenaeus walk with us in helping us to discern the difference. For, not surprisingly, the core beliefs we ought to defend even at the great sacrifice of unity are the same ones Irenaeus identified and worked so diligently and faithfully to defend in his day. The proof of his success in this effort is that, eighteen hundred years later, we read the story of Scripture in essentially the same way as he did. It's the greatest story ever told, and thanks in no small part to Irenaeus, we can still tell it today.

CHAPTER THREE

Perpetua's Confession

From then on we no longer placed any hope in this world.

—Perpetua of Carthage, *The Passion of Perpetua and Felicity* 4.

The story of our third saint, Perpetua, a young laywoman from Carthage, Africa, occurs in roughly the same period as that of Irenaeus. Nevertheless, the challenge she faced, through which she becomes a living saint for us today, is quite different. Whereas Irenaeus defended the faith from internal pressures with his words, Perpetua defended the faith from external pressures with her life. For Perpetua was a martyr, a person who was killed because of her faith.

The experience of persecution and martyrdom in Christianity, though foreign to many Christians today, begins, according to the book of Acts, almost immediately after the birth of the Church at Pentecost with the imprisonment and attempted silencing of the apostles and, a short time later, the public stoning of a man named Stephen.[1] The apostle Paul himself notes that, prior to his vision of the risen Christ and subsequent embrace of the gospel, he actively persecuted the Church in his role as a Pharisee.[2] Although Jews were the initial

---

1 See Acts 4 for the account of Peter and John's arrest and trial, mirroring Jesus's trial, before the Sanhedrin and Acts 6–7 for the account of Stephen's witness and martyrdom. According to Acts 12:2, Herod Agrippa had James, the brother of John, killed in these early years. Later in the same chapter, Peter is again imprisoned and likewise Paul in Acts 16 and the final chapters of Acts.

2 Galatians 1:13–14 and Philippians 1:4–6. These firsthand accounts are corroborated by Luke, a later companion and intimate of Paul, in Acts 7:58–8:3, 9:1–2 as well as his reports of Paul's sermons in later chapters.

agents of this persecution, the Romans quickly emerged as the most fearsome adversary to the Church.[3] The Roman historian Tacitus, for example, reports a horrific episode of persecution initiated by the emperor Nero in the mid-60s, which likely claimed the lives of Peter and Paul.[4] Although we should not think of Christians in these early years as living in constant fear and always meeting in secret—they, in fact, lived and met in the open for much of this period—the frequency of episodic outbreaks of persecution suggests that the fate of martyrdom was a real possibility for anyone who embraced the Christian faith.[5] Dietrich Bonhoeffer, a twentieth-century German theologian, famously wrote, "When Christ calls a man, he bids him come and die."[6] For early Christians, as well as for current Christians in many parts of the world, this sentiment is literal.

The reasons for these early persecutions vary. The initial Jewish persecution continues the antagonism between Jesus and the Jewish establishment, which brings to mind Jesus's remark to his disciples on the night he was betrayed, "If they persecuted me, they will persecute you" (John 15:20). Aside from Nero, who targeted Christians as a convenient scapegoat for the fire in Rome that he started, Roman persecution was due to the Christian refusal to worship pagan gods and goddesses, including the Roman Emperor himself. The Romans believed that their power was due to the favor of these deities,

---

3 The Jews by the mid-first century had their own problems with Rome. Decades of seditious actions by some Jewish factions led to war in the year 66. In the climactic events of that four-year war, the Romans marched into Jerusalem and destroyed the second temple, effectively ending the Judaism represented by the Old Testament (centered on the Temple and sacrifices). The Judaism that exists today descends from Rabbinic Judaism, which developed in the wake of the Temple's destruction and is centered on the Torah.

4 Although Scripture is silent on this episode, it does testify to persecution at the hands of the Romans as well. In the later chapters of Acts, for example, Paul is imprisoned by the Romans. In Acts 19, Roman citizens in Ephesus attempt to kill Christians. Additionally, the author of Revelation refers in his address to the church in Smyrna, which, at least a generation prior to Polycarp's leadership, experienced the martyrdom of a certain Antipas (Rev 2:13).

5 In telling the story of Irenaeus, we have already encountered several martyrs including Polycarp, Justin ("Martyr" is not just his last name), and Blandina and the other saints in Lyons. Tradition holds that all but one of the original apostles (including James, the brother of Jesus, and Paul) were martyred. Only John escapes this fate, although if he is the same John who records the vision of Revelation, he was at some point exiled on the island of Patmos.

6 Dietrich Bonhoeffer, *The Cost of Discipleship*, trans. R. H. Fuller (London: SCM Press Ltd.: 1959), 89.

and therefore pagan worship was a civic duty akin to voting in present-day democracies.[7] Moreover, since worshipping pagan deities involved paying temple taxes and purchasing idols for private use in the home, the neglect of this duty carried economic ramifications as well, as was already anticipated by the Acts 19 account of Ephesian persecution.[8] Official edicts issued in the later widespread persecutions, under Emperor Decius (249), Emperor Valerian (255), and Emperor Diocletian (303–311), all cite the restoration of the glories of ancient Rome as the reason for targeting the Christians.[9]

Christians found meaning in their experience of persecution and martyrdom by connecting it to discipleship. Jesus modeled the perfect life of faithfulness and was killed on the cross, so Christians who strive to follow his example should expect nothing else. Thus, to die because of your faith came to be seen as the ultimate act of discipleship, for it meant you were conforming to Christ not only in life but also in death. "Let me be food for the wild beasts," wrote the early-second-century martyr Ignatius of Antioch to the Roman Christians who were plotting to free him, "then I shall truly be a disciple of Jesus Christ . . . Allow me to be an imitator of the suffering of my God."[10] Although pursuing martyrdom was discouraged, if one was accused of being a Christian under threat of persecution or even death, the only faithful response was to confess. As Polycarp said when asked to recant his faith under punishment of death, "For eighty-six years I have been his servant, and he has done me no wrong. How can I blaspheme my King who saved me?"[11]

---

7 Around the year 112, the Roman magistrate Pliny the Younger wrote Emperor Trajan of his policy in dealing with the civil disobedience of Christians in his district. As he reports, he made Christians publicly sacrifice to pagan deities and curse Christ under punishment of execution. In his response, Trajan affirms the practice, adding only that Christians should not be sought out. Nevertheless, from these letters, it is clear that in the eyes of Trajan simply being a Christian was a crime punishable by death. For these primary sources, see John W. Coakley and Andrea Sterk, eds., *Readings in World Christian History, Volume 1: Earliest Christianity to 1453* (Maryknoll, NY: Orbis Books, 2004), 23.

8 According to Luke, Christian conversions in Ephesus had so disrupted the silversmith trade built up around the Temple of Artemis that the silversmiths organized a mob against the Christians, though a town clerk intervened.

9 The persecution under Diocletian was the longest and most brutal period of persecution and is referred to by historians as the Great Persecution.

10 Ignatius, *Epistle to the Romans* 4 and 6 in *The Apostolic Fathers*, trans. Michael W. Holmes (Grand Rapids, MI: Baker Books, 1999), 171, 173.

11 *Martyrdom of Polycarp* 9 in Holmes, *Apostolic Fathers*, 235.

Stories of faithful martyrs, like *Martyrdom of Polycarp* and *Martyrs of Lyons*, were widely read among early Christians for their ability to encourage faithfulness in the face of the same challenge and, more generally, to inspire a deeper life of discipleship among all Christians. The martyrs were the proto-saints of the Christian tradition, heroes who pointed other Christians to Christ through their Christlike actions.[12] However, these strange heroes were not the standard young, strong men who were common to Greek and Roman stories and society. Rather, they were those who were on the margins of Roman society, namely, youths, elderly people, slaves, and women. Such is the case with Perpetua.

She is known only through the account of her martyrdom,[13] likely written by an eyewitness, which comes down to us as part of a composite document that includes Perpetua's firsthand account of her experiences in prison written in the days preceding her death, the earliest writing in existence from the hand of a Christian woman.[14] Perpetua was born in Carthage, North Africa, around the year 180, into a noble Roman family. According to the brief introduction to the document written by the eyewitness, she was "a woman nobly born, educated in the liberal arts, and respectably married" (*PPF* 2). As Perpetua's own account reveals, hers was a close-knit family, which included parents and two brothers, although one had passed away prior to these events (the

---

12 Christians would often meet together at the gravesite of martyrs on the anniversaries of their deaths to remember their faithful examples. This early practice anticipated feast days in the Church's liturgical calendar that remember saints on the traditional day of their death. Wilken, *The First Thousand Years*, chapter 5. We will address these early burial spots, called *catacombs*, in the context of Christian art in chapter 6.

13 Later Christian writers, such as the third-century writer Tertullian and the fourth-century bishop Augustine, both of North Africa, refer to Perpetua as a model of discipleship, though it appears they, too, know of her only through the document.

14 The document also includes the personal reflections of another imprisoned Christian named Saturus, although Perpetua's account is much longer, and she remains the central figure of the story, as indicated by the traditional title of the document, *The Passion of Perpetua and Felicity*. Felicity is another of the arrested Christians, a slave, according to the editor, who becomes attached to Perpetua and, as we shall see, is her companion in martyrdom. We learn later in the account that Felicity is pregnant and gives birth while in prison. As a slave and a woman, Felicity also serves to highlight the heroic roles of the marginalized in Christian communities. However, for purposes of space, I will not dwell long on Felicity herself. In quotations of the work, I will use the accessible translation by Bryan M. Liftin, *Early Christian Martyr Stories: An Evangelical Introduction with New Translations* (Grand Rapids, MI: Baker Academic, 2014). Citations will be marked in the text as *PPF*.

living brother was with her in prison). Significantly, she had a close and loving relationship with her father, who, she reports, counted her as the favorite of his three children, a rather uncommon reality in a society centered on male heirs (*PPF* 5). He took a particular interest in raising her. Since professional tutors were reserved for sons, for example, he likely tutored her himself.[15] And he certainly was responsible for arranging her "respectable" marriage, a descriptor indicative of a union of high standing and prominence in the community. Perpetua's account also demonstrates her own genuine love and affection for her father. Her journal recounts near-constant thoughts of her father after her imprisonment, while her mother and husband receive no mention from her. For example, she writes that her "father's suffering hurt me as if I myself had been beaten" and that seeing his misery at her imprisonment "broke my heart" (*PPF* 6). Finally, the editor notes that Perpetua is a mother herself, having given birth to a son shortly before the events he recounts. As we shall see, concern for her infant son is the other great occupier of her thoughts in her final days. She is not only a loving daughter but also a devoted mother. By Roman standards, Perpetua has everything she needs—a wealthy and loving family, a respectable marriage, and a healthy son—to live a perfectly contented life.

At some point, however, Perpetua learns of the Christian faith. Unfortunately, the eyewitness does not include this fascinating and surprising detail in her story. As a noble woman with an education, she surely would have consumed the general Roman view of the nascent Christian faith as an unlearned superstition.[16] What changed her mind? Perhaps she had an occasion to hear some traveling preacher speak of the life-changing realities of the gospel, similar to the content we read in Paul's letters. Perhaps she became familiar with the Christian community in Carthage and was drawn to the evident love they shared or the acts of service they performed of the kind witnessed in Acts. Whatever the case, she embraced the faith, and at just twenty-two years of age, she is a catechumen on her way to baptism when she is arrested.[17]

---

15 So speculates Joyce Salisbury in her helpful work *Perpetua's Passion: The Death and Memory of a Young Roman Woman* (New York: Routledge, 1997), 8.

16 As Roman historians such as Tacitus or Pagan philosophers such as Celsus were fond of describing it.

17 In these early years, people who were drawn to the Christian faith first underwent a formal process of catechesis, or instruction, prior to baptism, which could take as long as three years. The reasons for this process, as Perpetua's story indirectly demonstrates, is that it takes time and deliberate instruction to understand how radically different the

From Perpetua's account, which begins when she is under house arrest, we learn that her father was perplexed by her decision to become a Christian. Who wouldn't be, given the circumstances? He was likely concerned when his only daughter first turned to this superstition and left behind their pagan religious traditions. Now her faith had landed her in prison, facing possible death. Perpetua reports his persistent attempts to persuade her to renounce her faith so that she could be freed to return to her former, noble life as a mother, a wife, and his daughter. But she does not renounce it. She reports one attempt to explain her resolve to him: "'Father,' I said, 'let me give you an example. Do you see this vessel lying here, this little pitcher or whatever?' 'Yes, I see it,' he replied. 'Could you call it by another name than what it really is?' 'No.' 'It's the same with me. I can't be called anything other than what I am: a Christian'" (*PPF* 3). Though this passage gives no insight into Perpetua's understanding of what a Christian actually is, it reveals a great deal about her conviction. She has so fully embraced this new faith that to renounce it would mean to become something she is not. For she understands that Christianity's claim on her has changed her identity, as opposed to being something she can add to her other identities as Roman daughter, wife, and mother. She writes that in response to this statement, her father "lunged at me like he was going to tear out my eyes" (*PPF* 3). He understands neither her faith nor her obstinacy.

It's hard for twenty-first-century Christians, for whom teenage rebellion has become a rite of passage of sorts, to fully appreciate the magnitude of this scene. In Greco-Roman society, noble daughters did not disobey their fathers. In the words of Lynn Cohick and Amy Brown Hughes, "The Roman familial system regarded the highest form of piety as that which honored the paterfamilias, the father of the family. A son or daughter's greatest responsibility lay with supporting their parents, especially the father."[18] Indeed, her father plays on her sense of duty as his daughter. After Perpetua is transferred to the local prison, he visits her, and Perpetua records his words: "Have pity on my gray hairs, daughter . . . Have pity on your father—if I am worthy to be called your father! With my own hands I tended you like a blossoming

---

Christian way of life is from that of the surrounding cultures. Perpetua is baptized while she is in prison.

18 Lynn Cohick and Amy Brown Hughes, *Christian Women in the Patristic World: Their Influence, Authority, and Legacy in the Second through Fifth Centuries* (Grand Rapids, MI: Baker Academic, 2017), 46.

flower. I favored you over both your brothers. So don't cast me aside now to be scorned by men" (*PPF* 5). His direct address of her as *daughter* intends to call to her mind her identity as his daughter and thus her duty to obey him; his reference to his old age and threat of being scorned plays on her sense of obligation to care for him as he had cared for her from when she was a young girl. This is the ancient Roman version of a guilt trip, only he stands on a stronger authority than his own hurt feelings or his daughter's pity. He stands on the authority of a society that found its very coherence and order in following the duties and obligations of one's role as part of a household.[19]

During this second visit, her father tries a different, though related, approach to persuade her to recant her faith: "Think of . . . your son! He won't be able to live without you" (*PPF* 5). A shrewd move! For just as her identity as a noble Roman daughter carried with it the duty of obeying and caring for her father, so, too, does her identity as a mother carry in that society the duty of caring for, raising, and passing on the noble Roman traditions to

---

19 The modeling of society on the order of a household, and the corresponding dependence of the former's harmony on the latter's order, goes back at least to Aristotle's *Politics*, where he developed "household codes" that spelled out the obligations between relationships, notably those of wives and husbands, children and parents, slaves and masters. Readers of the New Testament ought to be familiar with this convention as versions of the household codes appear in many places, most notably, Ephesians: "Wives, submit yourselves to your own husbands as you do to the Lord . . . Husbands, love your wives, just as Christ loved the church and gave himself up for her . . . Children, obey your parents in the Lord, for this is right . . . Fathers, do not exasperate your children; instead, bring them up in the training and instruction of the Lord . . . Slaves, obey your earthly masters with respect and fear, and with sincerity of heart, just as you would obey Christ . . . And masters, treat your slaves in the same way" (Eph 5:22, 25; 6:1, 4–5, 9 NIV). Nevertheless, these household codes have undergone a significant shift in the Christian community. Although Aristotle's codes emphasized the subordination of the first category of people (wives, children, slaves) to the second category (husbands, parents, masters), the writer of Ephesians subverts this understanding by commanding mutual submission of the partners in what is the first line of the code: "Submit to one another out of reverence for Christ" (Eph 5:21 NIV). Indeed, the specific command "to submit" is actually missing from verse 22, which, as Markus Barth argues, means that "the subordination of wives is an example of the same mutual subordination which is also shown by the husband's love, the children's obedience, the parents' responsibility of their offspring, the slaves' and masters' attitudes toward one another." Markus Barth, *Ephesians 4–6*, Anchor Bible Commentary, vol. 34A (Garden City, NY: Doubleday and Company Inc., 1960), 610. Incidentally, the subversion of this text is lost in many English translations, where v. 21 is separated from v. 22 by a subheading. While Ephesians 5's subversion of the traditional understanding of these relationships is notable, an even more radical subversion of these common cultural structures is at play in Perpetua's story.

her children. Perpetua scholar Thomas J. Heffernan notes, for example, that Roman women were required to bear and raise children "as part of their duty to the maintenance of the state, and they were celebrated for having done so."[20] Perpetua's steadfastness in regard to the abandonment of her son, then, was not only poor form but also illegal in Roman eyes. And given that her father is old and that her husband is never mentioned in the narrative, the remark that her son will not be able to live without her is not hyperbole. After all, the infant is still nursing. Perpetua, however, once again remains faithful, and her father leaves the prison defeated. Later, he shows up yet again at her public trial, the moment she is presented with the public choice to recant the faith and make the sacrifice or refuse and face death. Amid the likely raucous crowd, he appears, holding up her son. "Perform the sacrifice!" he yells. "Have pity on your baby!" (*PPF* 5).

While we might not appreciate the difficulty that came with disobeying her father, we can certainly recognize Perpetua's struggle when it came to her son. Our societies still recognize the obligations parents have to raise and care for their children such that our laws prosecute those who abandon children. Even more, those who have children know well the primal instincts involved in caring for and protecting our children. Perpetua has told us with her own hand that she has these instincts. When she had first been thrown into prison, for example, she describes the deplorable conditions of the "dungeon," including heat, suffocating darkness, and overcrowding, yet in all that time, she thought not of herself but her infant, who was not with her: "I was tortured by worry for my baby the whole time I was there" (*PPF* 3). When she is reunited with him during her imprisonment in order to nurse him, she writes, "All of a sudden the prison became like a palace to me. I wanted to be there more than anywhere else" (*PPF* 3). Here is a woman who loves her baby more than anything, who, beyond simply knowing her duties as a Roman mother, has evidently found great meaning in that identity. And now she sees him in her father's hands. He is probably crying amid the commotion of the crowd or out of hunger for milk that only she can provide. Perhaps Perpetua even experiences physical pain in her breasts as she had not nursed him for some time.[21] All she has to do is make the sacrifice, and she can return to her

---

20 Heffernan, *The Passion of Perpetua and Felicity* (Oxford: Oxford University Press, 2012), 30. He cites two such laws, *Lex Iulia* in 18 BCE and *Lex Poppaea* in 18 CE.

21 Later in her journal, Perpetua reports that God delivered her of this pain, known now as *mastitis*, though it is unclear if she had experienced it in this moment of her public

former life. Perhaps we think that's what she should do. Perhaps that's what we would do. Incredibly, at this climactic moment, Perpetua does not waiver. Even when the Roman governor Hilarian joins with her father in the pressure by calling on the same societal norms, saying, "Spare your gray-haired father! Spare your infant son. Just make a sacrifice for the emperor's well-being," she stands firm (*PPF* 6). In her words, "I replied, 'I won't!' 'Are you a Christian?' Hilarion asked. 'I am a Christian,' I declared" (*PPF* 6).[22]

Perpetua's faithfulness even in the face of death comes from her understanding of her new identity, what the book of Ephesians describes as the new nature given at baptism (Eph 4:21–24). Or as Paul says elsewhere, "Anyone who belongs to Christ has become a new person. The old life is gone; a new life has begun!" (2 Cor 5:17 NLT). Her faithfulness comes from her understanding that this new identity supersedes her Roman identity of daughter, wife, and mother and all the duties and expectations that went along with it. Because her situation is such that she cannot be both a Christian and a Roman, she chooses to be who she has become in baptism, the woman God created and called her to be. As Salisbury aptly notes, "The moment Perpetua identified herself as a Christian, she no longer belonged to Rome."[23]

Thankfully, we live in a time when our identities as sons and daughters, husbands and wives, fathers and mothers do not necessarily conflict with our identities as Christians.[24] Nevertheless, we still face the temptation to embrace competing identities that can blunt our Christian one. For example, the identities that come with our careers can conflict with our Christian identity, not only in demands to engage in immoral behavior but more commonly in the ways we understand ourselves and spend our time. In other words, many Christians today find their meaning and identity in their careers. Alternatively, the conflict may come from our nationalities. For example, a still-dominant assumption in the United States, at least from the part of the country where I live, is the synonymous meaning of the terms *American* and *Christian*. Yet the stories Americans tell ourselves in our histories, our political discussions, and our pageantry (think the Fourth of July) would cause us

---

trial or was simply concerned that she would due to the interruption of her breastfeeding (*PPF* 6).

22 The description of this trial accurately reflects Pliny's approach to Christians related above.

23 Salisbury, *Perpetua's Passion*, 91.

24 Although, as I mentioned above, this is not the case in all parts of the world.

to see those who live beyond our human-drawn borders as somehow other than us (even when those "others" are fellow Christians). In extreme cases, our nationalistic identities compel us to fight as Americans or Germans or whoever we are when our Christian identity tells us not only to love and pray for our enemies but also that Christians of a different nationality are closer brothers and sisters than our fellow citizens.

The choice of conflicting identities, however, rarely confronts us with such clarity. Most of us will never be faced with the life-or-death situation facing Perpetua. Rather, we are asked in a million small ways, every day of our lives, to choose whether we are a Christian or not. We often don't recognize these moments because we have domesticized our Christian identities by seeing them as compatible with the other identities we adopt, though, in most cases, they are not. Perpetua shows us a better way, not because she did not value or find meaning in her identity as a Roman daughter, wife, and mother but *in spite* of those values. This is what makes her choice a sacrifice and why sacrifice lies at the heart of what it means to be Christian. "'If any want to become my followers,' Jesus said, 'let them deny themselves and take up their cross daily and follow me'" (Luke 9:23).

Despite its brevity, her journal and the eyewitness's account of her martyrdom offer glimpses into her understanding, and that of the imprisoned Christian community, of the nature of the Christian identity she embraced. In the first place, it is clear she is recognized in the Christian community not as a daughter, wife, and mother but rather as a woman saved by the same grace. This is evident from the interaction she has with a fellow Christian after her imprisonment. In contrast to her father's emphasis on her roles as daughter and mother in his various addresses to her, this unnamed disciple addresses her as *domina soror*, or "Honorable sister, you are now greatly privileged" (*PPF* 4). Heffernan remarks that *domina soror* is a "term of formal courtesy and used to acknowledge her exalted status in this small, beleaguered community."[25] Accordingly, she is not asked to play the culturally defined roles in this new community; rather, though she is a female, young, and relatively new to the faith, Perpetua emerges as the leader of this small imprisoned band. For example, in a manner reminiscent of stories of Paul in Acts, Perpetua at one point convinces their guard to feed the imprisoned Christians better,

---

25 Heffernan, *Passion of Perpetua and Felicity*, 170.

which, surprisingly, he does (*PPF* 16). At another point, the guards let more people visit the prisoners because, in her words, "he recognized the spiritual power at work in us" (*PPF* 9). On the day of their martyrdom, which we will return to in greater detail shortly, the Roman authorities prepared to force the Christians to dress like priests and priestesses of pagan gods for extra humiliation. Perpetua refuses to wear the garments. In response, the commander relents, thus sparing the Christians this humiliation (*PPF* 18). The editor even suggests that the man in charge of the prison became a Christian because of such bold actions; perhaps he is the first in a long list of people so changed by Perpetua's faithful witness (*PPF* 16). Finally, she asks for and receives a series of visions, all of which confirm that she and the others will remain faithful in their ordeal of martyrdom.[26]

In the Greco-Roman culture, Perpetua would have never performed such radical actions because in that culture women simply did not do such things. As we have seen, their place was in the home, being obedient to their fathers, then their husbands, and finally in raising their children. This clear contrast to how the Christians viewed Perpetua demonstrates that the early Christian community understood the gospel to give meaning to women *as women*, not just in the tasks they performed in their traditional roles as daughters, wives, and mothers. Put differently, in the Christian community, Perpetua is honored not for what she can *do* but for who she *is*: a daughter of God. This contrast is reminiscent of the story of Jesus's interactions with Mary and Martha in Luke 10. When Jesus visits their home, Martha immediately moves into task mode, preparing the meal in the kitchen and doing other things expected of women in both Greco-Roman and Jewish cultures. In contrast, Mary sits at Jesus's feet, a place normally reserved for male disciples of a rabbi, and listens to Jesus's teachings. When Martha complains because Mary is shirking her tasks, Jesus replies, "Martha, Martha, you are worried and distracted by many things; there is need of only one thing. Mary has chosen the better part" (Luke 10:41–42). Jesus here redefines for Martha what it means to be a

---

26 The unnamed disciple who addresses her as *domina soror* encourages her to ask for the visions, which she does. While the content of the visions is fascinating, an analysis of it goes beyond our purposes in this chapter. Readers who are interested in the visions should read Liftin's translation of the *Passion* as well as the helpful interpretations by Cohick and Hughes, *Christian Women in the Patristic World*, 38–46, and by Salisbury, *Perpetua's Passion*, 92–112.

woman; the community in Carthage has grasped this redefinition, for they treat Perpetua in the same manner.[27]

Likewise, the eyewitness frames his account to make this same point about the countercultural, egalitarian nature of the Church. For in his introduction, he quotes the words of Peter at Pentecost, itself a quotation of the prophecy of Joel regarding the signs of the restored kingdom: "In the last days, God says, I will pour out my Spirit on all people. Your sons and daughters will prophesy, your young men will see visions, your old men will dream dreams. Even on my servants, both men and women, I will pour out my Spirit in those days, and they will prophesy" (Acts 2:17–18 as quoted in *PPF* 2). The Church is the community in which all human distinctions of race, gender, class, and so forth, distinctions that have created such violence and suffering and dehumanization throughout history, are abolished.[28] In the words of Paul, "As many of you as were baptized into Christ have clothed yourselves with Christ. There is no longer Jew or Greek, there is no longer slave or free, there is no longer male and female; for all of you are one in Christ Jesus" (Gal 3:28).[29]

Importantly, Jesus's redefinition of what it means to be a woman does not negate the God-given vocation of being a parent, for this, too, can be who we *are*. Recall that *after* her embrace of her Christian identity, Perpetua does not simply abandon her child as if she had been enlightened to some definition of womanhood that rejected the task of mothering; rather, she continues to

---

27 Men are not immune to defining themselves by what they *do*. As noted above, they often find meaning in their jobs and tasks of providing. Jesus in this passage, and Perpetua in her story, also speaks to men to focus on the one thing necessary, namely, who we *are* in his eyes.

28 I will return to this aspect of the Church in the context of race in chapter 12.

29 Although through much of Christian history, these hierarchical distinctions have marked the Church to the same extent as the culture, the early Church grasped this ideal, particularly in its honoring of women. Indeed, despite an occasional verse commanding women's silence, it is clear that women's fingerprints are all over this movement from its earliest days. Women were among Jesus's closest disciples and were by some accounts the only disciples who stayed with Jesus until the very end. Women found the empty tomb, saw the risen Jesus first, and were entrusted by him to relate the central message of Christianity—"He is risen!"—to the other disciples. Paul's first European convert was a woman, while another woman was, with her husband, entrusted to continue Paul's apostolic work in other churches. Women carried important letters, read and interpreted them to the churches, organized charitable works, were acknowledged as official leaders (apostles) of the movement, and were martyred for their faith. In later centuries, the importance of women (not to mention the other outcasts in terms of Greco-Roman society) is clearest in the martyrdom literature and, as we shall see in chapter 5, monastic literature.

deeply love and care for her infant even while she becomes a leader among the Christians. Her two vocations do not conflict. The difference is that for Christians, unlike Romans, the value of women is not *reduced* to this task but a part of a greater whole of what it means to be a woman. This explains why, as we shall see in a later chapter, Christians endorsed singleness as an honorable and complete way of life.[30] Christ has tasks for all of us to do, but Perpetua shows us that our primary calling is to him.[31] "I am the vine, you are the branches," Jesus said. "Those who abide in me and I in them will bear much fruit, because apart from me you can *do* nothing" (John 15:5, italics added). Perpetua again demonstrates this truth to us by remaining with Jesus, even though it meant forsaking her beloved task of motherhood, even though it meant her death.

Continuing the countercultural aspects of this work, the eyewitness describes Perpetua and the other Christians' day of martyrdom as "the day of their victory" (*PPF* 18). As the Christians were led out into the Carthage amphitheater for the public spectacle, they were cheerful, feeling as though "they were marching to heaven" (*PPF* 18). Perpetua exudes an inexplicable calmness and a "radiant countenance," a possible allusion to the first Christian martyr, Stephen, who, while being stoned, turned his face toward heaven and saw the glory of God (Acts 7:57–60).[32] She even starts to sing a hymn, and "the intense expression in her eyes made all the onlookers avert their gaze" (*PPF* 18). The implication is that Jesus is with them, as he promised his disciples he always would be. They have the peace that surpasses all understanding (John 14:27; Phil 4:7).

It is at this point that the guards attempt to make the Christians dress like priests and priestesses of pagan gods, but Perpetua's intervention spares them this humiliation. Instead, at the crowd's instigation, they are whipped, and the Christians give thanks to God that they, as stated in Bryan Liftin's helpful commentary, "participated in what their Savior had experienced."[33] Perpetua and Felicity are then separated from the men to be victims of a cow, "done to mimic the women's sex," the Roman hierarchy of relationships maintained even in death (*PPF* 20). The women are stripped bare, and Felicity, who has

---

30 See chapter 5.

31 I am indebted to John L. Drury for this language.

32 The radiance of martyrs' faces in death occurs frequently in this literature and in monastic literature. We will encounter another example of this phenomenon in chapter 5.

33 Liftin, *Early Christian Martyr Stories*, 105n20.

just recently given birth, is dripping milk from her breasts. The horrified spectators gasp, leading the guard to cover them with loose tunics. The eyewitness's descriptions of these details, in keeping with the greater point he has been making about the countercultural nature of the Christian community, relentlessly press home the fact that these delicate women, as perceived by the Roman crowd, are the real heroes.

The women are then knocked down by the cow, and after getting to her feet, Perpetua extends a hand to help up Felicity. The two women then stand side by side, clutching each other. Like Blandina before her, Perpetua calls to the other Christians and those watching to encourage them: "'Stand firm in the faith,' she urged, 'and all of you must love one another! Don't let our martyrdom be a stumbling block to you!'" (*PPF* 20). Like Christ himself, she is at the very end thinking only of others. Perhaps she thought, too, of her father and of her son. Perhaps she, like Jesus, had conflict even in this moment. But she remembers her new identity in baptism, and this allows her to stay faithful to the end.

That end, at least of her earthly life, finally comes when a Roman stabs her with a sword. Though it caused her pain, it was not a mortal wound until "she herself guided the young and inexperienced gladiator's wavering hand to her throat. Perhaps we might say that such a great woman, who was feared by the demon within the executioner, couldn't be killed unless she herself allowed it" (*PPF* 21). For in the context in which she lived, this was the necessary outcome of her new identity in baptism. Perpetua died a martyr and, in the haunting words of the eyewitness, "a true wife of Christ, beloved of God" (*PPF* 18).

However, according to the peculiar economy of God, rooted in the reality of resurrection, Perpetua is not dead. Rather, she is living among the great cloud of witnesses, watching us and cheering us on. Though the challenges that we face, at least in the Western world, are quite different from her ordeal of martyrdom, the peril to faithful discipleship is comparable. Perpetua reminds us, whatever our nationalities, careers, or familial identities happen to be, that we are above all else Christians and that identity matters for how we live in this world. May we, in all circumstances, adopt Perpetua's confession, "I am a Christian." And may her prayers to God on our behalf birth this faithfulness within us.

CHAPTER FOUR

Origen's Mind

*The treasure of divine wisdom is concealed in vessels
of poor and humble words.*

—Origen of Alexandria, *On First Principles* IV.1.7

Of all the figures in this book, Origen of Alexandria is perhaps the least likely to be considered a saint. For one thing, neither the Catholic Church nor the Orthodox Church recognize him as such.[1] More to the point from a Protestant perspective, Origen is an intellectual figure—dare I say a

---

1 This point brings up a few frequently asked questions, namely, who decides who gets to be a saint, and what is the process of that decision? In the first millennium, the process of recognizing saints was informal and often done by popular acclaim. Around the turn of the first millennium, the Catholic Church developed a more formal process of recognizing saints. Succinctly put, it involves nomination and attestation of one's life by their bishop, followed by an official inquiry into the evidence by the Congregation for the Causes of Saints, with the pope making the final decision. Full sainthood requires two verified miracles. See the description put out by the US Conference of Catholic Bishops, https://www.usccb.org/offices/public-affairs/saints. The Orthodox Church continues to lack the kind of formal procedures that Catholics have adopted, and generally speaking, right belief is preferred to verified miracles. While both churches are more liberal with their use of the title *saint* for all those in heaven, the presence of such formal and informal processes of recognition certainly implies distinctions, at least for those who are lifted up for models of disciples, and Origen has not made the cut. Neither Catholics nor Orthodox recognize as saints the three Protestant figures discussed in chapters 9, 10, and 12 either. But Origen is different from these figures in that he lived in the period prior to the division of the Church into different bodies.

philosopher(!)—and in recent years, there has developed in certain strands of Protestantism a suspicion of intellectuals. Christianity, some Protestants loudly claim, is a religion of love, and love is an emotion of the heart. It was Paul, after all, who said that "the foolishness of God is wiser than human wisdom, and the weakness of God is stronger than human strength" (1 Cor 1:25).

The genesis of such attitudes can be found in certain Christian responses to the Enlightenment, that period of intellectual history spanning the seventeenth and eighteenth centuries that witnessed the elevation of the individual over authorities such as Church and monarchy as well as that of reason over faith.[2] The effects of this profound shift are felt to this day, notably in the privatization of religion or the division of space into the sacred and secular, a distinction that was not recognized before the Enlightenment. Some Christians have responded with a sort of circle-the-wagons attitude and rejected participation in realms that are perceived as secular for fear of the expected challenge to their faith. This response manifests itself in, for example, denominations who reject any kind of medical intervention in favor of faith in God's miraculous healing. And in Christians who reject scientific data on such topics as evolution or climate change for its perceived contradictions to biblical truth.[3] And in Christians who are suspicious of secular universities and other institutions of higher learning. As an undergraduate professor of religion, I have spoken to many anxious parents questioning why our religion major, which is preparatory for seminary and the practice of ministry, includes the

---

2 This was the period in history, for example, that witnessed the toppling of centuries-old monarchies like France in the late 1700s. While religion was still prevalent among leaders and intellectuals of the time, such as the US Founding Fathers, it was more often Deism as opposed to traditional Christianity. Deism holds that a higher power created everything but then retreated and is no longer involved in the affairs of humanity. For a scholarly overview of this period, see Charles Taylor, *A Secular Age* (Cambridge: The Belknap Press of Harvard University, 2007), especially parts 1 and 2. For a more accessible introduction see, John Robertson, *Enlightenment: A Very Short Introduction* (Oxford: Oxford University Press, 2015).

3 Modern Christians, unfortunately, do not corner the market on such a rejection of scientific discovery. In the seventeenth century, the Catholic Church convicted Galileo Galilea of heresy for his views that the earth was not the center of the universe because this belief seemed to contradict Scripture's teaching that the sun "rises" and "sets." The Catholic Church has since admitted this mistake, and few Christians, if any, would now challenge this once controversial scientific discovery. One wonders if such will be the case in later generations regarding current controversial scientific theories.

study of both religion *and philosophy.* Many of them believe that the study of the Bible should be sufficient, not to mention safer.[4]

This anti-intellectual approach not only marginalizes the so-called secular realm and the knowledge on offer from its disciplines; it ill prepares Christians to meet the very real intellectual challenges that the life of discipleship sometimes presents. Christians who have not engaged the mind risk losing their faith at the most rudimentary of intellectual critiques, or at the experience of personal tragedy, or at the realization that the Scriptures seem to contradict themselves and include ideas (slavery, misogyny) that are clearly unjust. Small wonder that some Christians would rather just stick to the Bible, or rather those parts of the Bible that affirm their understanding of God as love.

In contrast to this position, however, Scripture is clear that Christianity has never just been about the heart. When asked to name the greatest commandment, for example, Jesus said not only to love God with one's heart but also with one's mind (Matt 22:37), implying not a tension but an integration between the two. Moreover, the same Paul who warned the Corinthians against the world's wisdom also told the philosophers at Athens that their learning ultimately pointed to God (Acts 17:18ff). Indeed, the Christian tradition has consistently affirmed that love is not just an emotion of the heart but of one's whole being. Consequently, the life of discipleship requires engagement not only of the heart but also of the mind. No Christian in history better modeled this holistic approach to discipleship than Origen.

Born in Alexandria, Africa, around 185, Origen was raised in the faith under the tutelage of his father, a prominent teacher in their local church. According to Eusebius, the historian we met in chapter 2, Origen's father supplemented his standard Greek education with lessons in the Scriptures, requiring him to learn and recite them by memory, tasks at which Origen excelled.[5] The defining event of his life occurs when he is seventeen. In that

---

4 This fear was dramatized in the 2014 film *God's Not Dead,* which is about an evangelical college freshman whose atheist philosophy professor required a disavowal of faith to pass the class. Despite its cartoonish portrayal of a philosophy professor who, in my experience in academia, nowhere actually exists, this film was widely hailed among certain Christian groups.

5 Eusebius, *Church History,* 6.2.7–9. Wilken observes how unique this biographical fact is among those figures regarded as Christian intellectuals or philosophers. Earlier, such figures, like the second-century apologist Justin Martyr, came to Christianity as adults after first having studied various philosophies. Origen learned the Scriptures as a

year, around 202, Roman Emperor Septimius Severus traveled through Alexandria and, at the request of a cadre of pagan priests, initiated a persecution of prominent Christians in the area. Origen's father was among those arrested and martyred while his young, devoted son looked on.[6] As he would relate in a sermon preached later in his life, the effect of seeing his father martyred deepened Origen's devotion to God and committed him to living a life of faithfulness that would honor his noble upbringing.[7] In the immediate aftermath, that commitment proved difficult as the government seized his family's property and wealth, leaving the large family—Origen had six younger brothers—destitute and his future uncertain.

Perhaps owing to his reputation as a faithful Christian and young scholar with promise, a wealthy Christian woman took Origen into her home and paid for his continuing education. Origen now focused his studies in philology, or Greek literature, which included a number of techniques aimed both at reconstructing ancient texts (copied by fallible scribes) and at understanding their meaning through close analysis of the words and grammar.[8] He also encountered numerous Jewish influences in Alexandria during this period, notably the works of the famous first-century Jew Philo, through which he first encountered the allegorical interpretation of Scripture.[9] He also learned Hebrew from a contemporary Jewish convert to Christianity, making him the first Christian to popularize the study of the Old Testament in its original language.[10] Most prominently, though, he pursued the study of philosophy. He became a disciple of Ammonius Saccas, an accomplished philosopher in

---

child and later turned to a more focused study of philosophy. Wilken, *The First Thousand Years*, 56.

6 The Alexandrian persecution occurs on the same imperial trip and in roughly the same time as the persecution in Carthage that claimed the life of Perpetua.

7 Wilken, *The First Thousand Years*, 56.

8 Eusebius, *Church History*, 6.2.15. Origen scholar Joseph W. Trigg describes four different stages involved in this intense training, including text criticism (reconstructing the original text), reading, interpretation or exegesis, and application. Joseph Trigg, *Origen*, The Early Church Fathers (London: Routledge, 1998), 5–6.

9 Philo was a Hellenistic Jew who lived and wrote in Alexandria from around 20 BCE to 50 CE. Besides his Jewish identity, he was a philosopher who read the Jewish Scriptures through the lens of Stoicism. His writings were influential on generations of Christians in the area, notably Clement of Alexandria, who lived and wrote in the generation prior to Origen.

10 To that point, Christians, including the New Testament writers, read the Old Testament in its Greek translation, called the *Septuagint*. Today, most English versions of the Old Testament are translated from Hebrew.

the Platonist tradition.[11] Origen's fellow student Plotinus would become the most important teacher and writer in a new era of Platonism, what scholars refer to as Neoplatonism. Origen again excelled in his philosophical studies, as evidenced by his own work and the testimony of Plotinus, who later wrote that he held Origen in the highest regard.

The goal of the Platonists was not simply the acquisition of knowledge but rather the cultivation of the good life achieved by using the wisdom of the masters to, in Joseph Trigg's words, "become like the divine as much as possible."[12] Origen's deep faith in God and solid foundation in the Scriptures, though certainly at odds with his teacher and fellow students, allowed him to engage in these studies without losing his faith. Indeed, Origen found common ground with the philosophers because he also sought wisdom. Origen simply had a different master. Trigg continues, "Origen did not accept Platonism uncritically, but only when it was consistent with the church's rule of faith . . . Origen therefore employed the study of philosophy, understood as an exercise involving moral purification as well as intellectual training as a necessary preparation for the study of Scripture."[13] For Origen, Scripture held the only true wisdom, and the divine to which he was conforming himself in his study was the God of creation and Israel as revealed through Jesus Christ.

For Origen, this moral purification involved the adoption of certain self-denying practices he believed would help him to better emulate the humble life of Jesus.[14] While he had been teaching students in literature during these formative years, he stopped in order to limit his distractions from the deeper study of Scripture. To make up for the loss of income, he sold his textbooks, a significant sacrifice to any serious student. He started fasting regularly, ceased drinking wine, and restricted his sleep to have more time to study the Scriptures. His youthful zeal even led him to the ultimate self-denying act of self-castration, apparently as a response to a literal reading of Jesus's reference to those who "made themselves eunuchs for the sake of the kingdom

---

11 Plato (428 BCE–348 BCE) was history's most influential Greek philosopher, and his writings spawned a tradition of interpreters that rivals that of the Christian tradition of scriptural interpretation.

12 Trigg, *Origen*, 13.

13 Trigg, *Origen*, 13.

14 These self-denying practices anticipate the kind of practices that monastic Christians would order their lives around. I will discuss the reason for such practices in more detail in chapter 5.

of heaven" (Matt 19:12).[15] (He would later regret that decision and counsel against such literalistic interpretations.) While twenty-first-century Christians might question some of these practices—self-castration in particular—we can certainly recognize the holy impetus to remove distractions and occasions to sin from our lives to better focus on and conform to Christ. Moreover, that the most learned man in Christian history found his discipleship not only in knowledge but in an obedient way of life gives lie to the modern antithesis of the mind and the heart. Origen demonstrates their integration in our embodied humanity as divine image-bearers.

Now in his early twenties, well-educated, and clear in his Christian convictions and vocation, Origen embarked on a career as a teacher and writer of theology (a word that properly means "the study of God" but comes to include a variety of topics related to God, Christ, and humanity as informed by Scripture) unparalleled in Christian history. First, he served as the lay head of a catechetical school in Alexandria, which operated independently of the bishop of Alexandria, the first of its kind.[16] Later in his life, Origen was ordained a presbyter in Caesarea, where he settled around 234 to the end of his life.[17] As both a lay theologian and presbyter, he wrote a prodigious number of books with the singular focus of illuminating the content of the Scriptures and instructing on methods of correct interpretation.[18]

The wide range of forms and topics of his works demonstrates his varied interests, scholarly abilities, deep faith, and, particularly in his role as presbyter, pastoral concerns for his fellow Christians. He wrote scriptural commentaries on nearly every book of the Bible, treatises on practical topics ranging from prayer to martyrdom, homilies, and, putting to use his skills as a philosopher, a comprehensive defense of Christianity against its biggest ancient critic, a man named Celsus.[19] He wrote what is widely considered the

---

15 Eusebius, *Church History*, 6.8.

16 Eusebius, *Church History*, 6.8.

17 This move angered the Alexandrian Bishop Demetrius as, in those days, one was only ordained in their home district. Some reports suggest that Demetrius initially barred Origen from ordination in Alexandria because of his self-castration.

18 Estimates place the number of his works in the mid-seventies. Unfortunately, many of these works have been either lost or intentionally destroyed, the reasons for which will become clear in the course of this chapter. Others survive mostly in a Latin translation, and a whole subset of Origen studies are devoted to deciphering Origen's true thought from the glosses of his Latin translator, Rufinus.

19 Perhaps Origen had worked out many of the arguments in the defense of Christianity he used against Celsus while he was a student under Ammonius Saccas.

first systematic theology, *On First Principles*, a thorough and learned analysis of the Church's core beliefs. In the preface, Origen lists these beliefs as (1) the oneness and transcendence of God; (2) Jesus Christ, the only begotten Son, who became human for our salvation; (3) the Holy Spirit, "united in honor and dignity with the Father and the Son," who has been poured out and is present and active in the world; (4) the inestimable worth and freedom of humans; (5) the existence of a spiritual realm; and (6) God as the creator of all things.[20] While Origen's theology certainly develops the teaching of the apostles in new ways, we recognize in these beliefs a continuity with the content of Scripture and earlier interpreters such as Irenaeus.[21] In all of these works, Origen did not reject the so-called secular knowledge he gained in his education but incorporated it into a Christian philosophy grounded in Scripture and illuminative of the nature of God. As such, he demonstrated, in Wilken's words, that "Christianity would be not only a community of faith but also a tradition of learning."[22]

Origen's singular contribution, however, is the method of scriptural interpretation that he both receives from previous Christians and codifies for future generations. He believed that the Scriptures were inspired, not only in their underlying message of salvation but in every paragraph and sentence and word down to the smallest preposition. The man who unfortunately took Matthew 19:12 literally fortunately took Jesus's words in Matthew 5:18 literally as well: "For truly I tell you, until heaven and earth pass away, not one letter, not one stroke of a letter, will pass from the law until all is accomplished." As Origen puts it, "The wisdom of God has permeated the whole of Scripture even to the individual letter."[23] It matters to Origen, then, that the Hebrew

---

20 Origen, *On First Principles* 1.Pref.4, trans. G. W. Butterworth, repr. (Christian Classics; Notre Dame, IN: Ave Maria Press, 2013), 4.

21 Origen explains this development by saying the Apostles taught only those doctrines they believed to be necessary for salvation but intended "the grounds of their statements . . . to be investigated by such as they should merit the higher gifts of the Spirit and in particular by such as should afterwards receive through the Holy Spirit himself the graces of language, wisdom and knowledge" (*FP* 1.*Pref*.2–3). While we may bristle at the elitism of this statement, we ought to grant Origen's point as all core doctrines have undergone development. The rub is determining which developments remain in continuity with Scripture and which go beyond it in unhelpful directions. In my view, this is the primary work of theologians in the Church today.

22 Wilken, *The First Thousand Years*, 55.

23 Origen, *Commentary on Psalms 125*, trans. Joseph W. Trigg, *Origen,* The Early Church Fathers (London: Routledge, 1998), 71.

text of Isaiah 7:14 states that a *young woman* will conceive, whereas the same text in the Septuagint states that a *virgin* will conceive.[24] It matters to Origen whether the Greek word *archē* in the first verse of John means "beginning" as in time or whether it means "principle" as in foundation.[25] It even matters to Origen the meaning of specific numbers, such as the cubits of the Ark given to Noah, or the presence or absence of a definite article, or the syntax of various sentences.[26] As a result, Origen's scriptural commentaries often stretched to multiple volumes. The first volume of his commentary on John, for example, covers only the first half of John 1:1. Such was the dignity, importance, and mystery of the Scriptures to Origen.

To aid in this careful study of the words of Scripture, Origen produced one of the most remarkable works of Christian history, a massive document that compiled six different versions of the Old Testament. Known as the *Hexapla*, this extraordinary and unique work was arranged in six parallel columns with the column to the far left containing the original Hebrew, followed to the right by a column with the Hebrew text spelled out in Greek letters to help Greek speakers pronounce the Hebrew, followed by four different Greek translations including the Septuagint.[27] This is the ancient equivalent of an interlinear Bible with several different English translations (NIV, NLT, etc.) or a Greek and English New Testament used by generations of seminary students and pastors. Paired with a basic knowledge of the original languages, these tools allow for a deeper reading of Scripture as well as richer and more engaging sermons. The *Hexapla* served as the basis for Origen's Old Testament scriptural interpretations, and its meticulous layout helped him apply the grammatical lessons learned in his philological studies to his study of Scripture.

---

24 Origen, *Against Celsus* 1.34–35, trans. Rev. Frederick Crombie, *Ante-Nicene Fathers*, vol. 4, ed. Alexander Roberts and James Donaldson, repr. (Peabody, MA: Hendrickson Publishers, 1999), 395–669.

25 Origen, *Commentary on John*, trans. Joseph W. Trigg, *Origen,* The Early Church Fathers (London: Routledge, 1998), Book 1.

26 Peter Martens provides a number of such illuminating examples. Peter W. Martens, *Origen and Scripture: The Contours of the Exegetical Life, Oxford Early Christian Studies* (Oxford: Oxford University Press, 2012), 54–63.

27 The *Hexapla* has been lost, probably because its massive size made it impractical to copy. This description of its contents follows the helpful reconstruction of Martens, *Origen and Scripture*, 45. Martens reports that while Origen never compiled a similar document for New Testament translations, he routinely performed the same sort of text-critical work in his New Testament interpretations.

Nevertheless, for Origen, Christian interpretation of Scripture can never stop at the level of the words, precisely because these words are "God-breathed" (2 Tim 3:16 NIV). As he writes in *On First Principles*, "Then there is the doctrine that the scriptures were composed through the Spirit of God and that they have not only the meaning which is obvious, but also another which is hidden from the majority of readers. For the contents of scripture are the outward forms of certain mysteries and the images of divine things. On this point the entire Church is unanimous" (*FP* 1.Pref.8).[28] In Origen's understanding, the Scriptures were not simply human writings that require the skills of a philologist to understand well. Rather, they were together a divine work whose primary author was the Holy Spirit. As such, the Scriptures not only contained the literal meaning intended by the human authors; they contained a deeper spiritual meaning intended by the Spirit that brought the disparate works into one story. The role of the interpreter, then, is to discern both meanings. The spiritual meaning, however, requires interpretive methods that go beyond those we have encountered thus far. In short, finding the spiritual meaning requires allegory.[29]

Allegorical interpretation is not as esoteric as it first sounds. It is simply the process of finding in a text a deeper meaning than what the words say. We actually engage in allegorical interpretation quite often. The story of the tortoise and the hare, for example, is not just that a slow tortoise improbably beats a faster hare in a race but rather that hard work and perseverance are more important to success in life than natural ability, or something of the sort. My guess is that most people would agree to this interpretation even though the words of the story never express this lesson. While the fairy tale's original author likely intended this allegorical meaning, sometimes we create allegorical meaning that was clearly unintended by the author. I recall vividly a few years ago watching the movie *Frozen* with my young daughters and pointing out to them that Anna's act of sacrifice, which saved her sister, Elsa, from death, is much like what Christ does for us on the cross. It seemed to me that they understood that lesson better than when I told them about Christ's sacrifice from the actual gospels! I should add that, though it hardly

---

28 For the remainder of the chapter, quotations from this work are taken from Butterworth's lucid translation and will be marked in the text as *FP*.

29 This may come as a shock to the reader since allegory was the interpretive method preferred by the Gnostics. As we will see, Origen's allegorical method distinguishes itself from the Gnostics' method in several important ways.

seems possible, this interpretation increased our enjoyment of *Frozen* all the more. In fact, the girls began to find different allegorical meanings in other Disney movies ranging from *Mulan* to *The Mandalorian*.[30]

We see, then, that allegory opens up texts to new and exciting interpretations, allowing readers to apply their lessons in ways that literal interpretations rarely allow. If you've ever heard someone express delight at finding something new in a text they've read numerous times before—this very thing happens all the time with Scripture—chances are you've encountered an allegorical reader. Indeed, the only time an allegorical interpretation does not work is when there exists no organic connection between the allegorical meaning and the words of a book or the images of a movie. While *Frozen* can be a movie about the saving power of self-sacrifice, for example, it cannot be one about how killing is an acceptable means of attaining power (Hans's approach) because everything in the movie would argue against it. This was precisely Irenaeus's point against the Gnostic use of allegory; the allegorical meaning they drew from Scripture was completely alien to Scripture's *hypothesis*. But allegory itself is not an unchristian way of reading; indeed, Irenaeus himself engaged it whenever he found Christ in Old Testament passages. Origen goes even further to suggest that allegory is the only properly Christian way of reading the Scriptures.

In the opening chapters of book four of *On First Principles*, Origen explains the different levels of meaning in Scripture, and the interpretive processes to draw them out, by likening the text of Scripture to the body, soul, and spirit of a human person. For Origen, the body of Scripture is the literal meaning of the words as intended by the human author and ascertained through the interpretive means of a philologist. The soul of Scripture corresponds to a moral level of meaning, which gives instruction for our formation. While moral exhortations exist throughout Scripture on the literal level (e.g., "Love your enemies and pray for those who persecute you"), the moral level locates moral exhortation in passages literally addressing something else. For example, passages in the Old Testament law that address specifics related to the nation of Israel, such as whether or not to muzzle one's ox, apply through the moral sense to all people regardless of whether they own an ox.[31] Finally,

---

30 This is the way. Let the *Star Wars* fan understand.

31 As Origen shows (*FP* 4.2.6), Paul reads this very law, Deuteronomy 25:4, on the moral level of interpretation: "For it is written in the Law of Moses: 'Do not muzzle an ox while it is treading out the grain.' Is it about oxen that God is concerned? Surely he says

the spirit of Scripture corresponds to the spiritual meaning, which while indicated by the words of Scripture, runs beneath them. Like the allegorical interpretation of the story of the tortoise and the hare, the spiritual meaning demonstrates that the Old Testament points to Christ (even though Christ is never mentioned by name in the Old Testament) and, thus, finds its resolution in the New Testament. The spiritual meaning demonstrates the fulfillment of the Old Testament prophecies in Christ (even though those prophecies are often literally fulfilled within the Old Testament itself). The spiritual meaning finds the Church prefigured in the people of Israel (even though the Church does not come into existence until many centuries after these writings), for Christians have been brought out of slavery to sin and given a new law.[32] And so on.[33]

Like the human spirit, the spiritual is the most important level of meaning because it is the meaning intended by Scripture's primary author, the Holy Spirit. As such, while anyone can interpret Scripture literally, the only way to discern the spiritual meaning is to be a disciple in communion with that same Holy Spirit. Origen writes, "While the whole law is spiritual, the inspired meaning is not recognized by all, but only by those who are gifted with the grace of the Holy Spirit in the word of wisdom and knowledge" (FP 1.Pref.8). Origen emphasizes this truth in many places, though none as beautiful as the image that comes at the beginning of his Commentary on the Gospel of John. Alluding to the description of that Gospel's assumed author in John 13:23, he writes, "No one can understand this gospel unless he reclines on Jesus's breast."[34] Only by the Spirit can disciples rightly discern that Jesus is the center of the Scriptures, the Old Testament pointing toward him and the New Testament reflecting on him. Only by the Spirit can disciples apply

---

this for us, doesn't he? Yes, this was written for us, because whoever plows and threshes should be able to do so in the hope of sharing in the harvest" (1 Cor 9:9–10). The moral level of meaning is a type of allegorical interpretation, though Origen singles it out for its focus on moral content.

32 It is not accidental that Matthew's Jesus, like Moses teaching the law, gives his most famous sermon from a mountain (Matt, chs. 5–7). The same set of teachings appear in Luke's Gospel from the very different setting of a level place (Luke 6:17–49).

33 Origen's three levels of meaning are the basis for what develops into a fourfold meaning of Scripture that dominates Western biblical interpretation throughout the Middle Ages. The fourth meaning that Origen does not address is the anagogical meaning, which finds in Scripture meaning regarding future events related to the afterlife. For Origen, such meaning would be included in the spiritual sense.

34 Origen, Commentary on John, 109.

those Scriptures, which on a literal level were written twenty-five hundred to nineteen hundred years ago, to our present context in order to live like Jesus. "He wants us to see [Jesus] with zeal, with perseverance, if need be in anguish and sorrow; to live with him ever present; to ask him questions and to listen to his replies: this, to Origen, is what the search for the meaning of Scripture really means," writes Catholic theologian Henri de Lubac.[35] This is why, for Origen, reading Scripture only according to its literal meaning is inadequate for Christians.[36]

This does not mean, however, that the spiritual meaning negates the literal meaning or that the literal meaning can be ignored; rather, the different meanings coexist in most passages. In his scriptural commentaries, Origen often engages both meanings, beginning with the literal and then moving to the spiritual. To cite but one example, in his *Commentary on Lamentations*, he rightly recognizes that on the literal level, the book is an extended lament over the destruction of Jerusalem and, in particular, Israel's first Temple in 586 BCE. But on the spiritual level, the work applies to the soul of a disciple who, though once was with God, has fallen away. The lamenting throughout the book, read spiritually, applies to our own suffering when we find ourselves distant from God just as the hope for a rebuilding of the Temple reflects our hope that we might return to God's presence.[37] Read in this way, Lamentations becomes a book for the Church and for the twenty-first-century Christian who might be lamenting their own context. Importantly, this allegorical meaning is not completely arbitrary but rather is born out of careful attention to the literal sense, in this case the meaning of particular words and images, as we saw was Origen's practice. He writes of Lamentations, "And is it not remarkable, if the perfect soul is not addressed as a house, a farmstead, or—better than this—as a village, nor even as a city, but is called Jerusalem, distinguished above all cities and honored by God, because she has been invested by wisdom and virtue with far greater renown than even the

---

35 De Lubac, "Introduction," in *On First Principles*, trans. G. W. Butterworth, repr. (Christian Classics; Notre Dame, IN: Ave Maria Press, 2013), xviii.

36 In contrast to assumptions that guide the instruction of biblical interpretation in universities and certain divinity schools and seminaries that form the Church's pastors. In that context, for example, the Old Testament is studied in terms of its literal meaning, apart from any reference to the New Testament. Indeed, it is no longer called *Old Testament* but *Hebrew Bible*.

37 Origen, *Commentary on Lamentations, Selected Fragments*, trans. Joseph W. Trigg, *Origen*, The Early Church Fathers (London: Routledge, 1998), 73–85.

greatest city, with all its multitude of buildings."[38] Moreover, the connection between buildings and souls finds support in other parts of Scripture, such as Paul's connection of the human body as the new Temple of God (1 Cor 6:19). Thus, allegorical interpretation cannot bring any meaning out of a text as the Gnostics mistakenly thought; rather, it is constrained by the particular words as well as the wider boundaries of beliefs provided by the core beliefs of the Church's rule of faith Origen addresses in the preface of *On First Principles*.

Yet Origen is also clear that while every passage of Scripture has a spiritual meaning, not every passage has a literal meaning. Here again, however, it is not for readers to make this decision according to their own sensibilities; instead, the text itself provides these clues. Origen writes, "The divine wisdom has arranged for certain stumbling-blocks and interruptions of the historical sense to be found therein, by inserting in the midst a number of impossibilities and incongruities, in order that the very interruption of the narrative might as it were present a barrier to the reader and lead him to refuse to proceed along the pathway of the ordinary meaning [and] might recall us to the beginning of another way" (*FP* 4.2.9). The most famous example of such a stumbling block comes in the Genesis account of creation. According to Origen, Genesis 1 should not be read literally because it in fact has no literal meaning. This is not because its account of creation does not correspond to scientific data (as is often the reasoning that leads modern readers to a nonliteral reading of Genesis 1) but because of the specific words of Scripture. "What man of intelligence," Origen asks, "will consider it a reasonable statement that the first and second and third day, in which there are said to be both morning and evening, existed without sun, moon, and stars, while the first day was even without a heaven?" (*FP* 4.3.1).[39] The same can be said of Genesis 2's anthropomorphic picture of God (God *forms* Adam with his hands and then *walks* with him). These "stumbling blocks" thus lead the careful reader to the deeper spiritual meaning of these chapters, where they will find a wealth of meaning about the power, character, and love of the Creator God.

Origen's scriptural interpretation, though perhaps initially foreign, particularly to Protestant ears, ought to serve as a model for our own readings.

---

38 Origen, *Commentary on Lamentations*, 75.

39 The difficulty with taking interpretive cues from scientific data is that we will then read all miraculous stories as metaphorical because science rejects the existence of miracles, particularly the idea that a person could rise from the dead. Nevertheless, the text in many cases assumes miracles are historical and therefore should be read literally.

Not only does it open the text to new avenues of meaning, which keep us going back to Scripture as a formative spiritual discipline, it avoids two pitfalls into which modern Protestant interpreters often fall. First is the practice of reading random passages divorced of any historical or literary context and applying the words directly to one's life. Such an approach fails to take the literal sense seriously and risks making the text mean something foreign. For example, when modern readers interpret Jeremiah 29:11 ("For surely I know the plans I have for you, says the Lord, plans for your welfare and not for harm, to give you a future with hope") as a promise that God will always give them what they want. However, the historical context of that passage, found on the literal level, shows that it is not about individual blessings but about the nation of Israel, who was in the midst of judgment in the form of exile. Second is the practice of interpreting the text only as a history book by focusing on ascertaining its literal meaning within its original historical setting. Such an approach fails to take the spiritual sense seriously and renders Scripture nothing more than a history book about the faith of other people. While both of these ways of reading have their place, by themselves they render Scripture as something it is not. The genius of Origen's scriptural interpretation is that he brings together both a literal and a spiritual approach. In Origen's hands, then, Scripture becomes the document it was intended to be: a human-written, Spirit-inspired testimony to the character of God and the salvific work of Christ, whose Spirit is still active in our midst through these living, God-breathed words of Scripture.

The end of Origen's story is tragic, somewhat appropriately, on two levels. In 249, after a relatively long life of faithful service to the Church, Origen was arrested in the first empire-wide persecution under Emperor Decius. Like other martyrs we have encountered thus far, he remained faithful in this ordeal, despite undergoing severe torture. Surprisingly, he survived and was released from prison.[40] His health was badly damaged as a result of the torture, however, and he died shortly thereafter, believing he failed to follow the faithful example of both his father, whom he idolized, and his Christ, whom he so dearly loved with all his heart, soul, mind, and strength. Perhaps more tragically still, some of his ideas were deemed by later Christians to fall into heresy.[41] The problem may lie more with Origen's interpreters than with

---

40 Eusebius, *Church History*, 6.39.

41 Among these include his somewhat deficient Trinitarian theology in relation to the official doctrine of the Trinity pronounced at the Councils of Nicaea in 325 and

the man himself, for some of his condemned ideas he recognized as either of a more speculative quality or implications of other sounder doctrines. One wonders how Origen would have responded had these controversies arisen in his lifetime. Nevertheless, his posthumous condemnation has precluded him from being recognized as a saint according to the official processes of those church traditions, Catholic and Orthodox, that honor saints with official titles.

One lesson of this book, however, ought to be that one's sainthood depends not on official pronouncements of other humans or institutions but rather on one's faithful devotion to God and holiness of life. For all the thousands of official saints recognized by the Church throughout history, there are surely many times that number of saints who have gone unrecognized for whatever reason, some of whom we will encounter later in this book. But these saints are known to God, and they serve as our witnesses, whether we recognize them or not. Among this group is surely Origen, of whom it can be said, in the words of one modern interpreter, "There is no father of the Church whose works are more profitable for study and whose temper and character are more worthy of our imitation."[42]

Constantinople in 381. Ironically, however, his writings on the eternal relationship of Father and Son provided the key argument for the Son's eternal nature and thus full divinity with the Father in the theology of these creeds. Moreover, the Church has typically not accused writers of heresy regarding doctrines that were defined after their deaths. If they did, the Church would have a lot more heretics in her history and a lot fewer saints. More problematic, however, was Origen's belief in the preexistence of souls and his belief that all beings would eventually be saved. Aspects of Origen's thought came under attack at various times following his death and culminated in his official condemnation at the Second Council of Constantinople in 553 CE.

42 G. W. Butterworth, "Translator's Introduction," in *On First Things*, trans. G. W. Butterworth, repr. (Christian Classics; Notre Dame, IN: Ave Maria Press, 2013), xxxix.

CHAPTER FIVE

Macrina's Freedom

You have released us, O Lord, from the fear of death.
You have made the end of life here on earth a beginning of true life for us.

—Macrina the Younger, *Life of Saint Macrina* 26.1–2

As we have seen in the first four chapters, Christianity's indigenous setting is characterized not by freedom from empire or cooperation with empire but rather by opposition to empire. Contrary to logic, however, Christianity thrived in such a setting, just as it is now thriving not in the West but in the Global South, specifically in areas where the adversarial relationship between Church and state remains.[1] In the ancient Roman Empire, Christians were persecuted into the early fourth century, when, following the Great Persecution under the Emperor Diocletian, a new emperor named Constantine assumed the throne. Constantine was raised by a Christian mother and was always sympathetic to Christians. In 312, on the eve of his own rise to power, he converted to Christianity and promptly made it legal, thus ending persecution in the Roman Empire.[2]

---

1 Timothy C. Tennent, *Theology in the Context of World Christianity: How the Global Church Is Influencing How We Think about and Discuss Theology* (Grand Rapids, MI: Zondervan, 2007), ch. 1.

2 Some reports suggest his conversion was the result of a vision of a *chi* and a *rho* (the first two Greek letters of the name *Christ*) occurring right before the battle that would make him sole emperor, which was interpreted for him as meaning "by this sign, you will conquer." The truth of this vision, like the sincerity of Constantine's conversion, is widely debated among scholars, though that discussion need not detain us. For those interested, I

While many Christians hailed this surprising turn of events as being God-ordained,[3] a significant number questioned it. The problem, as this minority group saw it, was the loss of Christianity's sacrificial nature. After all, Jesus had said, "Whoever wants to be my disciple must deny themselves and take up their cross and follow me" (Mark 8:34 NIV). If this was Jesus's definition of discipleship, then personal sacrifice was not just optional but constitutive of the life of a Christian. And how could a person, in a post-Constantine era, take up their cross? The answer comes in the emergence of what Wilken has called "one of the most enduring Christian institutions," namely, monasticism.[4]

Monastics are Christians who have chosen to live outside of society, removed from normal ways of life that entail things like employment, home ownership, marriage and family, and other activities. The first fourth-century monastics were solitary figures, folks like the Egyptian Antony, who, on reading Jesus's statement "If you wish to be perfect, go, sell your possessions, and give the money to the poor, and you will have treasure in heaven," left his family and job and went to live in the desert (Matt 19:21). Partly due to the popularity of a biography of Antony's life, written by the Alexandrian bishop Athanasius, large numbers of people went to the desert. Eventually, these hermits would find each other and form a common way of life structured around work and prayer and their lifelong vows of obedience, poverty, and chastity.[5]

The ideal that motivates these self-denying, or ascetic,[6] practices and best sums up the monastic project is detachment. To be detached from the things of this world—possessions, success, status, relationships, and the like—is to not find one's security or meaning in them. It is, therefore, to recognize that we are pilgrims in this world and that our true home is the kingdom of God,

---

recommend Peter J. Leithart's highly accessible work, *Defending Constantine: The Twilight of an Empire and the Dawn of Christendom* (Downers Grove, IL: InterVarsity Press, 2010).

3 Eusebius, for example, believed that the early struggle of Christianity triumphed not in the faithfulness of the martyrs but in Constantine's official recognition of Christianity and the Church's inheritance of the Roman Empire. Some Christians of the time referred to Constantine as the thirteenth apostle to signify this so-called triumph.

4 Wilken, *The First Thousand Years*, 100. Wilken rightly notes that monastic communities predated the fourth century, though it is not until after Constantine that monasticism comes fully into view.

5 Every monastic conforms their life to a written rule, one of the earliest and most influential of which was that of Benedict of Nursia, written around 530, which established the Benedictine Order. Through history, many different monastic orders have developed with different foci, though they all hold some version of these three vows in common.

6 This term comes from the Greek word *askēsis*, which means "exercise" or "training."

which, despite the rise of a Christian emperor or government, has not yet fully come. Such ascetic practices, which were adopted by certain Christian groups well before the fourth century, are rooted in Scripture.[7] Jesus himself lived such a life insofar as he never married and never owned much of anything. Likewise, his message often urged an ascetic attitude among his followers. He taught on the danger of money often, for example, telling parables about the need to store up one's treasures in heaven and saying, in one place, "No one can serve two masters. Either you will hate the one and love the other, or you will be devoted to the one and despise the other. You cannot serve both God and money" (Luke 16:13 NIV). Paul also adopted an ascetic lifestyle and, in particular, recommends the single life because married people have their interests divided between God and their spouses, while single people are "devoted to the Lord and holy in both body and the spirit" (1 Cor 7:34 NLT).

There is, of course, nothing inherently wrong with making money or being married or otherwise living and participating in a society. However, as any person with kids will attest, these normal activities and involvements can be distractions from our faith. In some cases, particularly with money, such activities can be occasions for sin. Thus, monastics willingly sacrifice these worldly goods and relationships in order to live holier and more focused lives of discipleship. Although the history of monasticism is not without its share of corruption, the ascetic way of life has produced some of the holiest, most influential saints in history. Foremost among these stands our fifth saint, Macrina.

As with the stories of most women in this early period, Macrina's comes to us by the hand of a man, namely, her younger brother Gregory, the late-fourth-century bishop of Nyssa.[8] His purpose in writing is to present her ascetic life,

---

7 For a scholarly account of the emergence of asceticism in the earliest centuries of Christianity, see Peter Brown, *The Body and Society: Men, Women, and Sexual Renunciation in Earliest Christianity*, repr. (New York: Columbia University Press, 2008), especially chapter 2.

8 The difficulty arising from this historical fact is ascertaining women's true voices from that of the men who tell their stories. We have already encountered this difficulty with Perpetua, though it was mitigated some by the preservation of her journal. Cohick and Hughes have helpfully addressed this difficulty in the specific context of Macrina's story. I concur with their assessment that the familial relationship between Gregory and Macrina, as well as Gregory's deep respect for his sister, makes it likely that *Life of Saint Macrina* can be trusted as a "limited preservation" of her. Cohick and Hughes, *Christian Women in the Patristic World*, 161. Gregory also wrote a letter that discusses Macrina and a second book, *On the Soul and Resurrection*, where Macrina is portrayed as a wise sage in

which he calls her "philosophy," as a model for others to follow.[9] Macrina was born around 327 in Cappadocia of Caesarea (modern-day Turkey), the oldest of ten children. Hers was a wealthy family, being the owners of several large land estates in the area, but, more importantly, a family with a strong legacy of Christian faith. Her father's parents were confessing Christians and had their possessions taken in the Great Persecution, while her mother's parents were both martyred in the same period.[10] Additionally, both her parents had reputations of deep faith and "uprightness of life" (*LSM* 2.2). Her mother, Emmelia, was herself drawn to an ascetic life at a young age, but the early deaths of her parents left marriage her only option.

Macrina, like all the children of this illustrious household, was raised in the faith. Emmelia served as Macrina's primary teacher and made the conscious decision to keep her from Greek literature because the portrayals of women lacked the virtue she desired for her daughter. Given the classical education of her brothers, this seems less a decision based in fear of secular learning, which we criticized in chapter 4, and more like the wise decision of parents to keep their young children from watching R-rated movies. In any case, Macrina's education focused solely on Scripture. Like Origen, she proved a capable student, eventually memorizing all of the Psalms. Gregory reports that from an early age, she "recited each part of the Psalter at the proper times of day, when she rose from her bed, performed or rested from her duties, sat down to eat or rose up from the table, [and] when she went to bed" (*LSM* 4.4). The Scriptures were her constant companion, and she internalized their words to better conform her life to their ideal. Moreover, Gregory's description

---

an extended dialogue between them that occurs on her deathbed. In my estimation, the problem of discerning Macrina's voice from Gregory's is particularly acute in the latter work, and, in any case, it adds no details of her life. Therefore, I will focus my account on *Life of Saint Macrina*, occasionally supplemented in the footnotes by the material from Gregory's letter. Quotations from *Life of Saint Macrina* will come from Kevin Corrigan's translation, *The Life of Saint Macrina* (Eugene, OR: Wipf and Stock Publishers, 2001), and will be marked in the text as *LSM*.

9 Anna Silvas calls this work a "'philosophical biography,' the intention of which is to illustrate an ideal through the account of a life," and notes several pagan antecedents of this genre. Anna Silvas, *Macrina the Younger, Philosopher of God* (Turnhout: Brepols, 2008), 103.

10 She was named after her maternal grandmother, Macrina the Elder, whom Gregory elsewhere credits with preserving the traditions of the faith that she had learned from the third-century bishop of Caesarea, Gregory Thaumaturgus, a student of Origen's. Silvas, *Macrina the Younger*, 12–17.

of Macrina's early spiritual practice intentionally foreshadows a monastic pattern of life, just emerging in this time, organized around the common recitation of Psalms at key hours of the day. We cannot know for sure, but perhaps Macrina's devotion to this practice speaks to a monastic vocation she experienced at a young age.[11]

That desire, if it did exist within her, was initially thwarted, for when Macrina reached marrying age, she was betrothed to a man chosen by her father. Gregory does not relate Macrina's personal feelings at this betrothal, although given her context as a young woman in an aristocratic household, she had little choice but to obey. As Cohick and Hughes write, "Roman marriage, especially of the aristocracy, was how power was allotted and shifted [so] the idea that a son or daughter would not participate in that structure at all was inconceivable."[12] Before they were married, however, her fiancé died. In response, Macrina determined that this betrothal had been her marriage and so vowed to remain single the rest of her life, a decision that, in Gregory's words, "was more firmly rooted than one might have expected in one of her age" (LSM 6.1). Despite the presence of many other suitors and her parents' resolve that she marry, she adamantly refused, claiming that the Christian hope of resurrection meant her betrothed was still living. Of course, it would have been proper for her to marry as remarriage after death was expected for aristocratic widows, and in any case, she had not actually been married. One sees in her obstinacy the shadow of Perpetua, rejecting cultural roles out of a singular devotion to Christ.

The pressure to marry ceased when her father passed away, an event that caused Emmelia to move her family to a large house on their estate in Annisa, which Gregory elsewhere describes as a remote location far removed from the city.[13] Though still just a teenager, as the eldest sister in a now fatherless

---

11 Given her own early predilections, Emmelia may have taken a special interest in an ascetic formation of her eldest daughter. Early in the work, Gregory describes a vision Emmelia had just after giving birth to Macrina of a sort of angel who named the baby Thecla. As described in the second-century work *Acts of Paul and Thecla*, Thecla was a companion of the apostle Paul known for her lifelong virginity. It is possible, of course, that Gregory fabricated this story as a means of linking her to the most famous ascetic woman of the time; however, these details at the very least make it plausible that Macrina's religious education had an ascetic flavor.

12 Cohick and Hughes, *Christian Women in the Patristic World*, 159. These structures reflect the same Roman societal structures we encountered in Perpetua's story in chapter 3.

13 Gregory, *Letter 19*, trans. Anna Silvas, *Macrina the Younger, Philosopher of God* (Turnhout: Brepols, 2008), 87.

family, Macrina assumed many household responsibilities including preparing the food, caring for the younger children, and tending to the financial care of all of the family's many estates. Even when her brothers and sisters all moved away for school or marriage, Macrina stayed with her mother. Gregory reports that Emmelia often said "that she had been pregnant with the rest of her children for the prescribed term, but as for Macrina she bore her always and everywhere, embracing her, as it were, in her womb" (*LSM* 7.1). The love and mutual devotion between mother and daughter, always a special one, matures in this period and anticipates the many examples of deep and fulfilling friendships among ascetics that throughout its history has been one of monasticism's loveliest features.[14]

Having essentially made a vow of lifelong virginity, Macrina's commitment to and practice of the ascetic life begins to have a profound effect on her mother, perhaps reawakening the ascetic vocation she had experienced prior to her own marriage. Gregory writes in one place that "by the example of her own life [Macrina] provided great guidance to her mother towards the same goal, namely that of philosophy, drawing her on little by little to the immaterial, more perfect life" (*LSM* 7.5). Notably, she convinced Emmelia to give up the family's materialistic way of life, and the hierarchical ranks that had marked the aristocratic landowning household for generations, in order to "share a common life with all her maids, making them sisters and equals instead of slaves and servants" (*LSM* 9.1). Given how established her family had been in this community, this reorganization is a stunning development that would have required much personal sacrifice for Macrina and her mother, not only of the money and status to which they had become accustomed but also the security that comes from bearing a new generation of descendants. Brown puts it this way: "Macrina presided over the disintegration of a civic dynasty."[15] Such personal sacrifice is only possible through an attitude of detachment grounded in the firm understanding that the passions, materials, and relationships of this earthly life are not where our contentment or our hope or our security is found. Such detachment is what allows ascetics to sell all their possessions or to gladly accept hardships such as living in the

---

14 These friendships occur among both members of the same sex and members of the opposite sex. Brown suggests that these deep friendships played an important role in encouraging ascetics to remain faithful to their vows, particularly that of chastity. Brown, *The Body and Society*, 265–66.

15 Brown, *The Body and Society*, 278.

desert or, in Macrina's case, renouncing her claim to the status and wealth that were rightfully her inheritance.

Emmelia was not the only family member to come under Macrina's immense influence. In addition to her profound effect on her brother Gregory, whom, among other things, she encouraged to keep fighting in defense of true doctrine,[16] we know of two other brothers whose spiritual direction and development owe to Macrina's intervention. First was her brother Basil, who, on returning from school at Athens, had become rather proud of his learning and exhibited an attitude of self-importance. Macrina could tell that her brother had begun to put his faith in and find his meaning in worldly things, the very attitude an ascetic rejects, and so took it on herself to teach him a different way of being. Gregory writes, "So swiftly did she win him to the ideal of philosophy that he renounced worldly appearance, showed contempt for the admiration of rhetorical ability and went over of his own accord to this active life of manual labour, preparing for himself by means of his complete poverty a way of life which would tend without impediment towards virtue" (LSM 8.3). Redirected by his sister, Basil himself became a believer in the value of asceticism. He would later enter the priesthood and eventually become the bishop of Caesarea, where his expert leadership was responsible for the expansion of monasticism throughout the area.[17]

Second was her brother Peter, the youngest of her siblings, born shortly before their father's death. Macrina brought him up herself, educating him

---

16 This episode occurs near the end of the work. Gregory visits Macrina on her deathbed and expresses discouragement at his work. Thinking not of her impending death but only of her brother, Macrina emboldens him in the work, saying, "Churches send you forth and call upon you as ally and reformer, and you do not see the grace in this?" (LSM 23.4). In Letter 19, Gregory writes more summarily of her influence on him, "We had a sister who was for us a teacher of how to live, a mother in place of our mother." Silvas, Macrina the Younger, 87. Gregory's dedication of two full books to Macrina is clear evidence of the effect she had on him.

17 Basil's writings on the Holy Spirit, moreover, which argued for the full divinity of the Spirit alongside Father and Son, were key in the development of Trinitarian doctrine that was formally adopted by the Church at the Council of Constantinople in 381. Also essential were the writings of her brother Gregory and their mutual friend Gregory Nazianzen (altogether known as the Cappadocian Fathers). In addition to her immense influence on the development of monasticism, her influence on Basil and Gregory ranks her as a crucial figure in the development of doctrine as well. For a scholarly account of the fourth-century Trinitarian debates and their key figures and councils, see Lewis Ayres, Nicaea and Its Legacy: An Approach to Fourth-Century Trinitarian Theology (Oxford: Oxford University Press, 2006).

in the same way Emmelia had educated her. Gregory writes, "She became everything for the child, father teacher, guide, mother, counsellor in every good, and she perfected him in such a way that before he left childhood, while he was still blossoming at the tender age of adolescent youth, he was lifted up towards the sublime goal of philosophy" (*LSM* 14.2–3). Peter, like his sister Macrina, became an ascetic and lived in her household for a time before becoming a priest and finally, around 380, the bishop of Sebaste in Armenia. Though arguably less well known than these three siblings, Macrina is the common source and constant thread of their faithful and influential lives just as she is the towering figure of fourth-century monasticism in Caesarea.

Indeed, under Macrina's guidance, the household, which included herself, her mother, and many former maidservants, developed into an organized monastic community committed to an ascetic way of life. With no distinction in rank, they held all of their possessions in common. They ate together at one table, worked together toward the same ends, prayed and worshipped together, and slept in common rooms. Gregory's rather long but poetic description of their way of life deserves to be quoted at length:

> And such was the order of their life, such was the high level of philosophy and the holy conduct of their living by day and by night that it exceeds the power of words to describe it . . . In them no anger, envy, hate, arrogance, nor any other such thing was seen; the desire for foolish things of no substance, for honour, glory, delusions of grandeur, the need to be superior to others, and all such things had been eradicated. Self-control was their pleasure, not to be known was their fame, their wealth was in possessing nothing and in shaking off all material surplus, like dust from the body; their work was none of the concerns of this life, except in so far as it was a subordinate task. Their only care was for divine realities, and there was constant prayer and the unceasing singing of hymns, extended equally throughout the entire day and night so that this was both work and respite from work for them. (*LSM* 13.3–5)

Macrina was the architect of this proto-monastic community, as well as its spiritual mother. She formed these women in the ascetic practices that shaped her own discipleship and had deepened her love and devotion to God. This work is all the more remarkable because there existed no kind of blueprint in her time for what a monastic community should look like. Yet the community she developed was extremely effective in forming faithful disciples and features all of the essential elements that would mark the more organized monastic orders up to the present day. And by the end of her life, through the work of her brother Basil, monastic communities devoted to Macrina's philosophy were thriving all over the area.

Protestants sometimes criticize monastic Christians, however, for the perception that they selfishly remove themselves from the troubles of this world and fail to live out Jesus's command to "go and make disciples of all nations" (Matt 28:19 NIV).[18] While such a criticism might apply to certain monastics through history,[19] Macrina's philosophy manifests no such selfishness. Rather, she embodies the integration of asceticism and service, Jesus's two greatest commands of love of God and love of neighbor, as central to the life of discipleship. Under her direction, the household frequently engaged in acts of service for the community. When the whole area was hit hard by a famine, for example, she and her brother Peter organized a large distribution of food from her estate's coffers, surely all the larger for the frugality that the house had practiced to that point, which fed people from all over the area. Additionally, she traveled the countryside and found "those who had been left prostrate along the roadways at the time of the famine; and she picked them up, nursed them, brought them back to health and guided them personally to the pure, uncorrupted life" (LSM 28.5).[20] Macrina shows, then, that detachment does not negate service to the world but in many ways makes it possible. For if she were attached to her possessions, she never would have given her food away in the famine or brought in more women to feed at a time when resources were limited. Additionally, her detachment allowed her not to rely on wealthy benefactors or even the local church but only on prayer and her faith that God would provide all their needs. For she did not

---

18 Protestant Christianity has no tradition of monasticism. The sixteenth-century Reformers who broke away from the Catholic Church and began the various Protestant churches viewed monasticism as a works-centered way of discipleship and rejected it as incompatible with the Scripture's teachings on justification by faith alone. There have been some attempts in Protestant traditions to revive monasticism, such as happened in the Anglican Church in the nineteenth century, but for the most part, Protestants continue to reject monasticism. I will return to the brief monastic revival in Anglicanism in chapter 12.

19 We will encounter this critique within Catholicism, and some resulting changes to certain orders of monasticism, in chapter 7.

20 According to Wilken, Basil followed Macrina's lead and insisted that monastics also be devoted to the well-being of the city. He writes, "The solitary life of prayer would be complemented by the active life. Contemplation and service would go hand in hand, and one of Basil's most enduring achievements was to establish hospitals for the sick and hospices to serve pilgrims." Wilken, The First Thousand Years, 105.

want her household to be in anyone's debt, to feel they owed anything to anyone, as debts could be an occasion to sin or compromise. Even when her mother died and she came into her large inheritance, she did not cling to it but, out of her detachment, gave her share to the local church. Nevertheless, as Gregory reports, her household was never in want for "God with His blessings secretly made the small resources from her good works grow like seeds into an abundant stream of fruitfulness" (LSM 22.6).

It bears noting as well that the monastic way of life is itself a form of service to countless numbers of men and women through history whose life otherwise had little hope or prospect. This is particularly the case with women in Roman society. As Cohick and Hughes observe, the ascetic life provided for women "a valid third category in addition to the two firmly established Roman categories of married and not married."[21] Likewise, Wilken writes that "monasticism allowed women to step free of inherited roles and expectations and opened up new vocations in the church and society . . . By adopting the ascetic life women became participants with men in the pursuit of holiness."[22] Indeed, Macrina's house welcomed women from all walks of life. On the outside, some were poor and alone, others rich but destined to a marriage they did not want. Within her walls, however, they were all equal and equally valued sisters in a common community moving toward holiness.

Though Gregory's portrayal of the household is an ideal one, Macrina's life was not without its trials. Notably, she experienced grief at the deaths of family members, specifically her beloved mother and her brother Basil at old ages and another brother, Naucratius, who died as a young man. Additionally, at some point in her middle age, she developed a tumor in her breast. These episodes demonstrate that the ascetic life is not some shelter against various forms of emotional or physical suffering. Gregory reports that at the death of Naucratius, for example, "her nature also experienced its own suffering; for it was her brother and her most beloved brother, who had been snatched away by death in such a way" (LSM 12.4). Macrina's prayers for healing from the tumor, moreover, brought her full nights of tearful prayer. Her commitment to asceticism did not save her from these sufferings but, rather, offered her a means of facing those sufferings without losing faith as so often happens to people in similar situations. For when one is detached from the things of this world and grasps the pilgrim nature of one's Christian identity, sufferings

---

21 Cohick and Hughes, *Christian Women in the Patristic World*, 159.
22 Wilken, *The First Thousand Years*, 106.

appear temporary. As Gregory writes of her response to her brother's untimely death, "She rose above nature and by means of her own reasoned reflections she lifted her mother up together with her and placed her beyond suffering" (*LSM* 12.5). And when she developed breast cancer, she refused to place her hope in medical treatment, though others pleaded with her to see a doctor. Instead, she turned to God in prayer, as she had all her life in response to any need. The tears from her prayers, in fact, formed mud at her knees, which she placed on her diseased breast. And when her mother made the sign of the cross over the spot, she was healed of the affliction.

Of course, one does not have to reject medical treatment to learn from or follow Macrina's faithful life. Nor does one need to join a monastic order or adopt an ascetic lifestyle. After all, even Paul, who wished that his readers could be single like him, had to admit that "each has a particular gift from God, one having one kind and another a different kind" (1 Cor. 7:7). Not everyone, in other words, has a vocation to monasticism.[23] Still, there are lessons from Macrina's philosophy that can be applied even to an active life, that is, a life marked by marriage and employment and home ownership and medical treatment.

Foremost among these lessons is the way we think about our possessions. As I mentioned at the beginning of this chapter, there is nothing inherently wrong with money or possessions. The sin comes rather in the attitude we take toward the things we own. Are they where we find our self-worth and meaning? Are they where we find our safety and security? Do we feel that the money and possessions are rightfully ours because we have worked for them? Such attitudes suggest that we are attached to our money or, to use Jesus's words, that it has become our master (Matt 6:24). This attachment makes it unlikely that we will give to others in need or use our money for any purposes other than for ourselves. And while it is rather convenient these days to criticize the supposed hypocrisy of rich Christians who own multiple houses, drive luxury cars, and the like, the truth is that this attitude can be present regardless of how much or *how little* we own.[24]

---

23 Though one wonders whether the lack of exposure to the monastic life among Protestant Christians has made it impossible for those who might have had such a vocation to recognize it.

24 Given Jesus's railing against money and his frequent teachings to give our possessions away, such displays of wealth among Christians are concerning and, I would argue, a potential manifestation of a sinful attitude toward possessions. Nevertheless, it

We can learn a better attitude toward our possessions from Macrina. She did not in fact sell all her things and give to those living in poverty to follow Jesus, but in her monastic vocation, she released her claim to them and so was never ruled by them. As a result, she was able to see the women who once were her servants as equal sisters in Christ as opposed to lower-class women who might take from her what was not rightfully theirs. She was able also to open her household's stores of food to a community in need and thereby sustain them through famine, though she herself was hungry and likely also uncertain of her prospects of survival. This attitude toward her possessions, a fundamentally ascetic one, can be pursued by all of us, regardless of whether we live an ascetic or an active life, regardless of whether we are rich, middle class, or poor. Through it, our love of God will be strengthened and our love of neighbor will be possible.

A second lesson we can take from Macrina applies to the way we think of our relationships. Friendship, marriage, and children are clearly God-given blessings and often the most beautiful things that we will experience in this life. For this reason, ironically, attachment to our relationships is an even greater temptation than attachment to our possessions because it is not immediately obvious how relationships can be occasions for sin. More to the point, it seems that attachment is just what is needed to make relationships thrive. How can I be a good husband, for example, if I adopt an attitude of detachment in my marriage? Certainly, there is truth in this question. Relationships where one or both parties are not fully invested will not long endure. Macrina's life, however, does not model a lack of concern or investment in relationships. Quite the opposite, Macrina was fully invested in all of her relationships. When her brother Basil was failing morally, she did not leave him to his own devices as someone who didn't care about the relationship would have done. Rather, she took him into her instruction and gave him her time, her patience, and her focus. The same goes for her mother, and for her other brothers Gregory and Peter, and for all of the women in her household. For all of Macrina's other virtues, she was an exemplary sister, daughter, and friend, the kind any one of us would like to have.

Instead, Macrina's detachment teaches us to prioritize our relationships better, that is, to live in such a way that our relationship with God is the most important one. This is not as easy as it first seems, and we will not acquire

---

is quite easy for middle-class and poorer Christians to criticize rich Christians without seeing the plank in our own eyes with regard to our possessions.

this ideal apart from concrete action. Putting God first means spending more time with God in spiritual disciplines of individual prayer, Scripture-reading, and the like, which necessarily means sacrificing time for other relationships. Putting God first means, at times, going against the advice or wishes of friends, family members, and even spouses. Macrina, for example, was a wonderfully obedient daughter until she fully embraced her monastic vocation, which led her to defy her parents' wishes that she marry. Putting God first may even require breaking off unhealthy friendships or, at the very least, changing the way we act in those friendships. These are sacrifices, to be sure; nevertheless, this well-ordered approach can actually foster our relationships, for, like Macrina, we will learn to love others as God loves us, putting their needs above our own. Put differently, we learn to be in relation to others as God is in relation to us. Conversely, when we put our human relationships first, not only does our relationship with God suffer but so, too, do those very human relationships we had prioritized.

This healthy ordering of our relationships, finally, might help the Protestant Church to recover the single life as a complete and fulfilling way of leading one's life and attaining holiness. As we have seen, this way of life has been honored since the earliest days of the Christian Church, but it is notably missing among Protestant communities, perhaps because our attachment to relationships suggests that the only way to be happy or fulfilled or complete is to be married and have kids. By contrast, Macrina's life was anything but incomplete. She had numerous chances to marry but believed not only that her faith would not be harmed if she remained single but in fact might be strengthened by the choice. Nor was her life devoid of deep relationship due to her singleness or her lack of children, for the women in her household were her children and God her husband.[25] As Gregory notes of Macrina toward the end of her life, "For it was really towards her beloved that she ran, and no other of life's pleasures ever turned her eye to itself away from her beloved" (LSM 24.5). So, too, should be our focus, regardless of whether we are single or married, part of a large family or an orphan, a person with many friends or few.

Macrina died in 380 in her mid-fifties. Gregory was by her side in her final days and notes how she faced her own death with the same detachment she

---

25 Gregory makes this point in Letter 19, writing, "Gathered around her was a great choir of virgins whom she had brought forth by her spiritual labour-pains and guided towards perfection with her consummate care." Silvas, Macrina the Younger, 88.

had displayed throughout her life. He writes, "For not even in her last breaths to feel anything strange in the expectation of death nor to fear separation from life, but with sublime thinking to philosophise upon what she had chosen for this life, right from the beginning up to her last breath, to me this seemed no longer to be a part of human realities" (*LSM* 24.3–4). Macrina died as she had lived, placing her hope and meaning not in the things of this life or in this life itself but in God, in whose presence lay her true home, the only place for which she longed. On her deathbed she uttered a prayer, some of the only direct speech we hear in the account, which encapsulates this lifelong desire she was now about to receive in full:

> You have released us, O Lord, from the fear of death. You have made the end of life here on earth a beginning of true life for us. You let our bodies rest in sleep in due season and you reawaken them again at the sound of the last trumpet . . . You who have cut through the flame of the fiery sword and brought to paradise the man who was crucified with you, who entreated your pity, remember me also in your kingdom, for I too have been crucified with you, for I have nailed my flesh out of reverence for you . . . May my soul be received blameless and immaculate into your hands as an incense offering before your face. (*LSM* 26.1–3, 14–15, 21)

Not long after this, Macrina breathed her last. In preparation for burial, the maidens placed a dark cloak over her body to mark the solemnity of the occasion. Gregory then notes a stunning detail. "She shone even in the dark mantle," he writes. "God's power, I think, added even such a grace to her body that . . . rays of light seemed to shine out from her beauty" (*LSM* 34.2). This occasion surely alludes to the numerous stories of martyrs who, in their final moments, like the "radiant countenance" of Perpetua, reflect the light of God's glory in their faces. Macrina is thus linked to the martyrs in her death, which suggests that her life should be understood as a sort of lived martyrdom, a means of sacrificial discipleship in a post-Constantine era. While, like me, most of my readers living after Constantine no longer have the option of martyrdom, we all have the option of a lived martyrdom. We have only to follow Macrina because, in so doing, we will ultimately be following him who said, "Whoever wants to be my disciple must deny themselves and take up their cross and follow me."

CHAPTER SIX

John's Eyes

*For since we are twofold, fashioned of soul and body,
and our soul is not naked but, as it were, covered
by a mantle, it is impossible for us to reach what
is intelligible apart from what is bodily.*

—John Damascene, *On the Divine Images* III.12

With our sixth saint, John Damascene (which simply means "a man called John from a place called Damascus"), we remain in roughly the same geographical location as Macrina but move into a different era of history. John lived from the end of the seventh century to the middle of the eighth century, which, for the first time, puts us in the Middle Ages (so named because it is in the *middle* of the ancient and modern ages), at least from a Western perspective.[1] From an Eastern perspective, however, John represents the conclusion of the ancient era (called the Patristic age, from the Latin *patres* for "fathers")[2] as

---

1 The boundaries of historical ages are murky and somewhat artificial. I am working with the traditional divisions that mark the end of the ancient period around 600 and the end of the Middle Ages, or medieval period, around 1500. Because the medieval period is so long, scholars subdivide the era into early (600–1050), high (1050–1300), and late (1300–1500) periods, which will be helpful for the following three chapters. See the preface of Kevin Madigan, *Medieval Christianity: A New History* (New Haven, CT: Yale University Press, 2015).

2 We have already seen that this title is a misnomer as women were highly influential in this early period, even if they did not leave a written record of their thoughts and service in the manner that men did. Nevertheless, the title *patristic* remains a useful designation

his work brings together and summarizes the doctrinal developments of the first eight centuries, after which, for reasons we shall see toward the end of this chapter, Orthodox Christians accept no new developments.[3] Thus, John Damascene stands as the representative *par excellence* for Eastern Orthodoxy, an ancient branch of Christianity of which most Protestants are largely ignorant.[4] Moreover, his writings introduce us to a spiritual discipline central to Orthodox Christianity, though largely misunderstood by Protestants, which can enrich our practice of the faith and intimacy with God.

Although the precise date of John's birth is unknown, some important biographical facts from his early years have come down to us.[5] His father, Sergius, for example, had a reputation as a faithful disciple and likely taught his son the ways of the faith.[6] But it was an odd time, to say the least, for Eastern Christians living in what by then was known as the Byzantine Empire.[7] For the beginning of that century saw the emergence of a new monotheistic (one

---

for this early period for its emphasis on the importance of early authorities in developing the truths of Scripture into a system of beliefs and practices.

3 For example, works such as *The Fount of Knowledge* and *The Orthodox Faith*. Nothing comes close to these comprehensive theological works in the West until Thomas Aquinas's *Summa Theologiae* in the high medieval period.

4 See the introduction to *Saint John of Damascus, Writings*, trans. Frederick H. Chase, Jr., Fathers of the Church 37, ed. Hermigild Dressler et al., repr. (Washington, DC: The Catholic University of America Press, 1999).

5 Biographical information for John comes from Theoganes's *Chronography*, a work detailing the history of Eastern Christianity written in the ninth century. See Chase, *Saint John of Damascus*, v–xviii. An eleventh-century work titled *Life of John of Jerusalem* about John is widely rejected as apocryphal. Unfortunately, John tells us next to nothing about himself in his writings.

6 Chase, *Saint John of Damascus*, ix.

7 During his reign, Emperor Constantine moved the Roman Empire's capital, as well as the army, riches, power, and prestige, from the Western city of Rome to the Eastern city of Byzantium, from which the Eastern Empire eventually takes its name (although he quickly renamed the city after himself—Constantinople). While this move strengthened the Eastern portion of the Roman Empire, it weakened the Western portion, including the city of Rome. As a result, Rome became vulnerable to non-Roman tribes and was eventually conquered in 476, leading to many different forms of rule in the West and, paradoxically, an elevation of the leadership role of the bishop of the city of Rome (a factor that led to the Catholic Church embracing the pope as its single authority). Although, as we will see presently, the ancient Roman Empire in the East was conquered in parts at various times in the ensuing millennium, it remained intact until 1453, when the city of Constantinople was overthrown by the Seljuk Turks, a Muslim Empire. They renamed the city Istanbul, by which it is known today.

God) religion, Islam, coming from the teachings of an Arabian man named Muhammad. He claimed to have received a revelation directly from God, which, according to the command of the angel Gabriel, who heralded the revelation, he began to recite.[8] His message was located in the Judeo-Christian tradition only in the sense that it spoke about the one God, the Creator, who had previously revealed himself to prophets like Abraham, Moses, and Jesus. Nevertheless, its content suggested that the previous monotheistic religions (Judaism and Christianity) had corrupted this one God's message. For, according to the Qur'an, "it is only God who deserves all praise. He has not begotten a son and has no partner in His Kingdom" (17:111). This language is clearly aimed at the Christian doctrine of the Trinity, for Muslims believed that the worship of Jesus is blasphemous, akin to the idolatry of Jews as recorded in the Old Testament. For all the similarities of the monotheistic traditions, therefore, Islam was at its core a new religion. And it spread very quickly. By the late seventh century, cities that had formerly been Christian—Jerusalem, Smyrna, Alexandria, and Antioch, to name a few—were now ruled by Muslim caliphates.

Muslim armies conquered Damascus in 635 and made it the capital of their vast Umayyad Empire.[9] Initially, Muslims did not have a policy of forced conversions. Christians were free to practice their faith so long as they abided by the new Muslim laws of the land.[10] Moreover, Christians were often tapped to serve in Muslim governments. John's grandfather and father both held high positions in the court of the caliph, and at some point in his early adulthood,

---

8 Muhammad was illiterate, so he did not write the revelation down. The name of the book of his spoken revelations, recorded by his followers, is *Qur'an*, which in Arabic means "recitation." Unlike Judaism and Christianity, which both find God's inspired word in human words (see chapter 4), Islam holds that the message Muhammad received was the literal word of God that he did nothing but repeat. God speaks, in other words, in Arabic. Though Christians often compare Muhammad to Jesus, this story suggests that Muhammad is more like Mary, who gives the Word to the world, as scholar of religion Stephen Prothero has noted. Stephen Prothero, *God Is Not One: The Eight Rival Religions That Run the World* (New York: HarperOne, 2010), 39.

9 Andrew Louth, *Greek East and Latin West: The Church AD 681–1071; The Church in History* vol. 3 (Crestwood, NY: St. Vladimir's Seminary Press, 2007), 4–5.

10 Wilken, *The First Thousand Years*, 294. Nevertheless, political and economic structures established by Muslims encouraged voluntary conversion. In particular, all non-Muslims in Muslim-controlled areas were required to pay an extra tax. Certainly, Islam gained many adherents in these years out of political expediency, similar to what happened to Christianity in the fourth century under Constantine.

John also went to work in the Muslim court, perhaps as a tax collector.[11] However, in 705, a new caliph named Al-Walid came to power in Damascus, and he proved to be less tolerant of his Christian subjects. Perhaps for this reason, John soon after quit public life and became a monk at the Monastery of St. Sabbas in the desert of Judea, some six miles east of Bethlehem. There he would spend the rest of his long life praying, studying Scripture, immersing himself in the great tradition of the Church, and writing theological works of unparalleled learning.

We saw in the previous chapter that monastics, though living an ascetic life often marked by solitude, were not unconcerned with the world. For Macrina, it was serving her fellow Cappadocian subjects during periods of famine. For Benedictine monks living under Benedict's rule, it was the duty of constant prayer on behalf of an active world population who could not pray unceasingly for themselves. For John Damascene, it was a "worship war" to rival anything that happened in 1990s Protestantism. In his day, churches were filled with icons—pictures of Christ, the Virgin Mary, and other saints—that were regularly used in worship services by the faithful.[12] Christians would often bow before them, pray to them, touch and even kiss them.[13] Louth notes that by John's day, such veneration of icons in worship had "become part of the fabric of Christian devotion, unreflected on, for the most part, simply because it was taken for granted."[14] It must have come as a shock to many Christians, therefore, when in 726, Byzantine Emperor Leo III issued a decree banning all icons from Orthodox churches. To put it in terms that Protestants will grasp, this would be as if some church authority suddenly banned all worship music from Protestant services. Many of us who find deep meaning in

---

11 The Acts of the Second Council of Nicaea (787) compare him to Matthew the tax collector because "he considered the following of Christ to be of more value than the treasures of Araby." Quoted in Chase's introduction to *Saint John of Damascus*, x.

12 Icons are marked by their distinct artistic style—two-dimensional paintings of full figures or head and shoulders on wood—which aims not at realism or individualism but conformity, for all icons are portraying the same glory of Christ.

13 I witnessed this firsthand while in the Church of the Holy Sepulcher in Jerusalem a few years ago. This church traditionally marks the place of Jesus's crucifixion and resurrection. Many Christians were prostrate before different pictures and objects, praying and crying loudly. On one of the crucifixes I saw, the feet of Jesus were almost worn away from disciples over the centuries who caressed them.

14 Louth, *Greek East and Latin West*, 46.

this manner of approaching God would see this as a terrible affront and feel deeply the absence of such hymns and choruses.

John saw the decree as an attack not just on a particular worship style but on the Christian tradition itself. As he wrote in one of his challenges to Leo's decree, "For what is small is not small, if it produces something big, so the slightest disturbance of the tradition of the Church that has held sway from the beginning is no small matter, that tradition made known to us by our forefathers, whose conduct we should look to and whose faith we should imitate" (*Treatise* 1.2).[15] He was right on this count, for the use of pictures in worship settings had a long history within the Church.[16] In fact, the earliest places of Christian worship still in existence, the third- and fourth-century Roman catacombs, feature numerous pictures painted onto their earthen walls.[17] These pictures include not only images of Christ but also depictions of Old Testament stories and, to a lesser extent, stories from Greek mythology. After Constantine legalized Christianity in the fourth century and Christians could begin building and meeting in their own buildings, they continued this traditional practice of decorating their churches with such pictures.

The pictures were not merely decorative but rather served a theological purpose, which the art on the walls of the catacombs demonstrate. The Catacomb of Peter and Marcellinus, for example, features a series of paintings from the story of the Prophet Jonah: (1) Jonah caught in the storm, (2) Jonah

---

15 For John's work in defense of the icons, which will be the focus of the remainder of this chapter, I will use Louth's translation, *St. John of Damascus, Three Treatises on the Divine Images*, introduction and translation by Louth (Crestwood, NY: St. Vladimir's Seminary Press, 2003), marking it in the text with the number of the treatise and the traditional paragraph number.

16 Although my summary of John's work will focus on icons, they are one aspect of a larger traditional emphasis on material objects in worship. For example, the earliest liturgical acts on record, namely, baptism and communion, both involve material objects that the faithful could see, touch, smell, and taste. These acts came to be called *sacraments*. In addition, seeing and touching relics and taking pilgrimages to see the places where Christ walked were all crucial parts of Christian piety because of the belief that such physical objects and places mystically connected Christians to Christ. As Wilken writes, "Christianity is an affair of things." Wilken, *The First Thousand Years*, 303. Such devotional practices remain central to many Christians today, as my trip to Jerusalem relayed above reveals. Madigan traces the development and corruption of this piety in the late Middle Ages. Madigan, *Medieval Christianity*, 327–342, ch. 21.

17 Wilken, *The First Thousand Years*, 49. The catacombs were underground burial sites where Christians buried their martyred brothers and sisters as a means of hiding their bodies from further desecration by the Romans.

tossed into the mouth of the fish, (3) Jonah spit out, and (4) Jonah resting on dry land.[18] The movement of the four paintings expresses the theological significance of resurrection—Jonah emerging from the fish to the shore, where he found rest—in the place where the hope of new life and rest in God's presence is most needed. Every time Christians went into the catacomb to bury the remains of a departed brother or sister, they would have been reminded of this hope. Put differently, these pictures were to the eyes what the reading of Scripture is to the ears.[19]

It is this theological function, then, that explains the ascendency of icons in the Church in the fifth century. For gradually, these pictures that were present in every church came to be used not simply as a passive means of expressing theological truth but as an active part of the worship experience. As "numinous" objects, to quote Wilken, the pictures came to be seen as physical manifestations of spiritual realities, a means of connecting worshippers to the divine realities depicted. They gave worshippers the sense that the saints were with them as they gathered around the Eucharistic table. They gave worshippers the sense that Christ was present as well and inspired within them the deep devotion that Christ deserves, for as Wilken again notes, "There is nothing more astonishing than a human face, and when painted on wood with piercing eyes it called for a response, a bow or a simple touch of the finger."[20] By John's day, however, no one had ever developed a theology to explain the scriptural grounding of this traditional practice. Rather, as Louth noted above, it was simply taken for granted.[21]

---

18 Robin M. Jensen, *The Substance of Things Seen: Art, Faith, and the Christian Community* (Grand Rapids, MI: Eerdmans, 2004), 27.

19 Jensen refers to these pictures as performing "visual exegesis." See the whole of chapter 2 in Jensen, *The Substance of Things Seen*. Indeed, the same method of reading Old Testament stories through the lens of Christ that we witnessed with Irenaeus and Origen is at play in the depictions of Old Testament stories. Small wonder that the most common Old Testament stories depicted in the catacombs—Jonah, Abraham's attempted sacrifice of Isaac, Moses hitting the rock in the wilderness—were ones where the connection to Christ was rather apparent.

20 Wilken, *The First Thousand Years*, 301.

21 This pattern of worship practices preceding theology is actually quite common in the first millennium. The technical name for the pattern is *lex orandi lex credendi* ("the law of prayer precedes the law of belief"). The greatest example is the doctrine of the Trinity. The earliest Christians worshiped Jesus alongside God, even while they remained monotheists (see, for example, Matthew 28:9, where the women left the empty tomb and, on seeing the resurrected Jesus, "clasped his feet and worshiped him"). Yet, as we have seen, it took the Church several centuries to work out the implied contradiction

As a result, some Eastern Christians at the time, known to history as Iconoclasts, believed icons were unbiblical and the displays of devotion to them idolatrous. They argued that God was revealed in Scripture as a transcendent being, in nature spirit (John 4:24), and completely different from and higher than the material world. For this reason, they argued, Moses had forbade Israel to make images of God (Exod 20:4–5). Unlike the pagan temples of the time, the Holy of Holies in Israel's Temple was empty. "Do not we worship this same God?" they asked. Moreover, they argued, pictures of the saints, which filled churches, could be nothing but idolatrous, for these were just humans. Finally, they argued that the Eucharist was the only authentic representation of Christ in the Church that Scripture allowed.[22] The perceived idolatry occasioned by the icons likely explains Leo's decree. Indeed, he may have associated the decline of his empire and its recent volatility with the loss of divine favor due to such idolatry.[23] Additionally, it was likely not lost on him that the Muslim faith, which was thriving in this period, strictly prohibited pictures of Allah. Perhaps he saw the prohibition as a means of keeping peace with the encroaching Muslims.[24] Perhaps he felt it was his job as emperor to restore the faithful worship of Christians in his churches to regain God's favor. Whatever the reason, the Iconoclasts certainly accorded him this power and supported his decision. The confrontation over icons thus had political ramifications as well. Who was the ultimate authority in the Church, the emperor or the bishop representing the tradition?

As a resident of Palestine, John was an Umayyid subject, rather far removed from the confines of the Byzantine Empire, where these policies were enacted.

---

by developing the doctrine of the Trinity. For those interested in the worship of Jesus in early Christian communities, see Larry Hurtado, *Lord Jesus Christ: Devotion to Jesus in Earliest Christianity* (Grand Rapids, MI: Eerdmans, 2003).

22 Robert Louis Wilken, *The Spirit of Early Christian Thought: Seeking the Face of God* (New Haven, CT: Yale University Press, 2003), 242. Sixteenth-century Protestant reformers used many of the same arguments in rejecting icons. John Calvin, for example, cited Exodus 20:4 and commented, "God's glory is corrupted by an impious falsehood whenever any form is attached to him." Quoted in Gesa E. Thiessen, ed., *Theological Aesthetics* (London: SCM Press, 2004), 137.

23 Leo had come to power after a quick succession of previous emperors, three in less than four years. Moreover, a catastrophic earthquake occurred in his empire earlier in 726 that Leo interpreted as divine judgment. Louth, *Greek East and Latin West*, 48–9.

24 Louth writes, "In some way, not easily discerned, iconoclasm was a way of negotiating the catastrophe experienced by the Byzantine Empire as a result of the rise of the Umayyads." Louth, *Greek East and Latin West*, 66.

However, he would have understood himself as a member of God's one Church present in all places and times. Indeed, his participation in the controversy itself is a witness to his understanding of the Church as distinct from various political communities; though living under Muslim rule, he was united in one body with his fellow Christian brothers and sisters living under Byzantine rule.[25] And this community is governed neither by a Muslim caliphate nor a Byzantine emperor but by bishops and pastors charged with maintaining fidelity to the great tradition founded on the confession that Christ alone is Lord. He writes, "I am not persuaded that the church should be constituted by imperial canons, but rather by patristic traditions, both written and unwritten" (*Treatise* 2.16). Elsewhere, he makes the distinction clear by citing Jesus's saying to render to Caesar what is Caesar's and God what is God's and commenting, "Political order is the concern of emperors, the ecclesiastical constitution that of pastors and teachers" (*Treatise* 2.12).[26] Seeing himself as one of these pastors—he was ordained a priest at some point—John wrote three different treatises against the Iconoclast argument.[27] By relying on Scripture and tradition, John developed for the first time a theology that supported the ancient practice of icon veneration. More significantly, John's work confirmed the Church's orthodox teaching of Christ as both fully human and fully divine.[28]

Because for John, at stake in this argument was not simply the appropriateness of icons; rather, the true issue was Christological. For the scriptural justification of icons, John argues, is the incarnation. Indeed, John agrees with the Iconoclasts that God by nature is "invisible" and that "it is impossible

---

25 John's perspective is a critique to twenty-first-century Christians who at best are indifferent and at worst revel at the problems experienced by denominations other than our own. If we believed, like John, that the Church was one body everywhere, then a wound to one part of the body would be a wound to the whole body.

26 Matthew 22:21.

27 The second treatise is a short reworking of the first, and the third is a reworking of the first two. The arguments of the three treatises follow essentially the same logic as well as the same scriptural and traditional arguments. In what follows, I will summarize John's main points using all three treatises.

28 After the Trinitarian controversies of the fourth century, the primary theological issue concerned understanding how Christ's divinity, established at the Councils of Nicaea and Constantinople, fit with his humanity that was clear from Scripture and, as Irenaeus had showed, was essential for salvation. The accepted position, defined by the Fourth Ecumenical Council of Chalcedon in 451, is that Christ existed as two natures (human and divine), united in one person, though it would be fought over the next three centuries.

to depict one who is incorporeal and formless, invisible and uncircumscrib-able" (*Treatise* 3.2). He grants, moreover, that to draw a picture of such a God would be a sin, as Moses's law confirms. However, when God unites himself to flesh in the person of the Son, he has "assumed the nature and density and form and color of flesh" (*Treatise* 3.8) and so becomes a material form that can now be drawn. John writes, "When you see the bodiless become human for your sake, then you may accomplish the figure of a human form; when the invisible becomes visible in the flesh, then you may depict the likeness of something seen" (*Treatise* 3.8). The prohibitions against images in the Old Testament Scriptures are not, therefore, applicable to icons of the incarnate Son. Rather, they prohibit graven images of the invisible God prior to the incarnation. Nevertheless, this does not signal a contradiction at the heart of the Scriptures; instead, the spiritual meaning of the Old Testament prohibitions "hidden beneath the letter" has nothing to do with images as such and everything to do with idolatry (*Treatise* 1.5).[29] He writes, "You see the single purpose [of these prohibitions] is that one should not worship . . . creation instead of the Creator" (*Treatise* 1.6). But that's just the point of the incarnation! Jesus is not a creature; thus, in drawing the incarnate Son and venerating his icons, the faithful are worshipping "the One who fashioned all" (*Treatise* 1.6).

To claim that venerating icons of Christ is idolatry, then, is tantamount to denying the reality of the incarnation. For the implication of the Iconoclast position is that the Son is not the Word who became flesh, as the apostle John (and Irenaeus) had argued, but a mere human being, a creature unworthy of worship. Or the alternative implication that God had not truly become flesh and so therefore cannot be drawn. Thus, we see why for John the question of icons cut to the very heart of the Church's understanding of Christ. For John, following the theology established at the Council of Chalcedon, the icon is neither a picture of a human nor an idolatrous picture of the invisible God but rather "an image of God who in his ineffable goodness became incarnate and was seen upon the earth in the flesh" (*Treatise* 2.5).[30] Put differently, the icon captures the person of Christ in whom divine and human natures are

---

29 This method of reading Scripture aligns with Origen's method. See chapter 4.

30 Nor even just his human nature, as the Iconoclasts would argue against icons in a later phase of the controversy. Such would be impossible given Chalcedon's definition of the uniting of the human and divine natures in one person (technically called "the hypostatic union" after *hypostasis*, the Greek word for "person").

unconfusedly united. As such, John can rightly proclaim in harmony with Scripture that "I do not venerate the creation instead of the creator, but I venerate the Creator, created for my sake, who came down to his creation without being lowered or weakened, that he might glorify my nature and bring about communion with the divine nature" (*Treatise* 1.4). With the full confidence in the reality of incarnation, John urged his readers to "depict him on a board and set up to view the One who has accepted to be seen" (*Treatise* 3.8).

For John Damascene believed, like Irenaeus, that "seeing God" was itself salvific as by this sight humans are brought back into communion with him.[31] Indeed, this theme is constantly present throughout the treatises. "I have seen the human form of God," he writes, "and my soul has been saved" (*Treatise* 1.22). "I will not cease from reverencing matter, through which my salvation was worked" (*Treatise* 1.16). Although this interpretation seems a blatant contradiction of numerous Old Testament passages—notably Exodus 33:20, where God says to Moses that "no one may see me and live"—John again looks to the spiritual meaning of Scripture. He finds that, despite particular injunctions against making images of God, the whole of the biblical narrative demonstrates God's use of the material to elevate humans to the immaterial realm. John references as examples Noah's ark, the rod, the golden jar that held the manna, the twelve stones taken from the Jordan, and most clearly, the Tabernacle adorned throughout with material objects (*Treatise* 1.17–20). The reason God uses such material things is that we ourselves are material and can thereby better understand divine things through the material. As Paul wrote of God's manifestation in creation, "The invisible things of God, since the creation of the world, have been clearly perceived through the things that have been made," on which John comments, "For we see images in created things intimating to us dimly reflections of the divine" (*Treatise* 1.11).[32] Most importantly, the incarnation itself follows this scriptural logic; as the Gospel of John says, "No one has ever seen God. It is God the only Son, who is close to the Father's heart, who has made him known" (John 1:18). The use

---

31 John's reference to being glorified and having communion with the divine nature is a particularly Eastern way of understanding what happens in salvation. As opposed to Catholic and Protestant models that are often forensic in nature (God forgives our sins and declares us justified), the Eastern view is a much more dynamic model where we are healed of the wound of death and become "partakers of the divine nature" (2 Pet 1:4). This is similar to Irenaeus's understanding briefly discussed at the end of chapter 2. We will encounter a Protestant version of a similar understanding of salvation in chapter 10.

32 John quotes Romans 1:20 here.

of icons in worship continues this logic: "If, in a way that bears analogy with us, we are led by images perceived through the sense to divine and immaterial contemplation and, out of love for human kind, the divine providence provides figures and shapes of what is without shape and figure, to guide us by hand, so to say, why is it unfitting, in a way that bears analogy with us, to make an image of one who submitted to shape and form and out of love for human kind was seen naturally as a man" (*Treatise* 1.33).[33] In other words, through the material images of Christ, we can be brought into spiritual communion with him.

The same argument, then, applies to icons of saints. In addition to being constant reminders that when we gather for worship, we are joining with the multitude of saints, a reminder sorely needed in many of our homogenous Western Protestant churches, icons of the saints also convey not their own glory but that of Christ. "If [the saints] are heirs of God and co-heirs with Christ and partakers of the divine glory and kingdom," John asks, "how shall not the friends of Christ be also fellow partakers on earth of his glory?" (*Treatise* 1.21). Thus, to deny images of the saints, particularly if one is willing to allow them of Christ (as some of John's opponents apparently were), is also to deny the reality of salvation, for no one less than "John the theologian, who leant on Christ's breast, therefore says, that 'we shall be like him'" (*Treatise* 1.19).[34] It is for this reason that Christ told his disciples that "he who receives you receives me," on which John comments, "So one who does not honor the saints does not honor the Lord himself'" (*Treatise* 3.49).[35] This is, the astute reader will note, essentially the same argument I offered in the introduction, namely, that in the stories of the saints, we see not them but Christ living in them. So, too, does the icon function. Or as John puts it, "What the book does for those who understand letters, the image does for the illiterate" (*Treatise* 1.17).

Of course, regardless of what the icons themselves convey, there remains the question of whether such shows of veneration—kissing, bowing down, and the like—are appropriate to offer material things. John argues yes by

---

33 So, too, I might add, is the logic behind all of the other material aspects of worship mentioned above, the sacraments in particular.

34 Orthodox writers are much stingier about the revered title *theologian*. In fact, there are only three such figures who earn that name, John the Apostle, the fourth-century figure Gregory Nazianzen, and the eleventh-century monastic Symeon, called "the new theologian."

35 John quotes here Matthew 10:40.

making a careful distinction between veneration, which is shown to icons, and worship, which is due to the Triune God, "who alone is venerable by nature" (*Treatise* 3.28). He writes, "Veneration offered out of fear or desire or honor is a symbol of submission and humility, but no one is worshipped as God, except the one who is alone God by nature, to all others what is due is reckoned for the Lord's sake" (*Treatise* 3.40). Indeed, there are many times in ordinary experience where we offer honor to another person in the form of a bow or a kiss. The same can be shown from Scripture: "Abraham venerated the sons of Emmor," John writes, "when he acquired the cave as a double inheritance for a tomb. Jacob venerated Esau his brother and Pharaoh the Egyptian, bowing in veneration over the head of his staff. They venerated, they did not worship. [Joshua] the son of Nave and Daniel venerated the angel of God, but they did not worship. The veneration of worship is one thing, veneration offered in honor of those who excel on account of something worthy is another" (*Treatise* 1.8). The honor that Christians show the icons is of this latter sort, not the worship due to God alone. Such veneration of icons is appropriate, moreover, precisely because of the divine images they portray. Jesus receives such actions as worship of *him*. In the words of the great saint Basil (whom we met last chapter), which John quotes many times through the treatises, "The honor given to the image passes to the archetype" (*Treatise* 1.25). Thus, the veneration of icons is not only appropriate but also facilitates true worship and devotion among the faithful.

If we return to our earlier analogy of worship songs, Protestant readers may grasp this final point. Songs, whether an old hymn or a new worship chorus, can be beautiful works of art in their own right and can, as such, draw out of us certain emotions that not every aspect of worship can. As a longtime Methodist, one of the aspects of Easter Sunday worship that I love most is the annual singing of Charles Wesley's unparalleled hymn "Christ the Lord Has Risen Today." I never fail to tear up when singing the words "Made like Him, like Him we rise. Ours the cross, the grave the skies," both because of the powerful words and the beautiful melody, often enhanced with organ, strings, and four-part harmonies. And stodgy Methodist that I am, I have similar reactions when I sing worship choruses like Bethel Music's "Slaves No More," particularly the bridge, "You split the sea so I could walk right through it. My fears were drowned in perfect love."[36] The artistic beauty of

---

36 This lyric, incidentally, is a wonderful example of allegorical exegesis. Here the Exodus story comes alive by referring to God's rescue of me from sin and fear.

these words and melodies leads me to experience emotions and a deep sense of devotion to God that I do not always experience in a sermon or a spoken prayer. Nevertheless, my praise is not of the poet or musician who penned the music, nor is it of the song itself or the band/organist playing it. Rather, it is of the Triune God to whom the words and music point me as I sing. And such is the case with the Byzantine icon. For Eastern Christians who encounter the icon of their Lord often experience a similar emotional experience, as a result of which they spontaneously kiss or touch the picture, in the same way that many Protestants may lift their hands in praise of the God of whom we sing. Jesus receives both displays as worship.

John's argument was persuasive. In 787, just a few decades after his death,[37] an ecumenical church council was convened at Nicaea, the site of the first ecumenical council some 450 years earlier, to discuss the matter of icons.[38] As with the previous six councils recognized as ecumenical, representatives from all major churches, both in the East and the West, were present. The council fathers agreed to restore the ancient practice of icon veneration, and their pronouncements largely followed John's arguments. Like John, they viewed the issue of icons as Christological; thus, the council came to be known as the Triumph of Orthodoxy. In Wilken's words, "The veneration of icons is the church's most palpable way of proclaiming that God appeared in human flesh in the person of Christ."[39] It also represented the triumph of the Church as an autonomous body against the Empire, both directly (as with the friendly Christian Byzantine Emperor, who tried to impose doctrine) and indirectly (as with the unfriendly Muslim caliphates whom some Christians tried to appease for the sake of peace).

The Seventh Ecumenical Council is significant, finally, for being the last council to be attended and recognized as authoritative, at least in theory, by all Christians. Because, for reasons that go beyond the scope of this chapter, the one, holy, catholic, and apostolic Church formed at Pentecost and passed down by the saints through the centuries would split in the eleventh century into

---

37 John died around 750, likely in his eighties.

38 In 754, Leo III's son, Constantine V, had called a council that upheld Leo's decree against icons and had, thereafter, purported to be the Seventh Ecumenical Council. Catholic and Orthodox Churches rejected the council as ecumenical, however, because none of the bishops of the primary churches (Rome, Constantinople, Antioch, Alexandria, and Jerusalem) was present. The initial iconoclastic fervor died with the death of Leo's grandson, Leo IV, in 780. Louth, *Greek East and Latin West*, 54–60.

39 Wilken, *The Spirit of Early Christian Thought*, 246.

two traditions, Western Catholicism and Eastern Orthodoxy.[40] And then in the sixteenth century, the Catholic Church would divide further into Roman Catholic and various Protestant bodies.[41] These formal divisions remain to this day, a sad commentary on the state of the Church. For if the cloud of witnesses shows us anything, it's that despite our many differences of races, cultures, and times, whether we speak Greek, Latin, German, English, or Chinese, whether we come from the East or the West, the eighth century or the twenty-first, we are one body in Christ. The same Christ who prayed for us on the night before his death, "that they may all be one. As you, Father, are in me and I am in you, may they also be in us, so that the world may believe that you have sent me" (John 17:21).

If Christians are to recover that unity for which Christ prayed, we must look, on a macro level, to what we share in common. Primary among these commonalities would be the Scriptures as interpreted through the creeds put forth by the Seven Ecumenical Councils. On a micro level, which is the level where real change can take root, we might open ourselves to reading folks from other traditions and other centuries. We might open ourselves to engaging other forms of spirituality, such as praying with the saints or putting an icon of Christ in our Protestant sanctuaries. Who knows? We may experience the same emotion and devotion from that picture as we do from our songs. We may even be moved to veneration.

If so, we have John Damascene to thank.

---

40 Historians often mark this "Great Schism," as it is referred to, at the year 1054, when the pope and the patriarch of Constantinople formally excommunicated one another. For those interested in the sad history of this occasion, see Louth, *Greek East and Latin West*, ch. 17. Because Catholics believe the pope is the primary authority in the Church, and councils called by him are ecumenical regardless of whether all Christians are represented, the Catholic Church went on to call fourteen more councils, the last of which, the Second Vatican Council, occurred in the 1960s. The Orthodox never embraced the bishop of Rome as pope, a factor that played a large part in their formal split, and so, after the Church was no longer one, they never embraced a new council as ecumenical.

41 I will address these sixteenth-century divisions in more detail in chapter 9.

CHAPTER SEVEN

Francis's Poverty

Thus, inwardly cleansed, interiorly enlightened,
and inflamed by the fire of the Holy Spirit,
may we be able to follow in the footprints
of your beloved Son, our Lord Jesus Christ.

—Francis of Assisi, *A Letter to the Entire Order* 51

In telling the stories of the lives of the saints thus far, we have often encountered a lack of information about their lives. For our seventh saint, Francis of Assisi, we run into the opposite problem—too much information. Francis's life was so compelling to his followers and admirers that within three decades of his life, a whole host of legendary stories arose that have since entered into the public consciousness.[1] In fact, I am willing to bet that, with the exception of Mary of Nazareth, St. Francis is the best-known Catholic saint among Protestants. We hear his name often, we see statues of him on bird feeders or in gardens, and we even sing a hymn, "All Creatures of Our God and King," that is attributed to him. Yet for all this knowledge, and for all the legendary stories, we rarely encounter the real Francis, the man who battled illness and self-doubt and contradiction; the man who worried near

---

1 In scholarly parlance, such accounts are called *hagiographies*. A hagiography presents a figure as a saint and so often downplays or omits details that would detract from such a characterization and is thereby distinguished from biography, which includes all details. To this point, we have had to rely on hagiographies, notably Gregory's *Life of Saint Macrina*.

the end of his life that the movement he started had been corrupted; the man who, for all his influence on Christianity, died in his mid-forties. This is unfortunate because it is in the real Francis, not the one of legend, that we find the true saint, the man whose greatest miracle was walking the gritty road of servanthood initially forged by Jesus Christ.[2]

Francis was born in the small Italian town of Assisi in the early 1180s.[3] This was a time of great upheaval in the Catholic Church. As noted in the previous chapter, the Catholic Church was now formally separated from the Eastern Orthodox Church, though efforts at reunification continued. Unfortunately, at least to modern sensibilities, these efforts took the primary form of crusades, military efforts to defeat the Muslim forces that had taken over most of the Eastern world.[4] The prospect proved more daunting than originally

---

2 The primary biographical account I follow is Augustine Thompson, OP, *Francis of Assisi: A New Biography* (Ithaca, NY: Cornell University Press, 2012). Thompson's work does an excellent job of sifting through the legends and comparing them to Francis's actual writings, to which many biographers surprisingly pay little attention, in order to present the real Francis. He also includes a lengthy second section that includes the latest scholarship on the historicity of all of the various accounts of Francis's life, making helpful judgments on the reliability of these stories. Readers interested in a more accessible biography should consider G. K. Chesterton, *Saint Francis of Assisi*, repr. (New York: Doubleday, 2001), which my account references some. I have also consulted the early Franciscan Bonaventure's *The Life of Saint Francis* in *Bonaventure*, trans. Evert Cousins, The Classics of Western Spirituality (Mahwah, NJ: Paulist Press, 1978), a spiritual classic in its own right. For Francis's work, I will use the volume *Francis and Clare: The Complete Works*, trans. Regis J. Armstrong, OFM, and Ignatius C. Brady, OFM, The Classics of Western Spirituality (Mahwah, NJ: Paulist Press, 1982). Citations will be marked in the text with the title and paragraph number.

3 The astute reader will note that we have skipped ahead somewhat since our previous chapter. This is not to suggest that there were no saints in the years between John Damascene and Francis of Assisi nor that nothing of note occurred in the history of the Church in those years. Rather, the confines of this book necessitate hard choices, and St. Francis is as good a figure there is for understanding the Church and Christian spirituality in the high Middle Ages. Incidentally, we will encounter one other major gap like this, namely between chapters 9 and 10, and the same reasoning applies there.

4 Muslim armies were less successful in penetrating Europe primarily because of the strong kingdom of the Franks, which, in 800 under King Charlemagne, made a formal alliance with the Catholic Church, establishing the Holy Roman Empire. Wilken, *The First Thousand Years*, ch. 35. Nevertheless, the popes saw Eastern Christians as part of their flock. Thus, every crusade from 1095 to the latter half of the thirteenth century has as one of its stated purposes the deliverance of Eastern Christians from Muslim occupiers and, in some cases, persecutors. There is reason to doubt how much this was actually a factor, at least among the crusaders themselves. One of the most tragic events in all of Church history is the Fourth Crusade in 1204, when Western crusaders on their way to

conceived and resulted in almost two centuries of fighting between Christians and Muslims over the rights to lands of biblical significance. Francis himself would live through three different crusades, one of which, called the Fifth Crusade by historians, intersects with his biography.

Closer to home, the Church was still in a period of reform, known to history as the Gregorian Reforms after Pope Gregory VII, who initiated them. Since the disintegration of Charlemagne's empire in the mid-ninth century, the papacy had become a possession of sorts for competing noble families in different places of Europe to use at their discretion, which led to the buying and selling of clerical offices or the passing of offices from one generation to the next.[5] Immorality among the clergy had been high and spiritual care of the laity low, and in the helpful summation of medieval historian Kevin Madigan, "everywhere canon law was either unknown or ignored."[6] Pope Gregory VII put an end to this, enforcing clerical celibacy, insisting on the independence of the Church from temporal powers, and placing a greater emphasis on the importance of morality among clergy and laity. The reforms had the effect of elevating the office of the pope not only over the head of the Roman church but also over "the entire body of Christians, called Christendom," a salient point to understand for a later chapter.[7] More to the point for the current chapter, in the century prior to Francis's birth, there emerged a need for reform among the monasteries as well. Though there were numerous monasteries across Europe, the original ideals of the monastic life, as witnessed in Macrina's story, had largely been lost. Most monastics lived comfortable lives in wealthy monasteries disengaged from real people living in the harsh realities of the medieval world. Though one would not have guessed it from his early life, Francis would chart a new monastic path, which, in reality, was the recovery of a very old one.

Francis's father was a wealthy merchant in Assisi, meaning Francis was in line for a lucrative inheritance and, by medieval standards, a rather comfortable life. At the age of fourteen, after a rudimentary education, Francis began work as an apprentice to his father and quickly learned to enjoy the spoils of a profitable business. As a young teenager, he delighted in wearing

---

the Holy Land ended up sacking the Byzantine city of Constantinople, an event that set back Eastern and Western Christian relations for centuries.

5 Prior to the eleventh century, clerical celibacy was not enforced.

6 Madigan, *Medieval Christianity*, 79. Madigan's discussion of the ensuing reforms in chapter 8 is insightful.

7 Madigan, *Medieval Christianity*, 145.

the latest fashions. He attracted a group of friends and went everywhere with them—"in a pack," as my parents used to say—often throwing lavish dinner parties.[8] His actions in these years suggest a desire to be seen, to be noticed, and to stand out. Thompson notes that in these early years, "Francis's personality included a touch of vanity and narcissism."[9] Ironically, however, few stories from this period come down to us save for an account that manifests the opposite inclination. One day, a beggar wandered into his father's shop looking for handouts. Focused on the day's tasks and perhaps, in his vanity, perturbed by the man's appearance, Francis drove him from the store. Later that day, however, he was disturbed by this hasty dismissal, and he sought after the man to, in Bonaventure's telling, give him "generous alms, promising God that from that moment onward, while he had the means, he would never refuse those who begged from him for the love of God."[10]

Some time later, Francis joined a local militia, though not for the good of his city or out of a sense of duty but, according to Bonaventure, "to obtain the glory of knighthood."[11] Here again, he was motivated by his desire to be seen. He was, however, thwarted in his quest as his unit was badly defeated, leading to his capture and yearlong imprisonment in nearby Perugia. The episode resulted in a sort of crisis for Francis. Not only had his failures in battle robbed him of his hope for glory, but his health was also significantly impaired, leading to ailments that would plague him the rest of his life. Thompson, moreover, suggests that he suffered from a form of post-traumatic stress disorder, which stories of his troubling dreams and flashbacks to the war during this period corroborate.[12] By all accounts, his military failures were a low point of Francis's life, symbolic of his inability to gain the self-glory he craved. This period is perfectly captured by a statue that stands today in Assisi outside of the Franciscan monastery. Francis sits on a horse in military uniform, his head bowed in failure.

On his return to his hometown, he curved further in on himself, rejoining none of his former activities, spending his time at home, or wandering the streets aimlessly. He did not throw any of his former parties or connect with

---

8 Thompson, *Francis of Assisi*, 8.

9 Thompson, *Francis of Assisi*, 9.

10 Bonaventure, *Life of Saint Francis* 1.1 in *Bonaventure*, 186.

11 Bonaventure, *Life of Saint Francis* 1.3 in *Bonaventure*, 188. In medieval times, such skirmishes among rival cities were common.

12 Thompson, *Francis of Assisi*, 10.

any of his old friends. His lust for life, it seems, was gone. He made one more halfhearted attempt at attaining military glory during this period, riding out to join up with a militia. But in the end, he stopped, for reasons that remain unclear. Though early accounts suggest that he had a vision from God, his change of heart is just as likely a result of his aimlessness and confused state of mind. Either way, he turned back before he reached the militia, sold his horse and military garb to a merchant in another town, and walked back to his hometown, a lost and confused man.

At this, his lowest point, around 1205 or 1206, two events occurred that changed his life. All of the oldest hagiographies include both stories, though they notoriously differ on the order.[13] Such discrepancies suggest that we should understand them as two parts of the same phenomenon, namely, Francis's experience and embrace of his divine vocation to ministry. For one does not often hear and respond to God's calling to ministry in a moment; it rather happens gradually and as the result of many factors. In my own life, I experienced God's calling over a period of many months during my sophomore year of college. Like Francis, I was in a particularly low point in my life, stricken with a bad case of mono, lost as to what I wanted to do with my life (after three recent changes of majors), and newly single after the girl I had planned to marry had broken up with me. Oddly, during that very period, several different people told me I should consider ministry because I had the gifts for it. I initially found these comments laughable as, due to my rather low state, I was not exactly thriving in my discipleship. But the comments kept coming. Later that spring, in a moment of deep prayer and reconciliation with God, I, too, sensed that he was calling me to ministry. Although I felt incredibly unworthy and unequal to the task, I said yes, changed my major yet again, and set out on a path I had never anticipated to that point and for which I am eternally grateful to God. In reflecting on this long experience with a trusted mentor, he helped me to see that the external call I was hearing from others finally aligned with the internal call I experienced in prayer.

Such an interpretation helps us understand these two pivotal events in Francis's life. His external call came not in the form of others telling him he had gifts for ministry but in a seemingly random encounter with

---

13 Thompson helpfully sorts out this confusing timeline, though I have departed from him here and followed the more traditional accounts of these stories. Thompson, *Francis of Assisi*, 10–17.

a leper. Although there was a leprosarium—a leper hospital of sorts—on the outskirts of Assisi, they rarely roamed the streets, so the sight of a leper as Francis was riding through town would have been strange. Nor was Francis at all disposed to kindness toward the man. We have already seen that vanity was one of his shortcomings in his early years. Later in his life, he connects this vanity specifically to his aversion to lepers, writing, "While I was in sin, it seemed very bitter to me to see lepers" (*Testament* 1).[14] He wanted to run the other way as he would have done at any other time in his life prior, but again something stopped him. Perhaps it was his own lowly state reflected in his simple garb. Perhaps for the first time, he identified with the leper, feeling in himself the same spiritual disease that the leper manifested on his skin. Whatever the reason, Francis jumped off the horse, embraced the leper, and kissed him. In this moment, the man who had always desired to be seen finally sees another, and the glory he had always sought was found in utter indignity. The experience changed him. As he writes, "And the Lord Himself led me among [lepers] and I had mercy upon them. And when I left them that which seemed bitter to me was changed into sweetness of body and soul; and afterward I lingered a little and left the world" (*Testament* 2–3).[15]

Francis's reference to a short period of lingering is intriguing. Did he begin to doubt in the weeks that followed whether the life-changing experience was of God? Was he drawn again to just embrace his comfortable life and inheritance, which would ensure a safe distance from lepers? Or did he feel pressure from his father, for whom, at least officially, he still worked? Whatever the cause of the lingering, it finally ended in a rundown church two miles outside of town, the setting of the second pivotal event. During his low period following his military failures, Francis had taken to visiting the dilapidated church called San Damiano and praying in front of the crucifix. The ancient stories report that during one of these prayers, he heard the Lord speaking to him from the crucifix: "Francis, go and repair my house, which, as you see,

---

14 Francis dictated this work, known as *The Testament*, near the end of his life, and it is the closest thing we have to an autobiographical account of his life. In this short work, he uses his hatred of lepers to summarize his life of sin and, as we shall see shortly, his embrace of them to summarize the change he experienced.

15 Bonaventure and other early biographers make the leper a figure of Christ who disappears shortly after the incident. Bonaventure, *Life of Saint Francis* 1.5 in *Bonaventure*, 189.

is falling completely into ruin."[16] Here was his experience of the internal call. Francis sensed—heard?—God calling him to a ministry of church renewal in a similar way to the change in his principles he sensed in the encounter with the leper. And as he literally began rebuilding the broken-down San Damiano by hand, so, too, did he begin to lavish the same kind of attention on broken-down humans, serving often in the leprosarium and seeking out those who were poor to give alms.

Francis's change of behavior was so radical that many people took notice. His father, in particular, saw the profits of his business dwindling through Francis's extravagant generosity and grew concerned for its long-term viability. So he took his son to court, likely to protect his money. Showing none of his earlier vanity, though perhaps with a continued flare for the dramatic, Francis gladly renounced his inheritance. According to the early stories, he stripped off all his clothes except a hair shirt and placed them at his father's feet.[17] He was now free of the burden of his inheritance, and the indignant manner of his renunciation confirms that he no longer cared for the glory that once consumed him. He went into the woods, a lighter man, singing hymns as he went.[18] Like Macrina and the monastics of old, in this courtroom, he denied himself in order to take up his cross and follow Jesus.[19] He would forever describe it as the moment he left the world, for, from this point on, Francis embraced a life of poverty for the spiritual rebuilding of God's Church, of which his embrace of the leper was both prophetic and paradigmatic.

Though inconceivable to his father, and to most people both then and now, Francis's new, simple lifestyle proved attractive to some. For after a few years of rebuilding San Damiano, caring for lepers at the leprosarium,

---

16 Bonaventure, *Life of Saint Francis* 2.1 in *Bonaventure*, 191. Thompson doubts the historicity of this event though he believes Francis experienced a time of healing while praying at the church. Thompson, *Francis of Assisi*, 11–14.

17 The early stories paint Francis's father as a rather despicable character, but Thompson gives a much more sympathetic portrait. Certainly, he was perplexed by Francis's behavior, but he had a rightful duty to protect his business, which was his and his family's livelihood. Thompson, *Francis of Assisi*, 14–16. Still, the prospect of being taken to court by his own father had to be jarring for Francis.

18 Chesterton's account of the juxtaposition of Francis's precarious situation and joyful attitude is helpful: "He was penniless, he was parentless, he was to all appearance without a trade or a plan or a hope in the world; and as he went under the frosty trees, he burst suddenly into song." Chesterton, *Saint Francis*, 48.

19 Bonaventure uses this scriptural passage to interpret the leper incident. Bonaventure, *Life of Saint Francis* 1.5 in *Bonaventure*, 189.

and doing odd jobs around Assisi for food, two men came to Francis who, in Thompson's words, "had both been inspired by Francis's decision to leave the world, seeing in him an authenticity that had escaped most citizens of Assisi."[20] One is reminded of the fourth-century desert monastic Antony, mentioned in chapter 5, whose biography inspired thousands to go to the desert. The difference here is that these men hadn't read about Francis; they had seen him with their own eyes, an incarnational principle that forms the key aspect of Francis's genius, to which I will return shortly.

This development, however, may have been as much of a surprise to Francis as anyone, for there is no indication in the early stories that he had intended to start a movement. Indeed, Francis had no idea what to do with the men. He writes, "And after that the Lord gave me brothers, no one showed me what I should do" (*Testament* 14). The three men decided together to ask a local priest to perform what was called a *sortes biblicae*, a practice popular among the laity that entailed opening the Bible to random verses to reveal God's will for the inquirer. The priest agreed and opened the altar missal three times to the following verses:[21] (1) "Go, sell what you own, and give the money to the poor, and you will have treasure in heaven; then come, follow me" (Mark 10:21); (2) "Take nothing for your journey, no staff, nor bag, nor bread, nor money—not even an extra tunic" (Luke 9:3); and (3) "If any want to become my followers, let them deny themselves and take up their cross and follow me" (Matt 16:24). While this is certainly not a method of reading Scripture to follow regularly—indeed, I have already been critical of it in this book[22]—it worked for this small band of brothers, who took the

---

20 Thompson, *Francis of Assisi*, 22. As reported by the early stories, the men's names were Bernard and Peter. Bernard was a rather rich man, but Peter was poor, indicative of the varied demographic of people whom Francis attracted. Francis's most famous disciple in his lifetime, however, is probably Clare of Assisi, who approached him in much the same way and later began her own order of nuns known as the Poor Clares. They carried on a lively correspondence in his life, though they rarely saw one another. Clare is also recognized as a saint.

21 The missal contains readings for different days so is potentially less random than using the same practice with a full Bible. The missal Francis used on this occasion still exists and can be seen at the Walters Art Museum in Baltimore, Maryland. Thompson, *Francis of Assisi*, 23.

22 Thompson reports that theologians in Francis's day rejected this practice as little more than superstition. Thompson, *Francis of Assisi*, 23. That Francis pursued the practice and trusted it is indicative of both his lay status (he would be ordained a deacon later) and his simple faith. It is also a reminder to educated theologians to be open to the surprising work of God that often comes in ways that we reject as simple.

passages as confirmation of the life Francis had already inaugurated. He continues in his *Testament*, "The Most High Himself revealed to me that I should live according to the form of the Holy Gospel" (*Testament* 14). The brothers committed to live together a life of poverty and service out among their fellow humans. And so began one of the most important arms of Church renewal through the Middle Ages, namely, the Franciscan Order, provisionally approved by Pope Innocent III in 1209 and officially approved by Pope Honorius III in 1223.[23]

What made Francis's movement stand apart from other monastic movements of the time was its refusal to be cloistered, that is, to be located in a monastery and removed from the ordinary world of everyday people. Rather, Francis and his brothers would be among the people, living and working alongside them, caring for them and serving them, and when necessary, begging with them. "The brothers shall not acquire anything as their own, neither a house nor a place nor anything at all," wrote Francis in what would become the order's official rule. "Instead as pilgrims and strangers in this world who serve the Lord in poverty, let them go begging for alms with full trust" (*Later Rule* 6). This was revolutionary at the time, for the Rule of St. Benedict, which had more or less governed all monastic orders in the West until that point, required monks to be bound to their monasteries. Though we have seen the positives of this approach with Macrina's house, I noted above that in the early medieval period, it started to breed corruption in places due to the excess stores of money the monasteries would come to possess through gifts and inheritances. Moreover, it exacerbated an already perceived division between monastics and laity. Not so with the Franciscans. They were the Friars Minor (Lesser Brothers), as the order was known in Francis's lifetime. Their

---

23 Since all monastic orders needed the approval of popes, Francis and his brothers traveled to Rome in 1209 to gain an audience with the pope. Earlier hagiographies make much of the submission of Pope Innocent III, widely considered the most powerful pope in history, to the humble Francis. Bonaventure, for example, writes that the pope initially rejected Francis because of his poor appearance but later admitted him because of visions of a palm tree sprout that gradually grew to become a beautiful tree and a poor man who held on his back the Lateran basilica. "This is certainly the man," the pope said, "who by his work and teaching will hold up the Church of Christ." Bonaventure, *Life of Saint Francis* 3.10 in *Bonaventure*, 206. Thompson paints a more realistic picture of that meeting, suggesting that a bishop, rather than Francis, likely spoke to Innocent on behalf of the brothers and that Innocent's provisional acceptance of the order was due to skepticism that it would bear any fruit. Thompson, *Francis of Assisi*, 24–28.

habit (distinctive monastic robes) was the tattered rags of the beggar.[24] They were not just to consider themselves on the same level as all other humans but were to consider others above themselves. "None of the brothers should be administrators or managers in whatever places they are staying among others to serve or to work," Francis writes in an earlier, provisional rule. "Instead, they should be the lesser ones and subject to all who are in the same house" (*Earlier Rule* 7.1–2).[25] The Franciscans, therefore, were a mendicant (begging) order, and while there would be others—the Dominicans were established as a mendicant order around the same time, known for their work of preaching to laity and ceasing the spread of heresy—the Franciscans alone embodied the ideal of poverty.

The Franciscan Order, then, was initially modeled on Francis's life, which itself was modeled on the life of Jesus, "who, though he was in the form of God, did not regard equality with God as something to be exploited, but emptied himself, taking the form of a slave, being born in human likeness" (Phil 2:6–7). Indeed, this incarnational principle explains so much of Francis's life and thought as it developed after 1209. He was earthy, material, real. He advocated manual labor for the brothers. Instead of the typical picture of the medieval monk copying texts in a scriptorium, the early Franciscans had dirty hands, torn cloaks, and full hearts. The brothers were to in all things live like Jesus, turning the other cheek, walking the extra mile, giving away their cloaks. Stories abound of Francis giving his only clothes away, to the detriment of his own health and often to the consternation of his brothers, who kept having to find new cloaks for him.

In the same vein, the most important aspect of worship for Francis was not the sung Psalms of the Benedictine Order or the sermon of the Dominican Order but, rather, the Eucharist.[26] Like Francis himself, the Eucharist was material, a thing you could touch, hold, taste, and see. As such, the Eucharist alone manifested the true presence of Jesus among the people. Moreover, the

---

24 This habit came to be the plain brown robe of the Franciscans, unique for its non-descript appearance. In his lifetime, Francis's robe was literally a tattered, sewn-together grayish robe, which can be seen at the Franciscan monastery in Assisi.

25 Francis wrote this first rule, now known as *The Earlier Rule*, following the provisional acceptance of the order in 1209. It developed into the *The Later Rule* he wrote, with more input from experts in Canon Law, in 1223. *The Later Rule* remains the official rule of Franciscans. Thompson, *Francis of Assisi*, 103–4.

26 Like devotion to Mary, the centrality of the Eucharist is a common theme in all of the stories of the saints.

simplicity of the bread and wine, everyday items in his time as in ours, mirrored the humility of the incarnate Word. He writes, "See, daily He Humbles Himself as when He came from the *royal throne* into the womb of the Virgin; daily He comes to us in a humble form; daily He comes down from the bosom of the Father upon the altar in the hands of the priest" (*Admonitions* 1.16–18, italics original). For this reason, the manner in which the priest handled the elements required strict care, and as such, a surprising amount of his writings is dedicated to the proper honor owed the Eucharist. "It spoke to Francis's profound sense of God's presence in the concrete here and now," Thompson writes, "and in the most commonplace of things and events."[27] This is not to suggest, of course, that Francis did not value prayer. Indeed, he was a man of deep prayer and found in the regular discipline times of sweet communing with God. Bonaventure writes, "The servant of Christ Francis strove to keep his spirit in the presence of God *by praying without ceasing* so that he might not be without the comfort of his *Beloved*."[28] The difference between Francis's habits of prayer and those of other monastics of the time is that they did not take him out of the world or keep him from the world. Rather, prayer always drove him back to the concrete world as the place of God's presence.

This incarnational principle, then, is the proper lens through which to understand one of the better-known aspects of Francis's spirituality, namely, his love of nature. It was often said of Francis that he communed with nature and wildlife, seeing these as equal to humans in God's creation. Many of the early, legendary stories have Francis preaching to birds or his brothers preaching to wolves and fish. He did so not because he believed nature was divine in itself, but rather he believed that, as God's creation, nature contained the image of the divine within itself as humans did. Chesterton writes, "The whole point of him was that the secret of recovering the natural pleasures lay in regarding them in light of supernatural pleasure."[29] In other words,

---

27 Thompson, *Francis of Assisi*, 63.

28 Bonaventure, *Life of Saint Francis* 10.1 in *Bonaventure*, 272, italics original.

29 Chesterton, *Saint Francis*, 64. Chesterton frames his entire narrative on this aspect of Francis's biography. He argues in chapter 2 that Christianity had to downplay nature in its first millennium in order to distinguish itself from paganism, which had viewed nature as divine in itself. Francis, for Chesterton, is a turning point where theology, cured of the ancient paganism, was able once again to embrace nature as manifesting God's presence. As he writes at the end of chapter 2, "While it was yet twilight a figure appeared silently and suddenly on a little hill above the city, dark against the fading darkness. For it was the end of a long and stern night, a night of vigil, not unvisited by stars. He stood with

the whole creation manifested God's presence in an analogous way to the Eucharist within the Christian community. His final and most beloved writing, *The Canticle of Brother Sun*, is a hymn of praise to the glories of creation: "Praised be to You, my Lord, with all your creatures, especially Sir Brother Sun, Who is the day and through whom You give us light. And he is beautiful and radiant with great splendor; and bears a likeness of You, Most High One" (*Canticle of Brother Sun* 3–4).[30]

The primary lesson to be drawn from Francis's life in our own time goes beyond those we took from Macrina's life. While the same ascetic values are certainly present in Francis's ascetic life, they can be interpreted as somewhat self-focused, that is, as pursued for the strengthening of our *own* lives of discipleship. While there is nothing wrong with such lessons, they do not capture Francis's example. For Francis's life was wholly and completely others-focused. Taking up his cross daily for Francis meant not just a sacrifice of money and relationships; it meant a life lived for others. And not just in theory but in concrete ways, for everything with Francis is concrete. He did not just give money for a church to be rebuilt; he rebuilt it with his own hands. Nor did he give donations of clothes to a charitable organization; he gave his own cloak to the poor person he passed on the road. He did not just talk about the ideal of caring for the sick; he hugged and kissed lepers. He did not just read about Jesus's command to make disciples of all nations; he traveled to Egypt during the Fifth Crusade, crossed enemy lines, and spoke with Malik al-Kamil, the leader of the Muslim forces.[31] He did these things at considerable risk, and indeed, his sacrificial way of life led to his untimely death in his early forties. For incarnational living is never without danger, as the original incarnation shows us. As a professor of mine once said, incarnation always ends in death.[32]

---

his hands lifted, as in so many statues and pictures, and about him was a burst of birds singing; and behind him was the break of day." Chesterton, *Saint Francis*, 28.

30 This was the first poem to be written in the vernacular Italian. Thompson, *Francis of Assisi*, 123.

31 Thompson, *Francis of Assisi*, 66–69. This incredible story is not one of legend but history. He was received well by the sultan, though the latter did not embrace the Catholic faith. One is reminded here of the actions by Pope Francis I in initiating peace talks with Muslim leaders in 2019 and 2021, marking the first time a Roman pontiff has visited the homelands of Islam. Perhaps Pope Francis was inspired to such action by his namesake.

32 Dr. Darrell Whiteman in an anthropology class I took at Asbury Theological Seminary in 2002.

The example of St. Francis is the most challenging of this book because his way of life refuses to be domesticated or allegorized away. To follow Francis means to take the *real* road of sacrifice. While I hesitate to even suggest ways of walking this real road, primarily because I fail to walk it myself, there are ways if we would have eyes to see. For some, it might mean giving so much that it hurts your bank account, even though you are saving for your kids' college or a vacation. For others, it means spending extra time with that student who needs it or that colleague who is hurting, even though you are tired and want nothing more than to go home. For all of us, it should mean never passing the person who is crying on a bench or at a table even though there is a meeting to get to. Taking this hard road will mean real consequences, just as it did for Francis. Recall that most people thought he was crazy. Indeed, very shortly after his death, the Franciscan Order turned from his ideal and became a cloistered order; even those who submitted to his rule could not walk its narrow road.[33] If we truly desire to follow Francis, perhaps the best we can do as a first step is to seek to make our acts of charity more concrete than they usually are. We can stay engaged in the world—the real, hurting world full of lepers and beggars—as opposed to retreating to the safe Christian corners of our safe Christian neighborhoods. Then, perhaps, we will have caught a glimmer of the day breaking with St. Francis.

If we ever needed a saint's prayers, we need them for this.

The last years of Francis's life were not great. He was sick and often in pain. He underwent an incredibly painful medical procedure that didn't work.[34] He saw the gradual decline of the fervency of his order from the ideal of poverty and living among the people, which gave him a near-constant experience of anxiety. Finally, like Origen before him, he was saddened that he would likely now not achieve martyrdom, which had always been an ideal for him.[35] Ironically, however, it is during these years that Francis had a mystical experience

---

33 The story of the Franciscans after Francis's life is in many ways a tragic one for the strife among the brothers over Francis's legacy. In the end, the Franciscans would become another cloistered order, the most prominent of the monasteries located in Assisi itself.

34 Thompson notes that he had a condition called *ophthalmia*, an inflammation of the eyes that made them extremely sensitive to light. As a treatment, a doctor performed a painful procedure, which cauterized the flesh from his jaw to his weaker eye without the aid of anesthesia. Thompson, *Francis of Assisi*, 128–29.

35 Part of his motivation for traveling to Egypt was the hopes of becoming a martyr. Indeed there were several points of his life when he left Assisi intending to preach the gospel in foreign lands with an expectation that he would not return, but each time his efforts were thwarted.

that is both the most well-known and least understood aspect of his life. While in prayer on a solitary retreat, Francis received a vision of a six-winged seraph affixed to a cross as though crucified. The mystical nature of vision is not the sort of biographical detail one expects of this real, concrete man,[36] and Francis himself was disturbed by it. But as he left the mountain and returned to the world, as he always did, he realized he had nail marks in his hands and a bleeding wound in his side. For he was experiencing the wounds of Christ, known to history as the stigmata. This experience was not a mystical vision or a dream but a real experience. The wounds bled. They caused him near-constant pain. Indeed, because of the number of eyewitnesses to these marks and the blood-soaked handkerchiefs that remain from his attempts to conceal the wounds, most scholars consider his stigmata as real,[37] though it lacks any rational explanation, much less a coherent reason for its appearance.

Perhaps only a theological interpretation will do: this poor man had so perfectly conformed his life to Christ that in his final years, he manifested Christ's very wounds. Like the martyrs of the early years, he literally became like Christ. But in keeping with the mendicant spirit of his order, his Christ-likeness did not take him from the world but left him in the world. Like Christ, he remained among the humans and the nature he so dearly loved, even as he bled for them. And the experience was for him at once painful and glorious, as the narrow road of incarnational living must always be.

---

36 Though, in another sense, it is a fitting bookend to the vision of Christ speaking to him from the crucifix in San Damiano at the beginning of his ministry.

37 Thompson, *Francis of Assisi*, 116–117, 265–66.

CHAPTER EIGHT

Julian's Heart

*This beautiful word "mother" is so sweet and kind
in itself that it cannot be attributed to anyone but God.*

—Julian of Norwich, *Showings* 2:60

Francis's strange vision of the crucified seraph is actually not as anomalous as one might think. In the course of Christian history, there have been numerous examples of disciples who have experienced such visions, as we saw with Perpetua in chapter 3. Indeed, the high Middle Ages was a particularly fertile period for such visionaries, known to history as *mystics*, especially among those whose voices were typically not heard, namely women.[1] Chief among this extraordinary group is our eighth saint, Julian of Norwich, whose description of the visions she received at age thirty reveal a God whom medieval theology had otherwise overshadowed and who remains overshadowed in many Protestant traditions today. Hers was a vision of a God who loves his children as only a mother could.[2]

---

1 Prominent examples of medieval women mystics include Hildegard of Bingen (d. 1179), Catherine of Siena (d. 1380), Joan of Arc (d. 1431), and Teresa of Ávila (d. 1582).

2 Julian's account of her visions survive in two versions, referred to as the *Short Text* and the *Long Text*. The *Short Text* was written in the 1370s, shortly after she received the visions and, in its current form, includes an introductory paragraph by the scribe who copied it. The *Long Text* was written later in life after more theological reflection on what she saw. I will focus my account on the *Long Text*, using the translation by Mirabai Starr, trans., *The Showings of Julian of Norwich: A New Translation* (Charlottesville, VA: Hampton Roads Publishing Company, 2013), and will mark it in the text as *Showings* 2 with the chapter number.

Julian was born in 1342 in Norwich, a city on the eastern coast of England.[3] By this point in England, as in nearly all Western lands, local principalities were thoroughly Christian, and church and state enjoyed a mutually beneficial partnership.[4] While there were some negatives to this arrangement, as we saw in the previous chapter, it proved an effective means of instilling the faith in new generations. A place like Norwich in the fourteenth century, for example, would have organized the life of its citizens around the rhythms of the church year—daily mass; regular processionals through town marking births, weddings, and deaths; fasts and feasts on holy days; and various celebrations of treasured saints, both universal and local. The most prominent structure in town was the Holy Trinity Cathedral, whose ringing bells, which marked *lauds*, or morning prayer, could be heard in every corner of town.[5] The city was thick with religious imagery, and the vibrant colors of each liturgical season gave divine meaning to lives that were otherwise filled with hardship.

Like all children, Julian would have been bathed in this imagery and learned from a young age, almost by osmosis, to order her own life around the teachings of what she will later call "her mother, Holy Church" (*Showings* 2.46). God was a palpable presence in her life, necessary for her daily sustenance, a help in time of need, a judge of her faithful and unfaithful actions. By her own account, as a child she had an uncommon faith and desire to experience her Lord. She writes that she had once prayed for three gifts from God: "One, participation in his passion; two, a life-threatening illness; and three, the grace of the triple-wound (contrition, compassion, and unbearable longing)" (*Showings* 2.2).[6]

---

3 Unlike many of the saints we have encountered, Julian was not well known in her lifetime. The few biographical details that exist come from her own words and some external references from those who encountered her as an older woman. Modern biographies engage in much speculation about her younger years based on typical lives of women from the same place and time. Biographies I have consulted for this chapter include Veronica Mary Rolf, *Julian's Gospel: Illuminating the Life and Revelations of Julian of Norwich* (Maryknoll, NY: Orbis Books, 2013) and Amy Frykholm, *Julian of Norwich* (Brewster, MA: Paraclete Press, 2010).

4 This partnership did not, however, create a unity of Christian nations in the West. During all of Julian's life, Catholic England was engaged in a constant struggle with Catholic France in what is known as the Hundred Years' War (1337–1453). Another well-known medieval mystic and contemporary of Julian's, Joan of Arc, was on the other side of this confrontation.

5 Rolf, *Julian's Gospel*, 21.

6 The word *passion* in this context refers to Jesus's suffering and death on the cross.

If it was suffering she longed for, she received it soon enough. For in 1349, when Julian was just six years old, the Black Death that had been sweeping across Europe for two years finally reached Norwich. It was a combination of three related diseases—bubonic plague, septicaemic plague, and pneumonic plague—carried from town to town on the fleas of rats and, in the case of the third strand, by air.[7] It spread like "fire when it [came] into contact with large masses of combustibles," wrote one eyewitness, and it killed quickly and indiscriminately.[8] People would develop a fever or black swellings in their necks and armpits or large boils on their skin, and within a few days, they would be dead. Due to poor sanitation and lack of effective medical treatment, city populations were decimated.[9] In Norwich, at least half of the population died.[10] As a young girl, Julian would have seen death all around her, the bells of the cathedral drowned out by the ubiquitous sobs of her friends and neighbors. She would have experienced death personally, for the first outbreak likely took her father and, if she had any, her brothers and sisters.[11]

Questions naturally arose as to the reason for such devastation, and in such religiously saturated areas, that answer was theological. "The conviction reigned that God was punishing mankind for its sins," writes historian Norman Davies.[12] Indeed, certain medieval views on God, particularly as experienced by the laity who attended mass regularly, made such a conclusion inevitable. Due in part to the enormous influence of Augustine,[13] the fourth-century theologian most responsible for developing the doctrine of original sin,[14] homilies regularly emphasized human sinfulness. While the

---

7 Norman Davies, *Europe: A History* (Oxford: Oxford University Press, 1996), 409.

8 So wrote the Italian author Boccaccio. Quoted in Rolf, *Julian's Gospel*, 70.

9 Scholars estimate that the plague took around a third of Europe's overall population, some thirty million people. Davies, *Europe*, 412. The plague also had many recurring outbreaks in later years.

10 Rolf, *Julian's Gospel*, 73.

11 In her writings, Julian only mentions her mother, who sat by her bed during her illness.

12 Davies, *Europe*, 411.

13 Much of medieval theology as it came to be written in texts and taught in the universities that trained parish priests was interpretations of Augustine. Additionally, Rolf reports that Augustine's autobiographical book, *Confessions*, was read all over Europe. "We may assume that Augustine," she writes, "suffused the air Christians breathed . . . and that Julian would have been exposed to them all her life." Rolf, *Julian's Gospel*, 119.

14 Original sin is the belief that all humans inherit from birth Adam's sinful nature, which came as a result of his original transgression in the garden. Augustine developed this doctrine from the writings of Paul (see, for example, Rom. 3:23, 5:12–14) against

point of such an emphasis was to proclaim God's grace in saving us from that sin, it often had the opposite effect of making God seem like a righteous judge all too eager to condemn and punish. This impression was reinforced by the complex system of confession and penance that arose in the Middle Ages and was strictly regulated by the church hierarchy.[15] The faithful were expected to confess their sins to a priest at least once a year on penalty of excommunication and then do acts of penance to prove the authenticity of their repentant hearts.[16] Even death did not entail an immediate release from this wretched state, for the Middle Ages also saw the development of a belief in purgatory, an intermediate place where Christians went to be further purged of their sins and so be ready for eternal life in heaven.[17] From this perspective, the plague merely served to support what the Church had been telling Christians all along. As Frykholm writes, "The stink of the plague was as vivid evidence as they needed for the terrible odor of sin."[18] While Julian herself does not discuss the plague directly, she does reveal that the teachings she received through her childhood caused her to focus on her sins. She writes, "The ordinary teaching of Holy Church, plus my own sense of things, had me convinced that the guilt of our sins hangs on us always,

---

opponents who argued that humans could essentially be holy by their own proper use of free will.

15 The church hierarchy in many ways regulated one's entire relationship with God. Lay Christians heard the Scriptures read and interpreted by and received the sacraments from their priests, who in turn were under the authority of their bishops, who were ultimately under the authority of the pope.

16 Madigan, *Medieval Christianity*, 310. Yearly confession was officially made a part of canon law at the Fourth Lateran Council in 1215. This council is considered to be the twelfth ecumenical council by the Catholic Church, but as noted in chapter 6, it is not recognized as such by the Orthodox Church or the various Protestant churches.

17 Purgatory developed from a much earlier practice of praying for the dead. It was made official doctrine at the Council of Florence held from 1438 to 1445. The council fathers wrote, "If truly penitent people die in the love of God before they have made satisfaction for acts and omissions by worthy fruits of repentance, their souls are cleansed after death by cleansing pains; and the suffrages of the living faithful avail them in giving relief from such pains, that is, sacrifices of masses, prayers, almsgiving and other acts of devotion which have been customarily performed by some of the faithful for others of the faithful in accordance with the church's ordinances." See session six of the council at https:// www.ewtn.com/catholicism/library/ecumenical-council-of-florence-1438-1445-1461. This council is considered to be the fourteenth ecumenical council by the Catholic Church, though, like the Fourth Lateran Council, it, too, is not recognized by either the Orthodox Church or the various Protestant churches.

18 Frykholm, *Julian of Norwich*, 27.

from the original transgression of the First Man to the time we ascend to heaven" (*Showings* 2.50).

What Julian's sins might have been, we have no idea. Indeed, aside from the fact that she survived the plague, we know nothing of Julian's life during her first thirty years. She must have received some sort of education, for she could read and write in English, and the descriptions of her visions show knowledge both of Scripture and of certain theological writings, notably Augustine. Some biographers have speculated that she took monastic vows at some point before or after her visions.[19] However, she never mentions having lived in a monastery or having taken vows, and unlike other monastic writers of the time, she writes not for other monastics but for common Christians (*evencristens* in her Middle English) with whom she identifies. More likely, then, Julian was a lay Christian and remained one her whole life. As a girl, she was probably tutored by her mother.[20] Her knowledge of Scripture came from regular attendance at mass and, perhaps later in life, from reading an English translation.[21] She may have learned theology from the friars who frequently instructed parishioners in the local parishes and perhaps, again later in life, from a spiritual mentor from one of the monasteries.[22] Because of her writings, which display an intimate knowledge of the mother-child relationship, many biographers suggest that she was married and had at least one child.[23] If so, she would have lost them in a later recurrence of the plague.

---

19 Edmund Colledge and James Walsh, intro., *Julian of Norwich: Showings*, The Classics of Western Spirituality (New York: Paulist Press, 1978), 20.

20 Her own reference to herself as "unlettered" when she first received her visions does not mean she was illiterate but rather unable to read in Latin (*Showings* 2.2).

21 By this point, the Latin Vulgate was the only authorized version of Scripture in the medieval Catholic West. However, in 1384, a professor of theology at Oxford named John Wycliffe produced an English translation of Scripture rendered from the Latin Vulgate. Wycliffe was an outspoken critic of the Catholic Church who believed, among other things, that all Christians should be able to read Scripture in their own language. His followers, the Lollards, were condemned as heretics toward the end of Julian's life for their criticism of the pope and other Catholic practices. Rolf suggests that many Catholics in England, including Julian, may have read the English Bible without associating it with the Lollards. Rolf, *Julian's Gospel*, 165–66. This conjecture helpfully explains her deep knowledge of Scripture.

22 So speculates Frykholm, *Julian of Norwich*, 47–52. She connects this person to the member of Julian's "religious community" who visited her toward the end of her illness (*Showings* 2.66).

23 Frykholm, *Julian of Norwich*, 24, 126–27; Rolf, *Julian's Gospel*, 128ff.

Julian first appears in history in the year 1373, when, at the age of thirty, she received the illness she had prayed for as a child. She was confined to bed for four full days, her illness so serious that she was administered last rites.[24] She was in great pain, the kind that can only accompany death. She writes, "I kept thinking I was about to die, and everyone who sat with me thought so also" (*Showings* 2.3). But she was not sad about it. She had experienced suffering all her life, been surrounded by death since the time she was six, and had lost a father, siblings, and possibly her own husband and children. "I had an intense yearning to be delivered from this life and from this world," she writes, "I experienced a constant flow of woe here . . . I could find no pleasure in living or in performing my ordinary duties" (*Showings* 2.64). She was ready to die and be home with her Lord, but he had other plans for her.

On the fourth night of her illness, she received her visions, sixteen over the course of the night and into the next day. The priest who had administered last rites had brought in a crucifix, which, as she looked at it, began to radiate with light while the rest of the room became dark as night. As she stared at the strange sight, the intense pain she had been feeling vanished. Suddenly, she "saw the red blood trickling down from under [Christ's] garland of thrones" (*Showings* 2.4).[25] To her astonishment, she realized that Christ was showing this vision to her and, more incredibly, that "he was revealing himself directly, without anyone or anything between us" (*Showings* 2.4). Her whole life, Julian had needed intermediaries to experience God: the Church, whose teachings described the nature of this God; the friars, who read and interpreted the Scriptures to her; the priest to whom she confessed her sins and from whom she received pardon as well as the consecrated Eucharist. To that point, her understanding of God had been shaped by their interpretations, and she realized in this vision that they could have been wrong. As she writes later, "Because we do not really understand the nature of love, we create a multitude of intermediaries that stand between our souls and our Beloved" (*Showings* 2.6). Now here was Christ before her, speaking to her, revealing

---

24 Last rites, called *viaticum*, include three acts believed by Catholics to be sacraments, namely, confession, anointing of the sick, and final communion.

25 The role the crucifix played in inspiring Julian's visions recalls Francis's vision of Christ talking to him from the crucifix in chapter 7 as well as the emphasis on icons and other holy objects explored in chapter 6. We will see another example of such a vision in a material object in chapter 11.

himself directly to her. Not only did she understand this as a sign of Christ's great love for her, a feeling that would only intensify as the visions went on, she was also prepared to embrace a different understanding of God than she had heard about her whole life.[26]

Her first ten visions focused on Christ's passion. In addition to the vision of Christ's blood flowing from the crown of thorns, Julian saw the agony on Christ's face (vision two), the "lashing of his tender body" (vision four), his final pain, thirst, and cruel death (vision eight), and the wound in his side (vision ten; *Showings* 2.1, 24). In these visions, Julian is given another one of her childhood wishes, namely, "participation in his passion," for through them she is mystically placed at the cross to "experience the suffering of our Savior and of the compassion of his blessed Mother and of all his true lovers who witnessed the pain" (*Showings* 2.2). She includes now herself among those lovers and, in particular, begins to identify with Mary. Indeed, several of her visions feature Mary, and through them Julian sees her pain and feels the depth of her motherly love for her son—a salient point for the theological meaning she will bring out of the later visions.

Julian's visions of Christ's passion fit squarely within her time for medieval theology and piety, more so than the ancient period, focused on the suffering Christ. This was the age, for example, when crucifixes depicting Christ's suffering body still on the cross and passion plays that dramatized Christ's final days on earth rose to prominence.[27] The reason for this focus has, once again, to do with human sinfulness, for medieval theologians explained Christ's death primarily as the result, or penalty, of human sin.[28] Thus, the focus on

---

26 The lack of intermediaries between the mystic and Christ in the vision is a theme that runs through all mystical literature. For this reason, mystics have always been on the periphery of the Church, sometimes considered suspect by those who preferred the normal means of experiencing God that came through mass and sacrament. Julian is clearly conscious of this suspicion and so, at many points in her writing, insists that she accepts everything the Church teaches (*Showings* 2.9, 34). At the same time, she acknowledges the mystery that what she sees does not fully align with some of the theological emphases of the Church's teachings.

27 Madigan, *Medieval Christianity*, 303–8.

28 The classic work here is by the high medieval theologian Anselm (d. 1109), *Cur Deus Homo*. Using medieval, feudalistic terminology, Anselm argues that sin is an affront to our master God and robs him of his honor and for which he demands satisfaction. That satisfaction comes in the form of Christ's death. While the link between Christ's death and human sin is biblical, it does not rise to prominence until the Middle Ages. Earlier theories of how Christ's death saves humanity focused more on Christ as a ransom and his resurrection as a victory over Satan rather than as a penalty for human sinfulness.

Christ's passion and death on the cross reinforced in humans the problem of their own sin that put him there.

Julian, however, brings different theological meaning to Christ's suffering. Her visions of her Beloved in agony reveal to her not her own sinfulness but rather the enormity of God's love. As she summarizes in the middle of her work, "Divine love is boundless and will continue forever . . . This, in fact, was what the whole revelation was about, from beginning to end" (*Showings* 2.46). And as she wrote at the very end of her work, "Our Beloved gave these showings so that we would understand love better. Through this understanding he gives us the grace to love him and cleave to him. We are his divine treasure" (*Showings* 2.86). She writes in one place that Christ, in both his life and passion, "is the embodiment of this love" (*Showings* 2.40) and in another place that "He is eternally shaped like love" (*Showings* 2.43). In her tenth vision, she sees this embodiment firsthand when she is brought mystically into Christ's body through the wound in his side. There she saw "his sacred heart, cloven in two," a place "beautiful and delicious . . . ample enough for all humanity to rest in peace and love" (*Showings* 2.24).

Christ did not submit to his passion, then, because of our sin but rather because of his love for us. "The love that made him suffer his passion is greater than all his pain," she writes (*Showings* 2.22). This thoroughly biblical truth— "For God so loved the world that he gave his only Son" (John 3:16)—had been lost in the overemphasis of sin in medieval theology. Consequently, many Christians feared more than loved God and saw the cross as an ugly sacrifice that would not have happened if we had just been good enough. By contrast, Julian's emphasis on God's love for humans engendered in her a reciprocal love for God and paradoxically made the cross a beautiful image, for it is the most tangible example of God's love for humanity. "Greater love has no one than this," Jesus had told his disciples, "to lay down one's life for one's friends" (John 15:13 NIV). Or as Julian heard Christ say to her in the midst of a vision, "If I could suffer more, I would suffer more." She comments, perhaps after many years of reflection on the profound locution, "He did not say, 'If it were absolutely necessary, I would suffer more.' Because even if it weren't necessary, he would do this over and over again for our love" (*Showings* 2.22).

For a helpful discussion of these different atonement theories, see Mark D. Baker and Joel B. Green, *Recovering the Scandal of the Cross: Atonement in New Testament and Contemporary Contexts*, 2nd ed. (Downers Grove, IL: IVP Academic, 2011).

As a medieval woman reared in the theology of the Church, Julian was as surprised by this change of emphasis from human sin to divine love as anyone. So much so, in fact, that through the course of her visions, she kept asking God to show her more about sin so she could understand it better and why humans always struggled with it. But she was shown no vision of sin. She writes, "I did not see any sin. I believe that sin has no substance, no particle of being, and cannot be detected at all except by the pain it causes" (*Showings* 2.27). This is not to say that no one sins; quite the opposite, "sin is inevitable," and she writes, "God reminded me that I'm bound to miss the mark" (*Showings* 2.27, 37).[29] But our sin should not be our focus. She writes, "For when I saw in a showing that God does all that needs to be done, I did not see any sin, and I saw that all is well. And when God did reveal something to me about sin, he assured me that 'All will be well'" (*Showings* 2.34). This, then, is the context for that most famous of Julian's quotations. God wants us not to fret over our sins but only to know that "all will be well and all will be well and every kind of thing shall be well" (*Showings* 2.27).[30]

All will be well, God assures Julian, because through Christ's death and resurrection, sin has not simply been defeated; rather, it has, like Christ's cross itself, been transformed from something ugly into something beautiful. "God showed me another thing," she writes. "Sin is a source of honor, rather than shame. While it is true that for every sin there is corresponding pain, we are blessed an equal measure of love" (*Showings* 2.38). Elsewhere, she writes, "Our shame will be transformed into honor and ever-greater joy" (*Showings* 2.39). This is a more compelling, and more loving, vision of forgiveness than simply sin's destruction. I am reminded once again of C. S. Lewis, who captures the same point in his superb allegorical vision of heaven and hell, *The Great Divorce*. In the course of the story, the narrator sees in hell a ghost of a man weighed down by a disgusting red lizard attached to his back. When an angel removes the lizard with great force (and much pain), not only is the ghost transformed back into a man, but the lizard is

---

29 Starr often translates *sin* as "missing the mark." Julian, therefore, does not minimize sin or pass over it as many modern Protestants do. Rather, as we shall see presently, the reality of sin for Julian serves to amplify God's love.

30 Incidentally, the things Julian does not see in her visions are just as instructive as the things Julian sees. In addition to not seeing sin, she notes that she never saw anything about hell or purgatory (*Showings* 2.33), penance (*Showings* 2.77), or God's wrath and anger (*Showings* 2.46–47).

transformed into a stallion, on which the man climbs and promptly rides out of hell.[31] Similarly, in Julian's interpretation, our most shameful sins become our greatest honors, for they are the very areas where God's love shows most clearly. Like Christ's enduring wounds in his resurrected body, which caused the apostle Thomas to proclaim, "My Lord and my God," our forgiven sins bring God the most glory (John 20:28).[32] What kind of God—who loves us to these depths, who willingly suffers for us, and who transforms our shame into honor—can this be?

Julian's answer? A Mother.[33]

While attributing feminine images to God would have itself been controversial in the Middle Ages,[34] Julian's extended meditation on the Motherhood of God in her later visions is even more disorienting because she identifies femininity with the Second Person of the Trinity, the Son. This particular identification is disorienting because, while God as a whole is spirit (John 4:24) and so transcends human gender, the Son becomes incarnate and is born as a man. Thus, if any person of the Trinity can legitimately be called male, it is the human nature that is joined to the divine nature in the person of the Son.[35]

---

31 C. S. Lewis, *The Great Divorce*, repr. (San Francisco: HarperSanFrancisco, 2001), 106–12.

32 This is a similar argument to one Paul makes in Romans, where he notes that "where sin increased, grace increased all the more" (Rom 5:20). Paul continues this sentiment with a warning that we ought not to sin *so that* grace can come (Rom 6:1–2). Julian writes a similar warning: "No man or woman should use the consoling teachings I have just offered as an excuse to say, 'In that case, I might as well go ahead and commit transgressions, because I will be rewarded for my bad behavior,' or even 'sin is no big deal.' Beware of this impulse to minimize the negative effects of missing the mark: such thinking is erroneous and comes from the spirit of evil" (*Showings* 2.40).

33 We have seen many biographers speculate that Julian was a mother prior to her visions. Additionally, we know from her own account that while she had lost every other family member by age thirty, her mother remained steadfast and kept vigil at her bedside during her illness. We have also seen that Julian had a deep devotion to Mary and seemed to grasp from her visions the intense love Mary had for her son. Any of these factors could have led Julian to explain God's love with the analogy to motherly love.

34 Rolf writes, "The entire feudal structure of the Middle Ages was built upon the undisputed foundation of the male as superior to the female in every way. Any publicly preached theology that presented God as *maternal*, or taught that there could be 'feminine' qualities manifested by Divine Nature, might challenge the concept of human male dominance." Rolf, *Julian's Gospel*, 512.

35 Indeed, sometimes the incarnation is used as an argument against using feminine images of God. But as Julian's work shows, this argument is faulty, not only because only the Son is incarnate (the Father and Holy Spirit do not unite with human flesh but remain spirit and so transcendent of gender) but also because the Son himself (or

But Julian, though never denying Jesus's literal manhood in the incarnation, feels the freedom from her visions to play with the language: "God chose to become our Mother in all ways, humbly and tenderly cultivating the ground of his work in the womb of a maiden" (*Showings* 2.60). Thus is revealed the analogical nature of Julian's language—the Son is not literally a female any more than the Triune God is literally male.[36] Rather, God's motherhood is expressed in Jesus's character, work, and, of course, love.

In developing this analogy, Julian is obviously working with medieval assumptions about innate feminine characteristics that are no longer normative; nevertheless, anyone with a loving and involved parent can understand the connection she makes. She writes, "I saw three ways to look at the Motherhood of God. The first is that she created our human nature. The second is that she took our human nature upon herself, which is where the motherhood of grace begins. And the third is motherhood in action,

---

herself?) retains a divine nature even in the incarnation, which also remains spirit and so transcendent of gender.

36 Because God is transcendent and not a part of our created order, all theological language is necessarily analogical. As developed by the greatest medieval theologian Thomas Aquinas, this means that human language can describe God positively (when we say, "God is love," we know what that means because we experience human love) but not fully or literally (God's love is infinitely superior to human love). *Summa Theologiae* 1.12–13. Everything we say about God, then, is an analogy. When we say God is a Father or a Mother, for example, we mean that he is *like* a human father or mother, even though he is infinitely greater than either concept. Nevertheless, theologians often forget this analogical quality of theological language, particularly in the area of gendered terms as applied to God. This explains in part the extreme resistance to using feminine language of God both in the medieval period and in today's context. See, for example, the essays in *Speaking the Christian God: The Holy Trinity and the Challenge of Feminism*, ed. Alvin F. Kimel Jr. (Grand Rapids, MI: Eerdmans, 1992). Roland M. Frye, for example, argues against feminine language applied to God on the basis of Scripture's privileging of masculine language. He notes that where Scripture speaks of God in feminine terms, such as Jesus likening himself to a mother hen (Matt. 23:37), it does so as a metaphor as opposed to direct application. Roland M. Frye, "Language for God and Feminist Language: Problems and Principles," in *Speaking the Christian God*, ed. Alvin F. Kimel Jr. (Grand Rapids, MI: Eerdmans, 1992), 17–43. This argument, however, neglects the truth that all theological language, even masculine images, is analogical. Indeed, one could argue that Julian's application of the Motherhood of God to the Son better reinforces the analogical nature of her language and makes certain that we will not slip into literal application as many do with masculine language. For a good contemporary theological argument for the appropriateness of feminine language applied to God, see Janet Martin Soskice, *The Kindness of God: Metaphor, Gender, and Religious Language* (Oxford: Oxford University Press, 2007), especially ch. 6.

in which she spreads herself throughout all that is, penetrating everything with grace, extending to the fullest length and breadth, height and depth" (*Showings* 2.59). Jesus is our Mother because he gives us life, not only at creation, as Irenaeus had noted, but at the cross, where he *births* us to new life. Julian writes, "In love, he labors to carry us inside himself, until we come to full term. Then he suffers the most painful blows and excruciating birth pangs that ever have been or ever will be endured, only to die in the end" (*Showings* 2.60). Thus, the surprising Motherhood of God of the later visions connects to Christ's passion of the earlier visions: Christ, whose motherly love for us is unbounded, sacrifices his own life so that we might live. "If I could suffer more, I would suffer more," Julian repeats the words of Christ to her (*Showings* 2.60).

Moreover, Christ continues to feed us, again like a mother, with his own body in the Eucharist, "the precious food of true life" (*Showings* 2.60). While the Eucharist is the primary means of such nourishment, Julian notes that Christ penetrates everything with grace, for "whenever a human mother nurtures her child with all that is beautiful and good, it is God-the-Mother who is acting through her" (*Showings* 2.60). This truth is not relegated to just biological mothers but, in fact, encompasses all acts of human compassion for others. As she writes earlier, "When I saw the compassion our Beloved has for our transgressions, my own heart was filled with compassion for all my fellow spiritual seekers" (*Showings* 2.28). Put differently, through the work of Christ, disciples are made mothers to each other and to the world. This connection is scriptural. The apostle John writes, "This is love: not that we loved God, but that he loved us and sent his Son as an atoning sacrifice for our sins. Dear friends, since God so loved us, we also ought to love one another. No one has ever seen God; but if we love one another, God lives in us and his love is made complete in us" (1 John 4:10–12 NIV). The incredible love Mother God has for Julian prompts in her the same love and compassion for her *evencristians*, fulfilling her third and final childhood wish.

Thus, when Julian miraculously survived her illness, she did not return to life as normal. She couldn't. The visions had left their mark and had changed not only her understanding of God but her whole life's purpose. Like Paul on the Damascus Road, she had seen Christ and needed to tell others. "I was moved by a deep love for my fellow spiritual seekers," she writes, "praying that they could all see what I was seeing, because I knew it would be such a comfort to them" (*Showings* 2.22). She first tried by writing and so produced the *Short Text* sometime in the years following the vision. The work is in

English, making Julian the first woman to write a book in that developing language. It is a good description of her visions and conveys the essentials that we explored in the *Long Text* above. But it wasn't enough.[37] She had more to say, and due to the constraints of everyday life in the medieval period, she couldn't find the time needed to say it. Perhaps this is the reason that, sometime by the early 1390s, she became an anchoress.[38]

The anchoritic life had been around for nearly four hundred years by that point. A version of the monastic life, anchorites pursued an enclosed, contemplative life removed from the concerns of the world (*anchorite* comes from the Greek word for "withdrawal"). But unlike monastics, they did not live in monasteries or follow the monastic routines of prayer and work and community; rather, they were enclosed in a single room typically attached or "anchored" to a local parish, in which their sole activities were prayer and contemplation and, for some like Julian, spiritual direction of parishioners.[39] Julian's room, connected to St. Julian's Parish in Norwich, was roughly nine by eleven feet and featured a window to the church, where she could view daily mass, and a window to the outside, where she could visit with guests.[40] Here she would spend the rest of her days, writing the visions that had so captivated her and meeting with and advising many *evencristians* who came to her for spiritual direction.

Although we have a firsthand account from one of Julian's mentees, we know little of the kinds of things she said in these sessions.[41] But having read her interpretations of her visions, we can guess. She likely told these medieval pilgrims, burdened by the weight of their own sins and fearful of a judgmental

---

37 There is, for example, little about the Motherhood of God in the *Short Text*.

38 There are four external references to Julian as an anchoress in various wills, which left money for her patronage, according to the normal means that the anchoritic life was supported. All of these wills date to after 1390. Rolf, *Julian's Gospel*, 188–89.

39 Madigan notes that the anchoritic life was often pursued by "older women, who had occupations not in convents but in the family home as wives and mothers and who, late in life, wished to pursue the intensities of the enclosed contemplative life." Madigan, *Medieval Christianity*, 149.

40 The church and room still stand today, though they were rebuilt in 1953. The original room was able to be measured during the rebuilding phase. Rolf, *Julian's Gospel*, 187, 614n41.

41 The fourteenth-century mystic Margery Kempe writes in her own account of her visions of having visited "Dame Julian" in 1413 to discern whether her visions were authentic. Julian believed they were, saying that "the holy ghost never moves a thing against charity," and urged her to be obedient. Rolf, *Julian's Gospel*, 192.

God, that they had it all wrong. She would tell them of the surprising reality of the God she had seen and that we need not fear him because he loves us as only a mother could. She would tell them that his suffering for them gave them new life and turned their shame into honor and glory. Likely those who sought her counsel walked away forever changed, just as Julian's own visions of the unending love of Mother God had changed her.

Julian died sometime after 1413 and was put to rest in an unmarked grave, indicative of how little known she was in her lifetime.[42] Although both versions of her work were copied and passed down among monastics, Julian's work was not widely read until the twentieth century.[43] The good news in the strange economy of God, however, is that Julian is known now. And from her place in the cloud of witnesses, she still speaks to all who have ears to hear, telling them the words Christ spoke to her as a much younger woman: "All will be well and all will be well and every kind of thing shall be well."

---

42 The scribal introduction to the *Short Text* mentions that Julian is still alive in 1413. Though she has never been officially canonized as a saint by the Catholic Church, she is unofficially considered one among most Catholics.

43 One wonders whether the events discussed in the next chapter would have turned out differently had more Catholic voices like Julian's been known in their time.

CHAPTER NINE

Martin's No

*My doctrine is this: that people should not trust in anything else
than in Jesus Christ alone, not in prayers, merit, or one's
own works because we are not saved by our running but
through God, who is merciful.*

—Martin Luther, Letter to Johann von Staupitz[1]

Around one hundred years after Julian's death, the Catholic Church underwent a series of divisions over some of the same theological issues Julian
was pressing in her visions. This period is called the Reformation because
of the widespread need for theological and ecclesiastical reforms that occasioned the divisions and spawned the various Protestant denominations.
Although the Reformation was not a singular event, but rather featured
simultaneous reformations in many different parts of Europe,[2] the catalyst

---

1 Herman Selderhuis, *Martin Luther: A Spiritual Biography* (Wheaton, IL: Crossway,
2017), 106.

2 Some examples of other reformation movements include the English Reformation,
from which the Church of England (Anglicans), Episcopalians, and Methodists descend;
the Anabaptist movement, from which Baptists, Mennonites, and other more sectarian
denominations come; and the Swiss Reformation, from which Presbyterians and other
Reformed denominations were born. The Catholic Church itself underwent a period of
reforms, producing, for example, the Council of Trent and a new monastic order called
the Jesuits. The Reformation only affected the Western Church; the Orthodox Church in
the East has remained essentially one body since the eleventh century.

of the movements was a monk, pastor, and theology professor from Germany named Martin Luther.[3]

Martin was born in 1483 in Eiselben, Germany, and baptized on the feast of St. Martin, for whom he was named.[4] This was a world very similar to Julian's, although Martin's posterior perspective made it seem even more hopeless. The plague still lingered, a constant reminder that death could come at any moment.[5] Peasants on the bottom rung of this stratified society made up the vast majority of people and had little hope or opportunity of experiencing any change of station. Their political leaders provided no stability, moreover, as the waning feudal system meant an ever-shifting parade of authorities and seemingly interminable skirmishes into which the peasants were drawn. While the darkness of this period can be overstated—some of the most brilliant theologians and scientists the world has ever seen lived in these so-called Dark Ages—for most people, life was, in the famous words of the seventeenth-century philosopher Thomas Hobbes, "poor, nasty, brutish, and short."[6]

The only hope in such a world was that of a more abundant eternal life after death through the promise of the gospel. Though Europe was almost universally Catholic at the time, however, even this hope was in short supply. For eternal life meant being in good standing with the Catholic Church, and there were about as many ways to lose good standing in the Middle Ages as there were to die. The general focus on sin we saw last chapter had been codified by the Church into literal lists of sins, which were impossibly long and detailed. Richard Marius's description of a typical fourteenth-century catalog gives us a sense:

---

3 Of the numerous quality biographies of Martin Luther that exist, my account draws on three, namely Richard Marius, *Martin Luther: The Christian between God and Death* (Cambridge: The Belknap Press of Harvard University Press, 1999), Heiko A. Oberman, *Luther: Man between God and the Devil*, trans. Eileen Walliser-Schwarzbart (New Haven, CT: Yale University Press, 1989), and Selderhuis, *Martin Luther*. For Martin's writings, I will use translations from these works as well as the helpful compilation *The Reforming Treatises of Martin Luther*, trans. C. A. Buchheim, A. T. W. Steinhauser, and R. S. Grignon (Prague: e-artnow, 2019), which will be marked in the text as *RT*. For anyone wishing to read some of Martin's vast corpus, this compilation offers a manageable starting point.

4 St. Martin of Tours was a fourth-century monastic. For the origins of this liturgical calendar, see chapter 3.

5 Martin lived through three outbreaks of the plague in 1527, 1535, and 1539. Marius, *Martin Luther*, 9.

6 Hobbes, *Leviathan* 1.12. I am indebted to Randolph A. Miller for this apt quotation.

[There were] sins of thought, sins of words, sins of action, including acts against God and the neighbor and the seven deadly sins, sins with the senses of the various parts of the body—including sins of the head, the neck, the ears, the eyes, the nose, the mouth, the tongue, the gullet, the hands, the stomach, the genitals, heart, knees, and feet. Then there were sins of omission, sins against the twelve articles of faith, sins against the seven sacraments, sins against the seven virtues, sins against the seven gifts of the Holy Spirit, sins against the fruit of the Holy Spirit, and sins against the eight beatitudes of the Gospels.[7]

To ensure forgiveness and, thus, good standing with the Church, Christians had to confess their sins and do penance—actions that confirmed the authenticity of their contrition—the coveted result of which was an indulgence, a piece of paper confirming one had done the proper penance and so would not need to do so in purgatory. Perhaps good in intention, this system bred corruption as the scriptural practice of confession (1 John 1:9) became purely transactional and, ultimately, monetized. For, eventually, indulgences could be purchased, allowing the purchaser to bypass the true repentance the system was designed to engender. Moreover, the market for such indulgences was seemingly endless as a person could not only acquire one on their own behalf but on behalf of family members who had died and were already in purgatory.[8]

The fact that Scripture nowhere mentions such an intricate system of penance was no matter because, as we have seen, most people could not read the Scriptures anyway. The Hebrew Old Testament and Greek New Testament were translated into the Latin Vulgate in the fourth century and by the Middle Ages had become the only authorized version, despite the fact that Latin was no longer the common language.[9] The faithful had to rely on

---

7 Marius, *Martin Luther*, 10.

8 Recall from chapter 8 what the Council of Florence had said about purgatory: "The suffrages of the living faithful avail [those in purgatory] in giving relief from such pains, that is, sacrifices of masses, prayers, almsgiving and other acts of devotion."

9 Ironically, the original motive for translating the Scriptures into Latin was that by the fourth century, most people in the West no longer spoke Greek, so the Vulgate allowed people to read the Scriptures in their native tongue. In the sixteenth century, no similar effort to translate Scripture by Church authorities existed. In fact, those who did so were considered heretics. Last chapter, we met John Wycliffe, who translated the Vulgate into English. Though he escaped ecclesiastical punishment in his lifetime, church officials exhumed his body forty-three years after his death to burn his remains, asserting that, by his vulgar translation, "the pearl of the gospel is scattered abroad and trodden underfoot by swine." Cited in Mary Dove, *The First English Bible: The Text and Context of the Wycliffite Versions*; Cambridge Studies in Medieval History 66 (Cambridge: Cambridge University Press, 2007), 6.

their priests and bishops to tell them what the Scriptures said; therefore, if they were told they needed an indulgence to be in good standing with the Church, then they got an indulgence. Though this system was effective in gaining wealth for the Catholic Church, it was ineffective in either conveying the gracious and loving nature of the God of Scripture or forming faithful disciples. To cite Matt Jenson's lovely turn of phrase, "It crushed the earnest, and it sedated the complacent."[10]

Though Martin did not suffer the hopelessness of those among the peasant class,[11] he certainly was among the earnest crushed by the Church's penitential system. From a young age, he was profoundly aware of his sin, which drove him to experience God not as a gracious and loving Father but rather as a judge and punisher of sins. He understood God's righteousness, as referred to in Romans 1:17, for example, as an instrument of wrath for those like him who could not meet his standards. As Martin would later write, "I did not love God, but I hated this righteous God who punishes sinners."[12] The most famous example of this fear came in 1505 when, on a visit home to see his parents, he was caught in a violent thunderstorm and feared for his life. As many in a similar situation do, he bargained with God, promising through an invocation of St. Anne, the mother of Mary, that he would become a monk if she rescued him.[13] Such bargaining implies not a confidence in God's grace but a fear of eternal damnation. And what better place to commit to pleasing the wrathful God than a monastery, where one takes vows of obedience and spends every waking minute seeking to serve God? "That was, after all, our doctrine," he writes in retrospect. "Would you like to become holy and pious through penance? Then you should become a monk to torture yourself with fasting and prayer until God wants you to be his friend again. With that purpose in mind, I entered the monastery."[14]

---

10 Matt Jenson, *Theology in the Democracy of the Dead: A Dialogue with the Living Tradition* (Grand Rapids, MI: Baker Academic, 2019), 169.

11 Martin's parents were relatively comfortable—his father was a miner—and Martin had many opportunities for education and future employment. Selderhuis, *Martin Luther*, 25-26.

12 *Preface to the Latin Works* (1545), in WA 54:185–86, trans. Selderhuis, *Martin Luther*, 84.

13 The invocation of St. Anne is of note for our particular subject. St. Anne was the patron saint of miners, his father's occupation, so it was perhaps his vicinity to home that led him to call on her of all the saints. Marius, *Martin Luther*, 44.

14 Cited in Selderhuis, *Martin Luther*, 46. Readers will recall from the chapter on Macrina how different this motive was from the original purpose of adopting the ascetic

By all accounts, he was a model monk in this regard.[15] He fasted. He prayed. He went to mass. He confessed, often for several hours at a time. But neither this disciplined life nor the vows he took offered him release from his inner turmoil and struggle with sin. God remained a distant, righteous, and terrifying judge. "In the monastery I never thought about women, money, or possessions," he would write later, "but my heart trembled and pondered about the question of how I could gain God's grace."[16] No matter what he did, Martin could find no peace and no experience of God's grace and love in the means on offer by the Church.

Until, that is, he turned to Scripture.

Martin had heard the Bible read in mass his whole life. He had even read portions of the Bible while studying at the university in Erfurt. But he had never studied it, never chewed over its contents the way that Origen modeled, never saw the grace running through all parts of the economy as Irenaeus had found. In short, he had never read Scripture for himself. The monastery taught him to do that. "He read his Bible from front to back and then would start anew," writes his biographer. "Luther searched in the Bible, he 'knocked' on the texts, he shook them like a branch of a fruit tree, and then he listened to find words of comfort and reassurance to drive away his fears."[17] So began a great love affair with the Scriptures that would last the whole of his life. More importantly, his fresh reading of the Scriptures slowly began to change his understanding of God and of the meaning of faithful discipleship.

Martin's focus on Scripture intensified after he earned his doctorate in theology in 1512 from the university in Wittenberg and became its new professor of theology. He began to deliver lectures to his students on various books of the Bible, such as Romans and Galatians, which required hours of personal study. He would have read Paul's detailed arguments against the Pharisaic theology of the Apostle's day that maintained that one was made right with

---

life. While Luther's attitude is not explanatory of all the religious vocations experienced in this time, he is certainly not an outlier. This was, moreover, a change of direction for Martin. At the time, he was studying to be a lawyer, having obtained his bachelor's degree in 1502 and his master's degree in 1505.

15 He joined the Augustinian Order, which had a reputation for producing good scholars and university professors, and so was able to pursue theological studies. Oberman, *Luther*, 129–31.

16 Cited in Selderhuis, *Martin Luther*, 48.

17 Selderhuis, *Martin Luther*, 59.

God through following the law.[18] Passages such as Romans 3:21–22, "But now, apart from law, the righteousness of God has been disclosed, and is attested by the law and the prophets, the righteousness of God through faith in Jesus Christ for all who believe," would have resonated with him against his own efforts to gain righteousness through his actions. Or elsewhere: "There is therefore now no condemnation for those who are in Christ Jesus. For the law of the Spirit of life in Christ Jesus has set you free from the law of sin and of death" (Rom 8:1–2). And still elsewhere: "For all who rely on the works of the law are under a curse . . . no one is justified before God by the law; for 'The one who is righteous will live by faith'" (Gal 3:10–11).

These scriptural arguments must have been like salve to his tortured soul. Through them, Martin came to see that he never could be good enough to earn God's grace, that this, as Julian had seen in her visions a century earlier, was not the point. Rather, Christ was good enough for us, and through his work on the cross, God gifts us *his* righteousness.[19] Martin later writes, "The gospel reveals the righteousness of God, namely, the passive, through which God the Merciful justifies us through faith, as it is written: 'The righteous will live by faith.'"[20] Moreover, since it was God who not only demanded the standard of righteousness but also provided the means—Christ—by which that righteousness was possible, Martin's understanding of God began to change. He began to see God not as the distant, wrathful, and somewhat cruel judge waiting to snuff him out should he ever step out of line but rather as the loving, gracious, present God revealed most clearly in the cross, where God took the punishment for sin onto himself.[21] "I felt completely reborn," he continues, "and it was as if I had gone through the open gates of paradise itself."[22] Though Martin's understanding on righteousness as attained through

---

18 Whether this is actually what the Pharisees taught or what Paul was saying they taught are open questions in biblical scholarship, but those debates are not relevant to understanding Martin's interpretation.

19 In technical theological terms, this understanding is known as *imputed righteousness*.

20 *Preface to the Latin Works* (1545), in WA 54:185–86, trans. Selderhuis, *Martin Luther*, 84.

21 Martin's continued emphasis on sin's punishment distinguishes him some from Julian.

22 *Preface to the Latin Works* (1545), in WA 54:185–86, trans. Selderhuis, *Martin Luther*, 84. Luther's 1545 preface explains much of this inner transformation and the reasons for the steps that followed. An English translation of the document in its entirety can be found at https://www.bluffton.edu/courses/humanities/2/ml-1545.htm.

justification by faith alone would develop in the ensuing years, the key insight occurred during his study of Scripture from 1515 to 1517. And this understanding, known by the Latin phrase *sola fide*, would constitute the primary dividing mark between Catholics and Protestants in the sixteenth century.[23]

As all readers of Scripture do, Martin couldn't help but graft his own context onto Paul's. Thus, he equated the Catholic penitential system, with its focus on *doing* penance for indulgences, with the Pharisaic theology of Paul's day. Indulgences were works, the very thing that Paul had said were made obsolete in Christ. But such theology had become, it seemed, the foundation of the Catholic Church. If he needed a reminder, he had it because the Church had recently ramped up the sale of indulgences to finance the building of a new cathedral in Rome. Indulgence preachers were everywhere, folks like Johann Tetzel, peddling their wares with the same ferocity and ubiquity as modern-day Facebook ads. They even had catchy slogans: "When the coin in the coffer rings, a soul from purgatory springs!"[24] The faithful were led astray by this system; the coins, of which they had little, were dropped often. And so, as a faithful Catholic himself, a professor of theology and thus an authority on the Scriptures, he felt he had the responsibility to speak out. This conviction explains his actions on October 31, 1517.

Every good Protestant knows the story. A renegade monk nailed his 95 Theses, exposing the corruption of the Catholic Church, to the doors of the Castle Church in Wittenberg, and so began Protestantism. While the history of the event is slightly less dramatic—there are no indications that Martin intended with this action to break from the Catholic Church, much less to make his theses public[25]—the significance of the event cannot be denied. The

---

23 While there remain differences between twenty-first-century Catholics and Protestants on the question of justification, both traditions have come to see that they are not as far apart as originally thought. A 1999 ecumenical dialogue between Catholics and Lutherans produced the extraordinary document the *Joint Declaration on the Doctrine of Justification (JDDJ)*, which reveals a surprising amount of agreement between the two traditions on this core doctrine. This agreement should not be interpreted as a result of Catholics changing their position so much as recognizing their much older position that they were not able to see in the heat of the polemics of the sixteenth century. Those interested in reading *JDDJ* can access the full text here: https://www.lutheranworld.org/sites/default/files/2019/documents/190603-joint_declaration_on_the_doctrine_of_justification_20_anniversary_edition-en.pdf.pdf.

24 Marius, *Martin Luther*, 135.

25 He more likely posted the theses for a debate within the academic department at his university. The form of the document as theses and its Latin text, as opposed to German,

95 Theses were quickly translated into German, copied, and thanks to the recent invention of the printing press, widely distributed to a public desperate for a different message, for a message of hope.[26]

That hope came in the form of a full-scale attack on the practice of selling indulgences. The 95 Theses denied that buying an indulgence did anything of eternal value, such as forgive sins against God or shorten years in purgatory (theses 3, 4, 32). More seditiously, they denied the pope any power to remit punishments save for the ones that he himself imposed (thesis 5) and limited the pope's role to one of intercession for sinners and the dead, as opposed to possessing the keys to eternity (thesis 26).[27] They accused the Church of greediness and of exploiting the poor faithful for its own monetary gain. "Why does not the pope, whose wealth is to-day greater than the riches of the richest, build just this one church of St. Peter with his own money, rather than with the money of poor believers?" (thesis 86, *RT* 28). Positively, the theses articulated what true repentance was. The opening thesis, for example, reads, "Our Lord and Master Jesus Christ, when He said *Poenitentium agite*, willed that the whole life of believers should be repentance" (*RT* 24).[28] Repentance cannot be reduced to a work, as the common practice of selling indulgences did, but is rather a disposition of the heart that one must have continually. Moreover, the good fruit of the repentant is not manifested in the acquisition of a piece of paper but in care for those who are poor and needy (thesis 46).[29] Finally, the theses contrast the poverty of indulgences to the treasure of the "Most Holy Gospel of the glory and the grace of God" (thesis 62), which is the only treasure the pope has the power to give (*RT* 27).

---

lend weight to this interpretation. Selderhuis, *Martin Luther*, 99–100. The famous story of the Wittenberg Castle doors likely originated with Philipp Melancthon, Luther's younger colleague and primary interpreter, some thirty years later after the Reformation was an acknowledged event in need of a definitive origin story.

26 Oberman reports that within two weeks, the 95 Theses had circulated all over Germany. Oberman, *Luther*, 191. The invention of the printing press the previous century is widely cited by scholars as one of the factors that made Martin's reforming movement successful in ways that previous ones, such as Wycliffe's, had not been.

27 Almost certainly an allusion to Matthew 16:18–19, which was the primary scriptural passage used by the Catholic Church to support the office of the pope.

28 The Latin phrase means "do penance" and is a quotation of the Latin translation of Matthew 3:2: "Repent, for the kingdom of heaven has come near." The original Greek word the Vulgate had rendered "do penance" is *metanoēte*, which means, more simply, "repent." Selderhuis, *Martin Luther*, 89.

29 The common belief, then and now, that Martin had no place in his theology for good works is overstated.

Though limited in scope, the 95 Theses struck at the very heart of the medieval Catholic Church. As Selderhuis has written, "With these questions, Luther undermined the foundations of a system that held enormous economic consequences for the church."[30] Moreover, they undercut the authority of the pope and contrasted the revelation in Scripture to Church tradition (in the specific form of the penitential system). Though it would take several years for the Catholic Church to respond with an official condemnation of Martin and even more time for the German professor to realize that the shape of his reforms would result in a church body separated from the Catholic Church,[31] the core of his reforming theology is all here.[32]

Two points of this theology, in particular, mark the Protestant churches that formed in the wake of his protests and continue to mark them today.[33] The first—justification by faith alone (*sola fide*)—we have already discussed. The second—his belief that Scripture is the primary authority in the Church—is worth dwelling on.[34] The Latin sentiment for this is *sola scriptura* (Scripture alone), though Martin did not mean by this phrase what most Protestants now mean (i.e., reading Scripture to the exclusion of tradition). In fact, Martin never advocated that Christians should read Scripture alone; he was, rather, a strong advocate for the importance of tradition, particularly Augustine—whose writings anticipated many of Martin's interpretations of Paul's understanding of sin and grace—and the ancient creeds. Martin was fully Trinitarian, for example, though we

---

30 Selderhuis, *Martin Luther*, 99.

31 This occurred at the Diet of Worms in 1521, where, on being asked to recant, Luther gave his famous speech protesting that he needed to be shown his errors from Scripture, not from councils and popes. "My conscience is captive to the Word of God. Thus I cannot and will not recant, for going against my conscience is neither safe nor salutary. I can do no other, here I stand, God help me. Amen." Cited in Oberman, *Luther*, 203.

32 Martin always desired to reform the Church while remaining within it. Only much later, after it was clear that this was not going to happen, did he work with others to form new politics and liturgies and hymns for a Protestant Church.

33 For those interested in the intricate historical details of the Reformation and the formation of Protestant churches, I suggest Owen Chadwick, *The Reformation*, repr. (London: Penguin Books Ltd, 1990). Although an older account, it is helpful for its concise yet comprehensive account of all of the different reform movements in the sixteenth century.

34 Both of these ideas developed in the years following the 95 Theses and reached definitive form in three treatises penned in 1520 in German, widely considered to be Martin's most important reforming works. They are *To the Christian Nobility of the German Nation, The Babylonian Captivity of the Church,* and *A Treatise on Christian Liberty*. I will use the first treatise in discussing Martin's belief in Scripture as primary authority.

have seen in this book that it is difficult to derive the doctrine of the Trinity from Scripture alone. More to the point, he continued to affirm beliefs and church practices that many Protestants today believe have no grounding in Scripture (for example, infant baptism, real presence of Christ in the Eucharist, and the perpetual virginity of Mary).

For Martin, Scripture as the primary authority meant only that it stands over and, in his day at least, against the pope. This was a revolutionary change in medieval theology, for, as noted, medieval theology held that the pope was the supreme authority in interpreting the Scriptures. In practice, this meant that for Catholics, whatever the pope said about matters of faith and doctrine were authoritative. Aside from the fact that the Scriptures say nothing about the office of the pope as such,[35] the problem with this system is that there was no guarantee that the pope would be a faithful man, in which case, the Church could easily be led astray. "Has not the Pope often erred? Who would help Christianity, in case the Pope errs, if we do not rather believe another who has the Scriptures for him?" (RT 42). He notes that, historically, councils had ensured the Church's fidelity to Scripture more effectively, though medieval Catholicism had forfeited even this structure because of the, again, scripturally baseless assertion that only the pope could call a council.[36] Rather, for Martin, the only authority over every human, whether peasant, priest, or pope, is Scripture, God's divinely revealed word: "If the Pope acts contrary to the Scriptures, we are bound to stand by the Scriptures" (RT 43). Martin felt that this conviction put him more in line with Church tradition than the idolatrous innovations that came from medieval theology.

If Scripture is the primary authority, however, this means that the pope and other church leaders are no more authoritative in their scriptural interpretations, and no more gifted by the Spirit to that end, than the average Christian. "We are all priests," Martin wrote, "and have all one faith, one Gospel, and one sacrament; how then should we not have the power of discerning and

---

35 Martin argues that Matthew 16:18–19 refers not to the pope but to the whole community and has nothing to do with doctrine or scriptural interpretation but with sin. As support, he cites Paul's confrontation with Peter over the issue of eating with Gentiles in Galatians 2 (RT 42–43). If Peter were a pope in the medieval understanding, Paul would not have had the authority to confront him in this manner.

36 Martin writes that Scripture stands counter to this doctrine as well for the so-called first pope, Peter, did not even call the council in Acts 15 that addressed the question of full inclusion of the Gentiles (RT 43).

judging what is right and wrong on matters of faith?" (*RT* 42).[37] Given what we have already seen in this book about the difficulty of interpreting Scripture, we might be prone to disagree here. Nevertheless, one does not have to deny Scripture's inherent difficulty to accept Martin's primary point—every Christian has the ability, as hard as it is, to discern Scripture's meaning through the presence of the Spirit and the aid of tradition.[38] For this to be possible, however, every Christian needed to read the Scriptures. To this end, Martin embarked on what might be his greatest contribution, namely, the translation of the Scriptures into German.

Written in the highly engaging prose for which Martin was known in his roles as professor and preacher, the Luther Bible quickly became a bestseller.[39] As a result, German Christians of all classes could for the first time read the Scriptures for themselves and discover the beauty of God's Word, the hope of the salvific story, and the grace and love of God's nature. Putting the Scriptures into the hands of the people made Martin's theoretical statements in 1520 a reality and did more for the momentum of the Reformation in Germany than anything else he did.[40] How many Macrinas were in that

---

37 In theological parlance, this is known as *the priesthood of all believers*, the corollary of which is that the pope is not closer to God than the average person is but that all humans are equal under Christ as our only mediator to God. Martin did not mean by this doctrine that there should be no priests or leaders but only that such vocations do not make a person holier or less sinful than any other profession and, as Julian saw, in no way mediate between humans and God. Certain readings of this doctrine demonstrate the origins of Protestant arguments against the saints outlined in the introduction.

38 Indeed, Martin's frequent claims that Scripture is clear and easy to understand should also be understood as more limited in application. For though there are many confusing things in Scripture, God's grace, love, and desire that we all come to him in repentance are abundantly clear. Such is Martin's point in contrasting Scripture's clarity to the intricacies of the medieval penitential system. One is reminded of Francis's simple and literal interpretations of the three verses that led him to his way of life that we saw in chapter 7.

39 The New Testament was completed in 1522 and installments of the Old Testament at different times over the course of the following decade. Both testaments were translated from the original languages. Book publishers of the time made a lot of money on these sales, though Martin refused any compensation for his work. Selderhuis, *Martin Luther*, 177. One discerns here Martin's heart for poor peasants that originally inspired his stand against indulgences.

40 Martin's was not the first German translation, though the quality of his translation quickly consigned the others to a forgotten footnote in history. Selderhuis, *Martin Luther*, 176–78.

crowd, now able to relish the German words of the Psalms as they went about their chores? How many Origens were there, captivated by Jesus's strange teachings in familiar words that set them on lifelong vocations of digesting the truths of Scripture? How many Julians, now able to think creatively about the nature of God they had encountered? Reading God's Word in one's own language not only makes it more understandable; it makes the incarnation an experienced reality. Here is a God who has come near, a God who has moved into our neighborhood and so speaks our language.[41] Moreover, we have seen in this book how profoundly traditional, not to mention life-altering, is the spiritual discipline of reading the Scriptures. Martin Luther made this possible for Germans once again.

The emphasis on Scripture's primary authority was greatly needed for church reform in the sixteenth century and remains needed in the twenty-first century. For while much has changed since the Middle Ages, the pervasive sinfulness of humans, including those humans who rise to leadership of churches, remains a constant. In both the Catholic and Protestant contexts, there have been far too many examples of moral and doctrinal failures among our leaders to doubt the wisdom of holding Scripture as authoritative over any human being or human institution. Yet if the average person could not read and interpret Scripture, such abuses may go unchecked, even more than they unfortunately already do. Scripture as the primary authority, by contrast, holds all humans accountable to a greater truth and refuses to be domesticated by a human Church all too prone to rejecting its radical teachings. For all the lamentable divisions the Reformation caused, this is its most important gift to the kingdom and its lasting legacy in the Church as a whole.[42]

For Martin Luther, however, this truth cuts both ways. For while the Reformer's personal faith, discipleship, and influence on theology are admirable and indeed saintly, many of his personal qualities are somewhat less so. He had, for example, a notoriously bad temper, and often in his polemics, he went beyond arguing for his position to personal attack and vitriol. As he got older, he grew more obstinate, which, unfortunately, made any

---

41 As Eugene Peterson's creative rendering of John 1:14 in the *Message* Bible states.

42 At the Second Vatican Council, the Catholic Church advocated the reading of Scriptures and the saying of the mass in the vernacular, which has led to a scriptural renaissance among the Catholic faithful. Though few Catholics would likely point to Martin Luther as the cause of this development, it is difficult to account for apart from Martin and the ongoing witness of Protestant churches.

prospect of rapprochement with the Catholic Church impossible. In fact, he came to believe that anyone who disagreed with him was of the devil, a sort of psychosis to be sure, and his later writings demonize his opponents instead of seeing in them a common humanity.[43] This character flaw had great consequences in the Peasants' Revolt of the mid-1520s, when many of Germany's poorest people rose up against the economic injustices I noted at the outset of this chapter. Luther had a lot of influence in this period and probably could have been a mediator. Instead, he sided fully with the German nobility and encouraged putting an end to the peasants' lawlessness, which resulted in mass casualties among the very people he had advocated for against unjust church policies.[44] Finally, and perhaps most notoriously, are his writings against the Jews, which advocate, among other things, that Jews were a sickness who ought to live in separate districts and have their synagogues destroyed.[45] Although this sort of hyperbolic rhetoric is indicative of Martin's work toward all his opponents (Catholics and Muslims as well) and was by no means rare in Christian medieval thinking in general, the danger of such words, even if intended metaphorically, as most scholars believe,[46] was made all too real in the twentieth century with the horrors of the Holocaust that began in Germany. How, then, do we reckon with such character traits present in a would-be saint?

If we accept Martin's understanding of justification by faith, as most Protestants do, this question has not to do with whether Martin is in fact in heaven with God, for the confidence we have in affirming that he is in heaven comes not from Martin's own righteousness or lack thereof but from that of

---

43 Selderhuis traces this devolution well. Selderhuis, *Martin Luther*, ch. 9.

44 Selderhuis, *Martin Luther*, 201–205.

45 Selderhuis, *Martin Luther*, 286–88.

46 Oberman, for example, makes a convincing case that Martin's writings against the Jews were not born of anti-Semitism so much as theological disagreement and, in the context of the Middle Ages, were actually quite progressive. Martin's ultimate point in assailing the Jews, Oberman maintains, was to demonstrate how Christians can fall under the same deception as God's chosen people had. Moreover, unlike many other medieval theologians, Martin and his followers never laid the blame of the crucifixion at the feet of the Jews but maintained that all sinners were to blame. Oberman, *Luther*, 292–97. While some accounts of Martin's writings against the Jews strike one as empty justifications, Oberman's argument has much to commend it. It is also worth mentioning that while Martin's writings may be linked, at least conceptually, to the Holocaust, so, too, did his writings inspire the German resistance to Hitler, as seen, primarily, in the writings of Dietrich Bonhoeffer.

Christ's. Despite troubling aspects of his biography, we can be confident of Martin's place in heaven along with other sinners saved by grace, such as the thief on the cross, whose final act of faith, despite an apparently sinful life, led Jesus to proclaim that they would be together in paradise (Luke 23:43). As Martin himself described the paradox of the Christian life: Christians are *simul justus et peccator* (simultaneously justified and sinners).[47] That is good news for those who still struggle with sin even after baptism, which, I take it, is every one of us.

The question, rather, regards whether the title *saint* is appropriate for him or whether it is reserved for those who displayed exceptional holiness on earth. Put differently, does the cloud of witnesses include everyone who has ever died in Christ? Some material in this book suggests an affirmative answer. We have already seen, for example, that no saint is perfect.[48] Moreover, we have also seen that there are likely saints in the cloud of witnesses whom the Church has not named. An additional point of Protestant theology, originating with Martin Luther, continues in this same trajectory, namely, Martin's belief that we are all equal in the eyes of God, regardless of our different vocations. If this is true on earth, there is no reason to think it should be any different in heaven or in the eternal restored kingdom of God. When we think of the saints, we often elevate them as being holier than most and, therefore, closer somehow to Jesus. Martin's understanding of the priesthood of all believers suggests a different picture of heaven, namely, a Eucharistic gathering with Jesus in the middle and all the saints around him. Or to use a more biblical image, of which Martin would surely approve, a wedding feast to which all have been invited and all are equally honored by virtue of the wedding clothes provided by the host. If this is the case, the cloud of witnesses is quite large indeed.[49] Despite his lamentable shortcomings and questionable rhetoric, then, Martin is a saint along with the rest at the table of God's grace, the table that we mysteriously join every time we partake of the Eucharist and every time we engage the saints in our discipleship.

---

47 Oberman, *Luther*, 184.

48 Perhaps we would know more about these imperfections had earlier saints had biographies as opposed to hagiographies written about them.

49 This understanding of the cloud of witnesses, however, does not mean that we cannot elevate certain saints as better examples than others based on their earthly lives. Practically speaking, we have to do that; otherwise, engaging the saints becomes an overwhelming task, just as the writer of Hebrews did not name every faithful Israelite in his litany of the saints in Hebrews 11.

Personally speaking, I do not see Martin as a manifestation of Christ the way I see Perpetua and Macrina and Francis. Nor do I invoke Martin in my prayers the way I do Mary and Irenaeus and Julian and others. This might be because of the troubling aspects of his biography. Or it might be a failure of mine to fully comprehend the radical restorative nature of God's salvific grace and love. Whatever the reason, I do try to think of Martin in the cloud of witnesses from time to time. I hope he is standing side by side and arm in arm with some of the very people he assailed on earth. I hope their embrace of him as a brother helped him to see his own errors that he did not see on earth. And I'd like to think that his Catholic opponents, in receiving him in the full fellowship that they never offered him on earth, saw through him their own failings. Perhaps, then, the saints can teach us even through their shortcomings. Perhaps the great cloud of witnesses is our best hope that unity among Christ's followers can yet be found.

CHAPTER TEN

Phoebe's Way

I long to be made a monument of what the grace of God
can effect on a once rebellious child of Adam.

—Phoebe Palmer, diary entry[1]

Christians who have lived for a while after their baptisms can become rather pessimistic about the possibility of attaining holiness. For one thing, patterns of sinfulness are difficult to break. For another thing, it is challenging to sustain the kind of spiritual fervency and focus one has in the youth of faith. Like a marriage, we cannot always *feel* that sense of euphoria or being in love that comes at its beginning; life and all its trials and mundanity and mediocrity can beat it out of us or cause its slow, barely perceptible drain. In the face of this reality, Martin Luther's understanding of Christians as simultaneously justified and sinners seems both comforting and empirically true. Unfortunately, it can also lead to complacency—something Martin himself never intended. If I am always a sinner, one might conclude, what's the point in pursuing holiness?

Thankfully, Martin's is not the only Protestant perspective on this question. Our tenth saint, Phoebe Palmer, is much more hopeful in her theology of holiness. Following the Methodist tradition in which she was formed, Phoebe believed that justification by faith alone produced in sinners a new birth (John 3:3), which empowered them to grow in their own holiness and to

---

1 Phoebe Palmer, *Phoebe Palmer: Selected Writings*, ed. Thomas C. Oden (New York: Paulist Press, 1988), 112–13.

truly conform to the perfect example set by Christ. This conviction not only transformed her life in a very dark and perilous period; it also transformed the religious landscape of the young nation of the United States of America. And this in a time when, in Methodism and nearly all denominations, women were not permitted to be teachers or preachers. Although Phoebe is not as well known today as she was in her lifetime, her powerful words and witness to holiness are as poignant to twenty-first-century Christians as they were to her contemporaries.

Phoebe was born in New York City in 1807 into a devout Christian family.[2] Years before, her England-born father, Henry Worrall, had been converted to Christianity while hearing the evangelist John Wesley preach.[3] Wesley (d. 1791) was a priest in the Church of England, which had separated from the Catholic Church in 1534. Although distinct from Roman Catholicism, the Church of England—or as it is more broadly known, the Anglican Church—was not exactly Protestant either. Rather, it sought to find a middle way (*via media*) between Catholicism and Protestantism.[4] This unique approach manifested itself in a number of ways, both in the sixteenth century and in current

---

2 Despite Phoebe's enormous influence on the Wesleyan/Holiness movement, relatively few biographies exist of her. I have drawn on the account written shortly after her death by Richard Wheatley, ed., *Life and Letters of Mrs. Phoebe Palmer* (New York: W. C. Palmer, Jr., 1876), which also includes excerpts of her journal and correspondence. Additionally, I consulted the comprehensive biography by Charles Edward White, *The Beauty of Holiness: Phoebe Palmer as Theologian, Revivalist, Feminist, and Humanitarian*, repr. (Eugene, OR: Wipf and Stock, 1986). For her own writings, which are voluminous, I will mostly rely on *The Way of Holiness: With Notes by the Way; Being a Narrative of Experience Resulting from a Determination to Be a Bible Christian*, 1843, repr. (London: Forgotten Books, 2012), which will be marked in the text as *WOH* with the book and section number. This work is her clearest account of both her own experience leading to holiness and her formula, of sorts, for others desiring to pursue this narrow path.

3 White, *The Beauty of Holiness*, 1–2.

4 Anglicanism's *via media* develops out of the historical circumstances of the English Reformation. The English king Henry VIII, though Catholic in his theology and practice, wanted to divorce his wife, Catherine of Aragon, because she failed to produce for him a male heir. Pope Clement VIII would not grant the divorce because, among other reasons, Catherine was the aunt to Charles V, the emperor of the Catholic Holy Roman Empire (and interrogator of Martin Luther at the Diet of Worms.) Thus, although Henry wished to remain Catholic in all beliefs and practices, he established, with the consent of parliament, the Church of England in 1534 and transferred all of the rights and duties of the pope to the English monarch. The following quarter-century saw much bloodshed as England swung back and forth between Catholicism and Protestantism based on the faith of the current monarch. The situation was resolved, at least initially, when Elizabeth I came to power in 1558 and established the compromise of the middle way, known as

expressions of Anglicanism in England and around the globe.[5] Anglicans, for example, retain the "smells and bells" of the Catholic mass while rejecting theologies of the sacraments that make clergy somehow higher than laypersons. Additionally, Anglicans retain a Catholic focus on traditional prayers and liturgy—notably the *Book of Common Prayer*—while lifting Scripture, in the vernacular, to the place of supreme authority within the Church.[6]

To give a more focused example that bears directly on Phoebe's story, John Wesley emphasized the importance of faith alone in the process of salvation to the same degree as Martin Luther and other continental Reformers, but he believed, like his Catholic brethren, that justification was accompanied by a new birth that enabled believers to grow in their own holiness. In other words, he rejected the Protestant notion that Christians are simultaneously justified and sinners and believed, rather, that justification must lead to holiness. He even allowed the possibility of what he called "entire sanctification," by which he meant complete perfection in intention and devotion to Christ such that sin no longer had any power in one's life.[7] This conviction, spurred on by a powerful personal experience of the Spirit, led him to preach widely in towns and fields.[8] The people of England came out in droves to hear him,

---

the Elizabethan Settlement. Her long reign of over forty years helped establish the *via media* as the core principle of the Anglican tradition. Chadwick, *The Reformation*, ch. 4.

5 Historically, the Church of England in the United States is the Episcopalian denomination, though, as with all Protestant denominations, it has experienced divisions in recent years with other US expressions of Anglicanism now growing.

6 For an engaging account of the development and subsequent importance of the *Book of Common Prayer* to the shape of Anglicanism, see Alan Jacobs, *The Book of Common Prayer: A Biography* (Princeton, NJ: Princeton University Press, 2013).

7 For an accessible account of Wesley's view of entire sanctification, see Kevin M. Watson, *Perfect Love: Recovering Entire Sanctification—The Lost Power of the Methodist Movement* (Franklin, TN: Seedbed, 2021), especially chs. 4 and 5. Watson shows that Wesley did not mean a person was perfect in regard to knowledge or mistakes; rather, it refers to full deliverance of willful sin. This was a controversial doctrine, both in Wesley's lifetime and today. But Wesley insisted on it in various sermons and in a tract entitled *A Plain Account of Christian Perfection*. I will say more about the doctrine below in the context of Phoebe's ministry.

8 Wesley, like the vast majority of Europeans in the eighteenth century, was a Christian from birth. Nevertheless, he experienced an evangelical awakening at age thirty-four while hearing Martin Luther's preface to his *Commentary on Romans* read aloud at a meeting at Aldersgate. He writes of the experience in his journal, "While [Luther in his book] was describing the change which God works in the heart through faith in Christ, I felt my heart strangely warmed. I felt I did trust in Christ, Christ alone, for salvation; and an assurance was given me that He had taken away my sins, even mine, and saved

and many believed in this short man's message, resulting in an evangelical revival fueled by a unique system of small groups that saw Wesley's followers, derisively called *Methodists* for their methodical practice of the faith, meeting in societies, classes, and bands to spur them to greater holiness.[9] This movement ultimately resulted in the Methodist denominations in both England and the United States.[10] And it was this movement, centered on the reality of lived holiness, that so captivated the young Henry Worrall. He became a committed Methodist, and when he came to the United States in 1792 along with his new wife, he joined the Methodist Episcopal Church.[11]

Phoebe was the fourth of their sixteen children. Like many of the saints we have studied, Phoebe displayed a deep faith and spiritual sensitivity from an early age. To cite just one example, she told a lie at age three that caused her so much grief, she later wrote, that she resolved from then on to always hedge her statements with the words *I think so* to avoid ever speaking untruthfully.[12] She received a strong religious education at home and, at age ten, sat

---

me from the law of sin and death." Wesley's Journal in *The Works of John Wesley*, 3rd ed. (Grand Rapids, MI: Baker Books, 2002), 1: 103. Wesley scholars debate whether this was a conversion experience or a recommitment to a deeper experience of the Christian faith—and Wesley's own writings are unclear—but either way, Wesley left Aldersgate a changed man, and the experience was an important catalyst to the revival that would come from his preaching and leadership.

9 Wesley was convinced in the power of social holiness, that is, that people become holy in the context of deep relationships with other Christians. Thus, he organized those who came to faith through his ministry into societies that would meet regularly outside of the official Anglican service. When the societies grew in numbers, he organized them into smaller classes of twelve people, which met regularly for prayer, Bible study, conversation, and acts of service. Additionally, some of these people would meet in even smaller groups of about three to five people called *bands*, which existed for the purpose of confession and accountability.

10 Wesley originally did not intend for these "Methodists" to be a separate denomination and encouraged members to continue attending Anglican services for Eucharist. But the Revolutionary War of the 1770s hastened the formation of Methodism as a distinct denomination in the United States.

11 Methodism officially began as a US denomination in 1784, making the Worrells just the second generation of US Methodists. By the time Phoebe was born, the United States was experiencing what has become known as the Second Great Awakening, where revival was moving from New York and New England to frontier settlements through camp meetings. Out of the Second Great Awakening, the Methodist denomination became the largest of US denominations because of its willingness to go to people on the frontier. Mark A. Noll, *America's God: From Jonathan Edwards to Abraham Lincoln* (Oxford: Oxford University Press, 2002), 165–70.

12 White, *The Beauty of Holiness*, 2.

through formal catechesis lessons by regular attendance at Methodist class meetings led by the famous Methodist leader Nathan Bangs.[13] At age eleven, she received her first Bible and began reading it faithfully. She wrote a poem on the inside of her Bible that channels Martin in her love of Scripture as well as Origen in her creative interpretation:

This Revelation—holy, just, and true—
Though oft I read, it seems forever new;
While light from heaven upon its pages rest,
I feel its power, and with it I am blest.[14]

At several points in her writings, she refers to having devoted her heart to Jesus "at such an early age that she could never remember when she had done it."[15] This reality actually led her at times to struggle with assurance that her faith was genuine, a struggle that plagued her into young adulthood. As she would later write, "Not to have an experience, like most others born into the kingdom of Christ, who are so fully able from the overwhelming circumstances of the occasion to state the precise moment, was a fruitful source of temptation, resulting in years of painful solicitude" (WOH 2.1). Yet, throughout the first part of her life, she was a devoted disciple regularly abiding in the spiritual disciplines of prayer, Scripture-reading, and church attendance.

Through these years, Phoebe displayed some of the ascetic qualities we witnessed in previous saints. Like Perpetua, Francis, and Julian, for example, Phoebe had several mystical experiences that she records. When she was thirteen, she heard a locution expressing God's tender love for her. She writes, "The place seemed to shine with the glory of God" (WOH 2.1).[16] Moreover, after coming of age, she had many suitors, all of whom she refused, to the consternation of her parents. Like Macrina, her head and her heart were

---

13 Elaine Heath, *Naked Faith: The Mystical Theology of Phoebe Palmer* (Eugene, OR: Pickwick Publications, 2009), 8. Bangs also lived in New York and served as the head of the Methodist Book Concern, an important role in early US Methodism. Additionally, he served as the most important early historian of Methodism. Russel E. Richey, Kenneth E. Rowe, and Jean Miller Schmidt, *The Methodist Experience in America*, vol. 1 (Nashville: Abingdon Press, 2010), 103–4, 120–21.

14 Quoted in White, *The Beauty of Holiness*, 3. Phoebe's writings are filled with similar short verses.

15 White, *The Beauty of Holiness*, 3.

16 Heath has helpfully explored the mystical aspects of Phoebe's theology. Heath, *Naked Faith*, especially chs. 2 and 3.

always elsewhere, and she did not view marriage as her life's accomplishment. However, at age nineteen, she met and fell in love with Walter Clark Palmer, a local physician and Sunday school teacher at the Allen Street Methodist Episcopal Church, where Phoebe's family were members. In her journal, she referred to him as "a kindred spirit . . . worthy of my love."[17] They were married a year later. Despite her ascetic leanings, Phoebe was now set to live a committed Christian life as an early American homemaker like so many faithful, nameless saints. But then tragedy visited her.

The Palmers' first child, Alexander, born a year after their marriage, died of illness at just eleven months old. Their second son, Samuel, was born the following year and lived only seven weeks. After giving birth to a healthy baby girl named Sarah in 1833, Phoebe birthed her fourth child, Eliza, in 1835. A year later, Phoebe was nursing Eliza when a friend came to visit. She put her baby in her crib and in the care of a nursemaid while she went to the other room. Later in the evening, the nursemaid foolishly attempted to refill the dimming alcohol lamp while the wick was still burning, causing it to catch fire and burn her hands. In a panic, the nursemaid threw the lamp, and it landed in the baby's crib quickly setting it ablaze. At the sound of her baby's screams, Phoebe ran into the room and drew her from the flames. But the damage had been done; Eliza died after only a few hours.[18]

The premature deaths of three of her first four children were crushing to the young mother. After Samuel's death, she could barely form the words for her intense grief. She writes in her journal, "I will not attempt to describe the pressure of the last crushing trial."[19] Eliza's death was the most difficult to bear as it came as the result of a careless and completely avoidable act. She might have done any number of things at this point; one could hardly blame her if she doubted the goodness of God or rethought her priorities, centered as they were around devotion to this God. Instead, she turned in grieving faith even more fully to God. In her book *Guide to Holiness*, she writes that as she was crying out to the Lord to help her understand why he would allow this to happen, she felt led to pick up her well-worn Bible. In a scene reminiscent of Francis's story, she opened it randomly and landed on the conclusion of Romans 11, "O the depth of the riches and wisdom and knowledge of God! How unsearchable are his judgments and how inscrutable his ways!" (Rom

---

17 Quoted in Wheatley, *Life and Letters*, 22.

18 White, *The Beauty of Holiness*, 5–8.

19 Quoted in Wheatley, *Life and Letters*, 26.

11:33). As she read the words, she heard the Holy Spirit whisper to her soul that "if I would only look at the all-loving hand of my Heavenly Father, in this afflictive dispensation, and not at second causes, that just in *proportion* to the magnitude of the trial, in all its peculiarities, the result would be glorious."[20] She immediately felt an overwhelming sense of the love of God and, as White describes the scene, "a new closeness to her departed child and knew Eliza was in the presence of Jesus."[21] Here was, to be sure, a mysterious God whose ways were unknowable, but he was still an all-loving Father who brought her comfort even in her unimaginable grief. This realization caused Phoebe not to remain paralyzed but to keep moving, keep seeking, keep praying. This resilient attitude would eventually change not only her life but also the lives of the thousands she would impact with her faith. As she wrote in her journal, "And if diligent and self-sacrificing in carrying out my resolve, the death of this child may result in the spiritual life of many."[22] Or as she writes later in *Guide to Holiness*, "In connection with the saving of souls, it was the beginning of days with me."[23]

As we saw with Francis's story, however, Phoebe's sense of divine calling did not move her immediately. In fact, the following year, she continued to doubt the sincerity of her faith as she had at various times throughout her childhood. She writes in summary fashion of this tendency of hers through her young life: "Though this was in a measure blest to her soul ... and tended to assure her heart more confidently of the gracious designs of Infinite Love toward her, yet the impression soon passed away and she relapsed into her former habits of reasoning and unbelief" (*WOH* 2.2).[24] This doubt is, on the surface, difficult to understand. How could a person who had experienced such tangible examples of God's love ever have cause for doubting? Yet they are indicative of the difficulties life presents in pursuing holiness of heart and life, the struggles that cause us to lose our spiritual fervency and fall back into our well-worn patterns of sin. If I am honest, such doubts are all too

---

20 Quoted in White, *The Beauty of Holiness*, 8, italics original. In her journal entry of the same account, she notes that she heard the words "Your heavenly Father loves you ... He doth not willingly grieve or afflict the children of men. If not *willingly*, then he has some specific design, in this, the greatest of all the trials you have been called to endure." Quoted in Wheatley, *Life and Letters*, 31, italics original.

21 White, *The Beauty of Holiness*, 8.

22 Quoted in Wheatley, *Life and Letters*, 32.

23 Quoted in White, *The Beauty of Holiness*, 9.

24 In *Way of Holiness*, Phoebe often speaks of her experiences in the third person.

familiar to me. Through my life, I have had significant experiences of God's love and felt clear answers to prayer, but these real experiences have not made me somehow immune against times of doubt and spiritual dryness. In matters of faith, often the most recent feelings or experiences speak the loudest. Phoebe's witness, moreover, shows that it is not only the significant moments of tragedy that can be detrimental to our faith and sapping of our spiritual fervency but also, and perhaps more so, the mundane struggles of everyday life, of working and raising children. The death of Eliza had caused her to turn more fully to God; perhaps the daily care of Sarah had unintentionally taken her from God.

But on July 26, 1837, a day which she would from then on refer to as her "day of days," Phoebe had an experience that put an end to her waffling and resulted in a firm commitment to lived holiness and a renewed focus on the sense of calling she received after Eliza's death. It was not, however, a mystical experience. She did not, like Perpetua or Julian or even herself in former times, hear a voice or see a vision. Nor did she, like John Wesley, feel her heart strangely warmed. Rather, in a somewhat ordinary manner, she sensed in prayer the Spirit leading her to make a greater commitment to God than she had before. In her journal, she described this commitment as "a solemn, most sacred, and inviolable compact between God and the soul." She continues, "I was to be united in eternal oneness with the Lord my redeemer, requiring unquestioning allegiance on my part, and infinite love, and everlasting salvation, guidance, and protection, on the part of Him who had loved and redeemed me, so that from henceforth He might say to me, 'I will betroth thee unto me forever.'"[25] Although she had been a faithful Christian her whole life, she had never before grasped the totalizing nature of the commitment God desired, which had likely been the cause of her past equivocations and doubts. She now saw that God called her not to a relationship that one flits in and out of or enters like a cold swimming pool on a hot day, one toe at a time to alleviate the temperature change. This was a marriage, Christ the bridegroom and she his bride, and like a human marriage, the commitment required to make it work could be nothing short of complete. So on this "day of days," she finally jumped in with nothing more than the promises of Scripture to catch her.

Surprisingly, Phoebe came to believe that in this prayer of consecration, she had experienced the "entire sanctification" she would have heard about often

---

25 Quoted in Wheatley, *Life and Letters*, 39.

as a Methodist. I say this is surprising because it departed from the normal ways that Methodists of her day interpreted entire sanctification. Although John Wesley himself had insisted the experience could be instantaneous,[26] it was for him the goal of the Christian life, the finish line, as it were. As this played out in the vast majority of people who claimed to have been entirely sanctified, it came at the end of life following a long journey of gradual growth in holiness. By contrast, Phoebe claimed it as the starting point for the journey, the singular commitment to the Lord, "entire, absolute, and unconditional," as she refers to it in her journal.[27] Put differently, it is the vow one makes at a wedding ceremony that solidifies the lifelong union. Moreover, her previous periods of doubt gave no evidence that she had attained some new level of holiness that would validate a claim to be entirely sanctified. How would this experience be any different from her previous mystical experiences that had not expelled the doubts? Only that she trusted God's Word fully. In this prayer, she asked whether she could know if the Lord received her. As in her prayers over Eliza, Phoebe was again directed to the Scriptures, where she received her answer. She writes, "In gentle whispers, the Spirit replied. 'It is written, I will receive you.'" She reflects of the experience, "I had thought of the doctrine of faith as difficult. Now I saw that it was only to believe *heartily*, what in fact I had always professed to believe, that is, that the Bible is the Word of God just as truly as though I could hear Him speaking in tones of thunder from Sinai's Mount, and *faith is to believe it!*"[28] So often I hear fellow Christians wishing to hear a word from God like God's people of old. So often I have wished to hear God's voice myself. Phoebe shows us that God's words are waiting for us in Scripture, if we would only receive them as the miracle they are.

Phoebe's claim to be entirely sanctified, then, rested on her full commitment to God and God's full commitment to her to make her holy: marriage

---

26 In his sermon "The Scripture Way of Salvation," for example, Wesley wrote that entire sanctification is "a divine evidence and conviction that [God] is able and willing to do it now . . . We may therefore boldly say, at any point of time, 'Now is the day of salvation.' 'Today if ye will hear his voice, harden not your hearts.' 'Behold! all things are now ready! Come unto the marriage!'" *The Works of John Wesley*, 6: 52–53. The point of such an emphasis is that Wesley believed that entire sanctification was as much a gift of faith as was justification.

27 Quoted in Wheatley, *Life and Letters*, 40.

28 Quoted in Wheatley, *Life and Letters*, 41, italics original. Phoebe always sought to ground her visions or impressions in prayer in Scripture and often used Scripture to give words and meaning to her impressions. This is what she means when she refers to herself as a "Bible Christian."

vows. Only by faith can marriage vows be said, for we know not what "in sickness and in health" or "for richer, for poorer" mean until we experience those times. By faith, Phoebe claimed to be entirely sanctified, believing in the promise of her Lord to make it so.

Just as marriages most often occur in the presence of others to serve as witnesses to the union, so Phoebe wanted others to know of her experience. Like Julian, Phoebe told others mostly through writing. In 1843, she published her most influential work, *The Way of Holiness*, where, using Scripture and her own experience, she developed a means of growing in holiness for others to follow.[29] She called it the "shorter way," not to indicate the length of time it took to become holy but rather to indicate that the journey toward holiness can commence at once.[30] Like Martin, she realized there was not some level of holiness one must achieve prior to acceptance by God, an assumption that would surely necessitate a much longer way. Instead, Phoebe's shorter way involved just three steps, the same three witnessed in her own experience of entire sanctification above, namely, (1) consecration, (2) belief in God's acceptance and assurance to fully sanctify his bride, and (3) bearing witness to the experience. Unlike Martin, however, she believed this gracious acceptance must result in holiness because "God requires present holiness" (*WOH* 1.1).[31] At the same time, *shorter* does not indicate easier. The way of holiness is, in fact, not an easy road but one that requires, in Phoebe's words, "*no less devotion* of spirit . . . than that which bore the martyrs through the flames," for, as Phoebe's own life attests, this world can present its own trials that weigh against our commitment (*WOH* 2.4, italics original). The reference to the martyrs indicates the depth of sacrifice required to consecrate oneself at the start of the way.

---

29 The work is divided into two parts. In the first, she outlines her altar theology and the three steps of the shorter way, aspects of her work I will engage shortly. In the second, called "Notes by the Way," she includes her own experiences, often in the form of journal entries. The book was initially printed anonymously because Phoebe did not think a woman should become a public figure. White, *The Beauty of Holiness*, 28. Additionally, as we have seen, her modesty led her to write of her personal experiences in the third person.

30 Heath, *Naked Faith*, 92.

31 One of the difficulties with Martin's theology of humans as simultaneously justified and sinners is the clear emphasis in Scripture on the importance of holy living. Writers such as Paul and John speak often of the possibility of living free from sin. See, for example, Romans 6:1–7 and 1 John 3:1–10. For an argument that grounds entire sanctification in Scripture, see Watson, *Perfect Love*, ch. 7.

Thus, the foundation of the shorter way is what scholars have called her "altar theology."[32] The image of the altar pervades Phoebe's writings. It not only brings to mind the marriage metaphor she has been developing—for marriages are consecrated at the altar—but more importantly, the attitude one needs to bring to the marriage. For the altar is the place of sacrifice, first in the Old Testament, as prescribed by the Levitical laws, and then of Christ, through which the Father restored the world as testified by the Spirit. She writes, "The altar, thus, provided by the conjoint testimony of the Father, Son, and Holy Spirit, is Christ. His sacrificial death and sufferings are the sinner's plea; the immutable promises of the Lord Jehovah the ground of claim. If true to the Spirit's operations on the heart, men, as co-workers with God, confess their sins, the faithfulness and justice of God stand pledged, not only to *forgive*, but also to *cleanse from all unrighteousness*" (WOH 1.9, italics original). Christ's sacrifice on behalf of the world makes him the altar. And the only response from sinners so justified is "to consecrate all upon the altar of sacrifice to God . . . and then acting in conformity with this decision, *actually laying all upon the altar* [believing] *that the sacrifice became the Lord's property*" (WOH 1.9, italics original). Significantly, Christ the altar makes sinners holy by grace before any growth in holiness has occurred for "the altar sanctifies the gift" (WOH 1.9). Phoebe believed that humans descended from Adam were sinful. However, having laid themselves on the altar, such persons, like Old Testament sacrifices, are sanctified, literally set apart from the world they inhabit. In Paul's words, they become "a living sacrifice" (Rom 12:1), a life verse of sorts for Phoebe.[33] Even so, Paul's emphasis on a living sacrifice meant that "one act of faith is not sufficient to insure perseverance in the 'way of holiness,' but that a continuous act was requisite" (WOH 1.9). Just as the marriage vows are said once in faith but then daily renewed in actual life, so the offerings at the altar need to be daily renewed as living sacrifices. One must continually keep oneself on the altar. This is precisely why holiness is a *way* and life a "pilgrimage" (WOH 1.1).

Just as Phoebe herself embodied certain ascetic qualities, so also her altar theology and shorter way demonstrate many affinities to ascetic theology, notably, Macrina's. The shorter way required nothing less than laying one's

---

32 Heath, *Naked Faith*, 95.

33 Notably, this verse lies in close proximity to the verse (Rom 11:33) she turned to when grieving the death of Eliza.

life on the altar, putting one's relationship with God before all other relationships and one's possession of the gospel above all other possessions. Like the martyrs and monastics of old, Phoebe gave God her whole life and radically trusted that God accepted her and would perfect her, the first two steps of her shorter way.

However, in the third step, witnessing to others, Phoebe breaks out of the ascetic mold cast for her. For she did not, like Macrina and Francis, feel compelled to leave her life to answer this call. Unlike Julian, she did not have to confine herself to a room to write her book. She couldn't. She was a mother with a child who demanded her time and attention.[34] She was a wife with a husband who needed her. So Phoebe remained as she was when entirely sanctified, a lay wife and mother, and simply began faithfully witnessing to the way of holiness in the midst of her ordinary life. In the words of Paul, she would forever "remain in the situation [she was] in when God called [her]" (1 Cor 7:20).

Phoebe, thus, sets an important example to all people who sense the call of God on their lives to share their stories, namely, that witnessing to the power of the gospel can happen effectively in any station of life. Like the shorter way, the work of witnessing does not need to be put off until one is officially trained or authorized by some church body. In Phoebe's time, in fact, women were not yet able to preach or serve as leaders within Protestant churches. There was, in other words, no clear place for her to bear witness. Yet, whatever the Church said, she believed that God ordained the "ministry of *all* Christ's disciples" and that "she was divinely commissioned and ordained by the great Head of the church for the special work which she felt impelled to do."[35]

Despite the challenges of raising a family and lacking an official place to serve in her Methodist church, Phoebe's faithful work for the kingdom and in the service of holiness is incredible.[36] In addition to her many publica-

---

34 Phoebe would go on to have two more children, Phoebe in 1839 and Walter in 1842. Her daughter Phoebe Knapp would become a composer, writing many of the tunes to beloved church hymns including "Blessed Assurance."

35 As quoted by White, *The Beauty of Holiness*, 194.

36 The barrier against ordained ministry does not face women in many Protestant churches today. Phoebe's Methodist Church first ordained women in 1956. Although Phoebe never argued specifically for the ordination of women, in 1859's *Promise of the Father*, she argued against the position, then standard, that women should not serve as leaders within the Church. In the work, she takes on the two passages commonly used in favor of this position, namely, 1 Corinthians 14:34 ("Women should remain silent in the churches. They are not allowed to speak, but must be in submission, as the law says")

tions, read by thousands in the Methodist world,[37] Phoebe was an influential teacher. In 1838, she started preaching at camp meetings, an important tool for evangelism on the prairie.[38] Perhaps because of the fruit of this work, a year later, she became the first woman appointed to lead a Methodist class meeting of men and women. "This appointment gave official sanction to a woman to teach and lead men as well as women," writes Heath.[39] In 1840, she took over leadership of the Tuesday Meeting for Holiness started by her sister Sarah Lankford four years earlier. Originally designed as a gathering for Methodist women to share their stories and so encourage faithful living, the meeting was transformed under Phoebe's leadership. Notably, she led the meeting's first male attendee, Thomas C. Upham, a congregational minister and professor at Bowdoin College, to experience entire sanctification. Upham would subsequently write two books about his experience and publicly identify his work with Phoebe, lending prestige and credibility to her writings. This led many more people, men and women, pastors, bishops, and homemakers, to attend her Tuesday Meetings. One prominent attendee was Nathan Bangs, the influential Methodist leader who had taught Phoebe as a child. Methodist historians Richey, Rowe, and Schmidt note that "by the 1850s the meeting had become broadly evangelical, drawing ministers

---

and 1 Timothy 2:12 ("I do not permit a woman to teach or to assume authority over a man; she must be quiet"). The first passage, she argues, relates to the specific church in Corinth and was not meant as a universal law, while the force of the second passage is not that women should not teach but that they should not do so in a way that usurps the pastor's authority, or in other words, they should not teach the wrong way. Moreover, the powerful witness of women leaders in Scripture, such as Deborah, as well as in history, such as herself (though she is too modest to so say), is proof enough of a woman's ability to preach and teach the gospel. For more on these arguments, see White, *The Beauty of Holiness*, 190–93. Today, many different Protestant denominations ordain women. While the Eastern Orthodox Church and Roman Catholic Church both continue to reserve ordained priesthood to men, there are numerous ways for women to serve in ministry in those faith communities, as we have witnessed in this book.

37 White reports of *The Way of Holiness*, her most influential work, that fifty-two thousand copies were sold in America and 100,000 were sold worldwide. White, *The Beauty of Holiness*, 29.

38 Camp Meetings were typically weeklong events where farmers and other rural dwellers would travel to and set up camp for the week, attending religious services through the days and evenings. They often resulted in conversions and ecstatic spiritual experiences. They were also less regulated by church officials, which explains Phoebe's ability to preach in these settings as opposed to churches.

39 Heath, *Naked Faith*, 10.

and laypeople from almost every Protestant denomination."[40] Countless Christians were thus affected by Phoebe's holiness theology, and it helped to birth many new holiness denominations in the United States, including the Church of the Nazarene, the Salvation Army, the Church of God, and the Pentecostal-Holiness Church.[41] Not only did it spread Phoebe's ideas, but it also popularized John Wesley's belief that personal holiness is best achieved in the context of small groups of people, an idea that still finds purchase in the small group movement of Protestant mega churches and the resurgence of the band meeting in parts of Methodism.

This was all from a woman who, in the face of tragedy, laid her life on an altar, believed in God's goodness and power to make her holy, and opened her mouth to bear witness.

Phoebe would live into the 1870s, nearly four decades after her day of days, keeping up her busy schedule of raising children, writing, traveling, preaching, and teaching. She continued her leadership of the Tuesday Meeting for Holiness for over thirty years, a record nearly unmatched by any minister. Faithful work. Daily sacrifice. Staying on the altar. Phoebe showed in her work and in her life that holiness in this life is possible. She died in 1874 of kidney disease, a loving wife and mother and a faithful disciple who kept her vows to the end.[42] We proclaim in hope that her beloved bridegroom kept his. May Phoebe pray for us as we experience our own trials and mundanities of this life in our efforts to grow in holiness and faithfully witness to God's transforming work.

---

40 Richey, Rowe, and Schmidt, *The Methodist Experience in America*, 130.
41 Heath, *Naked Faith*, 26.
42 White, *The Beauty of Holiness*, 101–3.

CHAPTER ELEVEN

Thérèse's Flowers

All the flowers He created are beautiful. . . .
If all the little flowers wanted to be roses,
nature would lose its springtime adornment,
and the fields would no longer be sprinkled with little flowers.

—Thérèse of Lisieux, *The Story of a Soul*, 2–3

As inspiring as the lives of the saints are, their holiness and radical efforts on behalf of the kingdom can sometimes make them hard to identify with and even seem unapproachable. Personally speaking, I will probably never be martyred like Perpetua or inspire a new form of Christian life like Macrina or sell all of my possessions to give to the poor like Francis. Most days, it feels enough to get my kids to school on time without yelling at them or swearing in a fit of road rage. Compared to the remarkable lives of the saints, our lives can seem, well, ordinary and can give our more mundane efforts at discipleship a feeling of inadequacy. A fair question to ask at this point in our study of the saints is whether faithful discipleship requires the accomplishment of such extraordinary acts.

The answer to this question comes in the witness of our eleventh saint, Thérèse of Lisieux. As far as the earthly lives of saints go, Thérèse's was a rather ordinary one. She was just an average Frenchwoman who entered a relatively unknown convent at age fifteen, lived a faithful but inconsequential monastic life, and died of tuberculosis at the tender age of twenty-four. Her autobiography, *The Story of a Soul*, written at the request of her superiors, focused mostly on a happy though ordinary childhood filled with the innocent pleasures of youth and marked by the sincere efforts of a girl intent on living faithfully. Though she desired to be a missionary and even a priest, she focused on faithfulness in what she called "little things"—helping fellow nuns, being nice to those she did not like, and so forth—simply because these were the only options of faithfulness available to her. By all accounts, this unremarkable Christian should have been forgotten upon her premature death. But quite unexpectedly, *The Story of a Soul* became a bestseller precisely because of its focus on faithfulness in little things, which resonated with ordinary Christians who could never do the "big things" typically identified with saints. Known as the Little Flower, from the humble way she refers to herself throughout her autobiography, Thérèse demonstrates that faithfulness, and even sainthood, comes in all shapes and sizes and is open to all who pursue it with love.[1]

Born in 1873 in the French city of Alençon, Marie-Franciose-Thérèse Martin was the youngest child of a devout Catholic family.[2] She was named after the sixteenth-century Spanish mystic and monastic figure St. Teresa of Ávila, known for her contemplative prayer life as well as her reforming efforts of the Carmelite Order, originally founded in the twelfth century. These reforms resulted in a new order, the Discalced ("without shoes") Carmelites, widely considered to be one of the primary arms of the sixteenth-century Catholic Reformation addressed in chapter 9. Thérèse's parents chose the name with intention. In her autobiography, Thérèse recalls as a child hearing a priest talking about St. Teresa and her father whispering to her, "Listen, my little

---

1 There are many versions and translations of *The Story of a Soul*. I have used the version that I first read in 2008, near the beginning of my journey with the saints. *St. Thérèse of Lisieux: The Story of a Soul, A New Translation*, trans. and ed. Robert J. Edmonson, *Christian Classics* (Brewster, MA: Paraclete Press, 2006). Quotations will be marked in the text as *SS* with the page number. For details on her life, I have consulted the first authorized biography by August Pierre Laveille, *The Life of St. Thérèse of Lisieux*, trans. Rev. M. Fitzsimons, OMI (Notre Dame, IN: Christian Classics, 1929), which benefits from interviews with many who knew Thérèse, as well as the more critical account by Guy Gaucher, *The Story of a Life* (San Francisco: HarperSanFrancisco, 1987).

2 France was still reeling from the French Revolution of the late eighteenth century, which turned many people away from Catholicism to embrace an antireligious atheism. However, these realities did not have much effect on Thérèse and so will not factor into our story. For a good account of the effects of the French Revolution, as emblematic of modernity, on Christianity more generally, see Mark Noll, *Turning Points: Decisive Moments in the History of Christianity*, 3rd ed (Grand Rapids, MI: Baker Academic, 2012), ch. 11.

queen, they're talking about your Patron Saint" (SS 36). As she notes with affection, Thérèse always listened to her father, and the details of her life will show she was surely listening at this point.

Thérèse's first four years of life, what she calls the "first period" of her existence, were quite happy (SS 6). As the youngest child, and likely because she had nearly died in infancy,[3] Thérèse was the favorite of the house. As her sister Marie wrote in a letter, "Everyone in the house showers affection on her."[4] Perhaps as a result of this attention, Thérèse had a temperamental disposition in these early years. As her mother recalls in several letters,[5] Thérèse could be difficult. "She's a child who easily gets emotional," she writes (SS 9). Elsewhere, she expands, "When things don't go the way she wants them to, she rolls on the ground like a madwoman who thinks all is lost. There are times when it gets so strong that she loses her breath" (SS 14). For her part, Thérèse recalls being overly emotional as a child. Nor would such behavior change just with age. When she was well into her teens, Thérèse recollects, "if it happened that I involuntarily gave a slight amount of trouble to a person I loved, instead of taking the high road and *not crying*, I increased my fault instead of reducing it, by *crying* like a baby. And when I started to become comforted by the thing itself, I *cried because I had cried*" (SS 102).[6] While Thérèse identifies this as a negative trait, it also more benignly suggests that she was a sensitive person who experienced and expressed her emotions with intensity, a quality that remained to the end of her life. Indeed, the most frequent causes of her intense emotions were her experiences with her faith and the deep love she felt for her family.

Thérèse also experienced an early awakening of love for God, no doubt cultivated by the faithful religious practices she imbibed in the Martin household. The family attended mass daily, said prayers together, fasted, kept the Sabbath, and observed the liturgical calendar of feast days. Theirs was a

---

3 Due to her inability to nurse from her mother, Thérèse spent the first year of her life living with a wet nurse in the Normandy countryside, the likely origin of her strong connection to nature and, in particular, flowers. Gaucher, *The Story of a Life*, 15.

4 Quoted in Laveille, *Life of St. Thérèse*, 50.

5 These letters were preserved by Thérèse's sister Pauline, who served for a time as prioress of Thérèse's convent under the name Mother Agnes and was the first to ask Thérèse to write down her recollections of her childhood, which form a core part of *The Story of a Soul*. Thérèse includes portions of her mother's letters in recounting her childhood.

6 All italics in quotations of SS are original.

generous household, moreover, often visiting the sick and dying, welcoming homeless people to their table, and, at least once, arranging for their shelter.[7] Through such practices, Thérèse developed an intimate connection with God; she would often speak of God to her mother and sisters in a familiar manner, displaying a knowledge that was, in her mother's words, "quite unusual at her age" (*SS* 19). She continues, "All she talks about is God; she wouldn't miss saying her prayers for anything . . . There's something so heavenly in her look that we're quite taken by it!" (*SS* 21). Her sister Pauline had already committed to a monastic vocation, and Thérèse's admiration for her older sister initially drew her to the same path: "Without knowing too much about what that was, I thought, *I'm going to be a nun, too.* That's one of my earliest memories, and ever since, I've never changed my resolve" (*SS* 10).

But Thérèse's happy childhood was not to last as, in just her fourth year of life, her mother died of a fibrous tumor originally caused by a childhood injury.[8] This tragic event marked a turning point, ushering in the second period of Thérèse life, what she would later describe as "the most painful of the three" (*SS* 26). Out of financial necessity, their father moved the family to Lisieux to live with his sister-in-law's family. This move brought with it some unexpected joys, including the fostering of a bond with her father and sister Pauline. Thérèse and her father took long walks together and spent time in the garden he made for her, cultivating and admiring flowers. Pauline became Thérèse's surrogate mother in numerous ways, most significantly, in the area of religious instruction. Under Pauline's tutelage, Thérèse's faith developed significantly. As she describes the second period in retrospect, "In the same way as the springtime flowers begin to germinate under the snow and begin to open at the first rays of the Sun, even so the little flower whose memories I'm writing about had to pass through the trial of winter" (*SS* 23).[9]

When Thérèse was nine, Pauline joined the convent in Lisieux.[10] Though she would visit Pauline often, the nature of their sisterly relationship changed,

---

7 Gaucher, *The Story of a Life*, 20–21.

8 Laveille, *Life of St. Thérèse*, 56.

9 She writes of her religious experiences in this period with emotional intensity. To cite one of many examples, she writes of her first confession, "When I left the confessional I was so happy and so light that I've never felt so much joy in my soul" (*SS* 35).

10 The Carmel convent of Lisieux was established in 1838 by two Carmelite nuns from Potiers, Mother Elizabeth and Mother Geneviève, along with two novices from Lisieux. Laveille, *Life of St. Thérèse*, 151–52. Mother Geneviève was still alive when Thérèse entered, and she recounts many fond memories of the saintly old nun. She writes

and this marked a significant trial for Thérèse: "I was going to lose my second *mother*. . . Oh! How can I tell you of the anguish in my heart?" (*SS* 54). In the midst of her grief, however, Thérèse received clearly her own monastic calling:

> Then you (Pauline) explained to me about the life at Carmel that seemed so beautiful to me. As I was going over in my mind everything that you had told me, I felt that Carmel was *the desert* where God wanted me as well to go and hide. . . . I felt it with so much strength that there wasn't the slightest doubt in my heart. This was not the dream of a child who lets herself be carried away, but the *certainty* of a Divine call. I wanted to go to Carmel, not for *Pauline*, but for *Jesus alone*. (*SS* 55)

What had, prior to this moment, been faint stirrings in her heart were now clarified for her with the vision of a life spent devoted to love of God in worship and service of others in prayer, particularly for priests, which was the focus of the Carmelite Order.[11] Pauline encouraged her sister's newly clarified vocation and, soon after, took her to see the prioress, who, though recognizing the child's sincerity, informed her that she would have to wait to join Carmel until she was older.

Her inability to enter Carmel immediately was another sorrow for Thérèse, compounded by her separation from Pauline and, sometime later, her oldest sister, Marie, who also became a Carmelite nun. More trials would come in the next few years including unexplained periods of dryness in prayer and, most significantly, an illness that overtook her from the end of 1882 to spring 1883. What started as a persistent headache culminated in a period of uncontrollable shakes, fever, and delirium, leaving her bedridden for the better part of a month. The doctor was perplexed, never having seen such a serious illness in a young child. The situation looked dire; indeed, her sisters thought she was going to die. The family prayed unceasingly for a miracle and tried to bring her comfort. They placed in her room a statue of Mary that had belonged to her mother, and Thérèse writes that gazing at it did bring some relief. One day, as she was praying to Mary, she received a vision through the

---

of her, "God, who had already given me so many graces, wanted me to live with a *Saint*, not one I couldn't imitate, but a Saint who was made holy through hidden and ordinary virtues" (*SS* 190). As we will see below, this is a good summation of Thérèse's own "little way" of faithfulness.

11 As Thérèse describes it, "How beautiful is the vocation that has as its object to *preserve the salt* that is destined for souls! That vocation is Carmel's, since the only objective of our prayers and our sacrifices is to be *the apostle of the apostles*, praying for them while they evangelize souls through their words and especially by their examples" (*SS* 134).

statue: "Suddenly the Blessed Virgin seemed *beautiful* to me, *so beautiful* that I had never seen anything so beautiful. Her face was breathing inexpressible goodness and tenderness, but what penetrated right to the depths of my soul was 'the lovely smile of the Blessed Virgin.' Then all my sufferings melted away, and two big tears burst from my eyelids and streaked silently down my cheeks—but these were tears of an unadulterated joy . . . Oh! I thought, the Blessed Virgin smiled at me, how happy I am" (*SS* 65). Thérèse was instantly healed, never to experience that particular illness again.

This miraculous account echoes Julian's deathbed vision from the crucifix that was, likewise, the source of her healing. At the same time, this connection underscores the simplicity of Thérèse's experience; she heard no voice and saw no supernatural light or blood radiating from the statue. She simply had the impression that the Virgin was very beautiful and that her smile was meant for Thérèse: "I saw her *smile at me*" (*SS* 67). The simplicity is fitting for the Little Flower, whose visions even seem pedestrian when compared to those of other saints. Yet it was for her a source of healing grace that would always remain with her: "Yes, the little flower was going to be born anew to life," she later interpreted the experience. "The glowing *Ray* that had warmed her was not going to stop its blessings. It doesn't act suddenly, but sweetly, gently, it picked its flower back up and strengthened it in such a way that five years later it opened up on the fertile mount of Carmel" (*SS* 66).

Protestants reading this story might have pause that Thérèse's reflections on this episode suggest that she understood the source of her healing as Mary and not Christ, which seems to confirm the fears with engaging the saints as a spiritual practice. However, the explanation of praying to the saints I laid out in chapter 1 offers a better understanding of this account. Recall that when we pray *to* Mary and other saints, we are not asking that they give us gifts, miracles, or other blessings from their own persons or resources. Rather, we are asking for them to intercede for us to Christ that we might receive those blessings from him, the giver of "every good and perfect gift" (James 1:17, NIV). In other contexts, Thérèse recognizes this truth. She writes, for example, in one place, "It's Jesus alone who is acting in me" (*SS* 248). Elsewhere, she writes, "The road on which I was marching was so straight, so shining, that no other guide was needed for me than Jesus . . . I used to compare spiritual directors to faithful mirrors who reflected Jesus into souls, and I used to say that for me God didn't use an intermediary, but He would act directly" (*SS* 112). This image provides a great metaphor for understanding the work of Mary in Thérèse's life and more generally the work of the saints in our lives—Mary was not the source of Thérèse's healing but the conduit; she reflected *his* healing grace to her through a simple smile.

Thérèse's physical healing paralleled an equally miraculous spiritual healing, which occurred in this second period. For even after seeing the Virgin's smile, she continued to experience long periods of dryness, unanswered prayer, and a rather rough period of what she called "scruples," or an excessive fear of her own sinfulness (*SS* 86).[12] Her volatile temperament and easy tears persisted as well, resulting in much spiritual turmoil. But this all changed for her on Christmas Day, 1886, which marked the beginning of the third and final period of Thérèse's life, "the most beautiful of them all" (*SS* 104). She writes, "On that radiant night that sheds light on the delights of the Holy Trinity, Jesus the sweet *little* child, just one hour old, changed the night of my soul into torrents of light . . . On that *night when* He made Himself *weak* and suffering out of love for me, He made me *strong* and courageous. He put his armor on me, and since that blessed night I was never defeated in combat" (*SS* 102). These are powerful words, yet, here again, the simplicity of the account stands out. For there was no great miracle experienced, no vision seen, no locution heard. She only notes that, following a beautiful midnight mass, she was disappointed in overhearing her father's annoyance at the family's annual Christmas traditions. As was her custom, she ran upstairs, fighting away tears. But then, to her shock, she realized that she was not upset but maintained through her disappointment an inner joy. She was able to return to the family and enjoy the evening.

The reason this ordinary event was so significant for Thérèse is that it marked for her the end of her childhood. She found that she was no longer emotionally beholden to events that used to wreck her. She received, by God's grace, an equanimity, or, as we saw in the chapter on St. Macrina, that ancient monastic ideal of detachment. "In an instant," she writes, "the work that I hadn't been able to do in ten years—Jesus did it . . . I felt *charity* enter into my heart, the need to forget myself in order to please others, and ever afterward

---

12 Biographers often suggest that these scruples were the result of the influence of the heresy of Jansenism, which was particularly active in France at the time. Gaucher, *Story of a Life*, 56–56, 89. The story of Jansenism is a complex one, but the version active in France emphasized that God could only be pleased through hard acts of faithfulness, which could easily make one fear one's own sinfulness, as Thérèse did in this season. This theology is similar to what I described in the introduction to this chapter, namely, the belief that faithfulness required doing "big things" for God. As such, this bout of scruples likely influenced Thérèse's turn to the "little way" of faithfulness in the convent.

I was happy!" (SS 104).[13] Importantly, it was the child Jesus ("just an hour old") who released the Little Flower from her spiritual suffering and helped her "put an end to childish ways" (1 Cor 13:11). To paraphrase a theological statement we encountered in the chapter on Irenaeus, Jesus became a child so that Thérèse might become an adult. Following her Christmas grace, as she would come to call it, the Little Flower was now spiritually prepared to enter the convent.

Unfortunately, at just thirteen years old, she was still too young. Moreover, the prospect of leaving her dear father alone weighed heavily on her. Still, she pursued what she felt was her singular calling, informing her father the next spring of her intentions and winning the approval of her uncle,[14] who said she "was a little flower that God wanted to pick, and he would no longer be opposed to it!" (SS 120).[15] Church officials still demurred, among them the vicar-general, Father Révérony, who had the authority to allow her early admittance. Thérèse realized she would have to take her petition for early admittance to a higher authority. For Catholics, then and now, the highest spiritual authority on earth is the pope.

As it happened, she would get such a chance, for the following year her father took her and her sister Céline, along with a group of pilgrims from their parish, on a pilgrimage to Europe, the crowning moment of which would be an audience with Pope Leo XIII.[16] Thérèse resolved that she would petition the holy father, the vicar of Christ, to enter Carmel early. That she would have the audacity to consider such a request from her lowly station—both in age and stature—is incredible in itself. Moreover, the audience was only to pay

---

13 Readers from the Wesleyan tradition ought to recognize a kinship in this account to John Wesley's Aldersgate experience, the point when this committed though fearful Christian felt his "heart strangely warmed."

14 Her father was initially very grieved at the idea of giving over another one of his daughters to the convent, but eventually he reconciled himself to it. Families of monastics or missionaries or other disciples pursuing God's calling to unanticipated locations also endure a sacrifice.

15 This sentiment clearly resonated with Thérèse as she referred to it in the introduction to her autobiography: "It is for you (Pauline) alone that I'm going to write the story of the little flower picked by God" (SS 4). Perhaps she first began thinking of herself as God's Little Flower in this moment.

16 The pilgrimage was organized in honor of the fiftieth anniversary of Pope Leo XIII's ordination to the priesthood. It also served as a political statement in support of the pope against Italy's anticlerical government. Laveille, who was a pilgrim in the same group, describes in detail the situation as well as the events of the pilgrimage. Laveille, *Life of St. Thérèse*, 129–46.

honor to the pope, not to speak to him. Father Révérony, the leader of their group, explicitly "*forbade us to speak* to Leo XIII" (*SS* 151) right before they entered the room. Hearing the directive, Thérèse turned toward her sister, who knew her intentions. She said only, "Speak" (*SS* 151), and somehow, the Little Flower mustered the courage to do just that:

> A moment later I was at the Holy Father's feet and had kissed his slipper, and he was extending his hand out to me. But instead of kissing it, I joined my hands together and, lifting toward his face my eyes bathed in tears, I cried out, "Most Holy Father, I have a great grace to ask of you! . . ." Then the Supreme Pontiff lowered his head toward me in such a way that my face almost touched his, and I saw his *dark* and *deep eyes* fix on me and seem to pierce me to the depths of my soul. "Most Holy Father," I said to him, "in honor of your jubilee, allow me to enter Carmel at the age of fifteen!" (*SS* 151)

The account is comical for the power differential that existed between the pope, the most powerful figure in Catholicism, and Thérèse, an insignificant French girl. The scene is reminiscent of the humble Francis coming before Pope Innocent III described in chapter 7. Yet, even here, the simplicity of Thérèse stands alone, for she was not asking for a new monastic order or anything of much consequence, it would seem; she only wanted to enter a convent earlier than rules allowed.

After receiving clarification on the request from Father Révérony, who stood at his side, the pope initially told her to do whatever her superiors told her. Thérèse, however, persisted, knowing he was the ultimate earthly authority and could grant her request, regardless of what her superiors had decided. The pope finally said, "*You will enter if it is God's will*" (*SS* 152). The response was not necessarily the permission she had hoped for, but Thérèse was encouraged. More importantly, the interchange clearly had an effect on Father Révérony, for the priest, who had previously been against Thérèse's wishes, took an interest in her for the rest of the pilgrimage. By its end, he promised her that he would do everything in his power to grant her wish. In April of the following year, Thérèse entered Carmel early, at just fifteen. She took the name Sister Thérèse of the Child Jesus, likely a reference to the work of grace the child Jesus did in her heart in 1886 but also, perhaps, a prophetic name indicating the simple but profound witness she would have. For in the monastery, she would focus the remainder of her short life on being faithful in little things, a vision of spirituality she called her "little way."

In truth, the little way was a continuation of the manner in which Thérèse had been living at least since 1886 and, more than she herself admits, her entire life.[17] Because the little way needs no monastery to follow. For at its heart, it means faithfulness in the things we experience in everyday life: our jobs, our relationships with our family and friends, our interactions with strangers we encounter, and the like. In other words, the little way is faithfulness in places that are often unseen and unknown by other humans. As such, it is distinct from the manner of faithfulness celebrated in our culture and in Thérèse's own time, namely, those great, consequential acts done for God and for his kingdom. There is, of course, nothing wrong with doing such big things for God; many of the stories told in this book would qualify as such. The difficulty is when we restrict faithfulness, and sainthood for that matter, to the big acts. Or when we do big acts not for God but for the praise of others, as Jesus warned about in the Sermon on the Mount (Matt 6:1–4).[18] Or when we only seek to do the big things while failing to be faithful in the little things that present themselves every day.

In a letter to her superior, Thérèse describes her countercultural way of faithfulness as follows:

> You know, Mother that I've always desired to be a saint, but alas! I've always stated, when I've compared myself to the Saints, that there is between them and me the same difference that exists between a mountain the summit of which is lost in the sky, and an obscure grain of sand that is trodden under foot by passersby. Instead of becoming discouraged, I've told myself: God wouldn't know how to inspire desires that can't be realized. So despite my littleness I can aspire to sainthood. To make myself bigger is impossible; I have to put up with myself such as I am with all my imperfections. But I want to seek the means of going to heaven by a little way that is very straight, very short, a completely new little way. (SS 230)

---

17 Although space precludes a full description, many episodes from her third period of life, prior to entrance into Carmel, demonstrate this little way of faithfulness. Among these include her catechizing young children and her prayers for the soul of Pranzini, a notorious criminal in France at the time. Both of these examples prefigure the work she would do in the convent. For a greater description of these activities and others from this time, see SS, ch. 5 and Laveille, *Life of St. Thérèse*, ch. 6.

18 Thérèse referred to this passage in one of her earliest descriptions of the little way. She writes, "God let me feel that true glory is the one that will last forever, and that to obtain it, it isn't necessary to do outstanding works, but to remain hidden and to practice virtue in such a way that the right hand doesn't know what the left hand is doing" (SS 70).

This is no abstract theory of faithfulness but a description of her manner of living. While examples of her little way abound from her time in the convent, two must suffice. In one place, she describes a certain Sister St. Peter, an elderly nun who sat in front of Thérèse at evening prayers. The suffering from her old age made her rather contemptuous toward other sisters, and, thus, the job of taking her back to her room was one no one sought for its unpleasantness. "However I didn't want to miss such a beautiful opportunity to practice charity," Thérèse writes, "so I offered myself quite humbly to guide her—and not without some difficulty, I managed to get my services accepted!" (SS 281). Without being asked, and without seeking recognition, Thérèse took the undesired job, and despite often being chastised by the old nun for the manner of her service, not to mention the hardship involved in getting an immobile person to and from her room, she found joy and even the presence of God in this simple task.

In another place, Thérèse mentions a fellow nun she really didn't like. As she writes in her charmingly sanitized way, this unnamed sister "has the talent of displeasing me in everything: Her manners, her words, her character seemed to me to be *very displeasing*" (SS 250). Despite her personal feelings, Thérèse knew this woman "must be *very pleasing* to God" (SS 250). Therefore, she did the opposite of her natural feelings and "set about doing for this Sister what I would have done for the person that I love the most" (SS 250). She prayed for her every time she saw her and "tried to render her every possible service" (251). When she was tempted to speak harshly to her, she smiled and changed the subject. She was so nice to this sister that the sister came to believe she was Thérèse's favorite! Significantly, these were not artificial actions like we sometimes experience or do to others in our culture of niceness—what is often called being *two-faced*. For the little way is precisely about being faithful in little things that no one but God sees. Thérèse served and loved the unnamed sister truly and wholly because she sought to treat and think of her as Jesus did.

My guess is these examples strike most of us as insignificant. The reason for this impression is that we feel anyone can do such things. In other words, it doesn't take a saint to be nice to someone. But herein lies both the genius and the challenge of the little way. Such acts of faithfulness are indeed things that anyone can do, and they readily present themselves in our lives. Everyone knows a Sister St. Peter and likely more than one "displeasing" unnamed sister. But how many seek such people out to serve and to love? How many choose rather to avoid such people or, what is worse, to be antagonistic toward them? Thus, the little way turns out to be harder than first thought, even more so because such acts will largely go unseen. But such is the path that Thérèse faithfully pursued. What, then, compelled her to such faithfulness?

Not surprisingly, the answer is quite simple: love. "I have finally found my vocation," she writes. "My vocation is love" (SS 217). When a person is infused with God's love, serving and loving others come naturally. When a person is infused with God's love, being two-faced or indifferent toward others ceases to be an option because all people are seen as worthy of love. She writes, "When charity has cast deep roots in the soul, it shows on the outside" (SS 259). Moreover, love is necessary to faithfulness in all things because without love, even the big acts of faithfulness are meaningless. She writes, "I understood that without *love*, all works are only nothingness, even the most dazzling, such as raising the dead or converting entire peoples" (SS 198). Thérèse's words echo those of Paul, who, when cautioning the Corinthians on their preference for showy spiritual gifts like speaking in tongues, pointed them instead to the supreme spiritual gift given to all those who are in Christ: "If I speak in the tongues of mortals and of angels, but do not have love, I am a noisy gong or a clanging cymbal. . . . And now faith, hope, and love abide, these three; and the greatest of these is love" (1 Cor 13:1, 13). Thérèse lived her little way by love, the greatest of the spiritual gifts; she was faithful in all things because she loved people born of her deep love of God. What a simple yet saintly way of living.

As I noted in the introduction, Thérèse did not live a long earthly life. In 1896, she contracted tuberculosis. She suffered greatly in her last year of life, spending much of it bedridden in an infirmary. Nevertheless, she managed to write several letters to her superiors articulating her little way of faithfulness, as well as her vocation of love that animates it, which form the fitting conclusion of *The Story of a Soul*. Importantly, however, neither these letters nor her bodily death in September of 1897 would form the conclusion of her work on earth. For a crucial aspect of a Catholic theology of the saints is that the saints remain active in heaven, continuing to love and serve people, continuing to reflect Jesus's grace to people on earth. Formed in the Catholic faith, Thérèse believed this was possible. In the last months of her earthly life, she reflected some on the possibility that she, too, might be active from heaven, continuing to pursue her little way by sharing it with others. In a letter to her sister Marie, she writes of this possibility, referring to herself in the third person:

> Dazzling works are forbidden her; she cannot preach the gospel or shed her blood.... But what does it matter? Her brothers and sisters are working in place of her, and she, the *little child*, remains very close to the *throne* of the King and the Queen, and she loves in the place of her brothers and sisters who are going into combat.... But how will she bear witness to her Love, since Love is proved in works? Well, the little child will throw out *flowers*, she will use her *perfumes* to give a lovely fragrance to the royal throne, she will sing with her silvery voice the hymn of Love. (*SS* 220)

At another time, she repeated the sentiment to one of her sisters, saying that she would "let fall a shower of roses after my death."[19] And in her last days, she told her sister Pauline, "I feel that my mission is soon to begin, my mission to make the good God loved as I love Him, to give to souls my little way. If the good God grants my desires, my heaven will be spent upon earth until the end of the world. Yes, I will spend my heaven in doing good upon earth."[20] What a simple wish, not to heal people or appear to people or to do anything with the purpose of giving herself glory but only to give out flowers as a reflection of God's love. Yet, because of these sentiments, and because of the thousands of testimonies of Thérèse visiting people in the form of flowers, as she said she would, Catholics believe that Thérèse is one of the most active saints. While this idea may sound foreign to Protestant readers, there is actually nothing in the notion of active saints that conflicts with Protestant theology or that could not be incorporated in a Protestant understanding of the saints. For it testifies, better than anything, to the reality of the resurrection and to the love the saints in the cloud of witnesses have for those of us still running the race.

St. Thérèse was the first saint who opened my eyes to this possibility and, consequently, to the importance of saints to our lives of discipleship. In 2008, I was supposed to travel to Italy with my wife, Julie, her parents, and her great-uncle. Knowing we were going to be visiting pilgrimage sites in Rome, Assisi, and other locations, I wanted to read the autobiography of a Catholic saint to accompany me on the journey. One of my Catholic friends suggested *The Story of a Soul*, I think because of the prominence that Thérèse's pilgrimage

---

19 Quoted in Joseph F. Schmidt, *Everything Is Grace: The Life and Way of Thérèse of Lisieux* (Frederick, MD: The Word Among Us Press, 2007), 317.

20 Quoted in Laveille, *Life of St. Thérèse*, 317.

had in her story. I had never heard of St. Thérèse, and to be quite honest, I was not expecting much from this young French nun. But I started reading it on the plane at La Guardia as we waited to take off for the long flight to Italy.

Minutes from departing, my father-in-law alerted us that he was having a heart attack. Thankfully, Julie was able to stop the plane from taking off, and he was rushed to a New York City hospital for emergency surgery. He made it through the surgery, and though his recovery was not certain, my in-laws insisted, against Julie's protests, that we go on to Italy the next day. So with much hesitation and sadness, we did. It was good to be there with Julie's great-uncle, but the loss of not being with my in-laws and the worry that my father-in-law's recovery was still in question were crushing, particularly to Julie. She was often near tears and walked around the ancient lands with a persistent sadness and unrest in her heart.

On the third day of the trip, we drove from Rome to Assisi, home of St. Francis. By that point, I was well into *The Story of a Soul* and already captivated by St. Thérèse, but this day I was focused on St. Francis, whom I had already read some about. While we were driving, I regaled the car with the miraculous stories of St. Francis preaching to animals, experiencing the stigmata, and the like. Julie sat quietly in the backseat, as she had been to that point on the trip. When we neared the town, we could see the beautiful Franciscan monastery in the distance, sitting on a hill at the end of a large open field of green. The field was filled with beautiful bright-red poppies. It was so full, the green of the field was nearly swallowed up in the dazzling red of the poppies. I noticed the poppies, of course, but was more focused on the monastery, my mind fixed on St. Francis. But Julie was taken with the poppies, and that day I noticed she had changed, that she no longer seemed sad or burdened. I figured it was due to walking in the very places St. Francis had walked, seeing his relics, and praying together in his church. But later that evening, she told me it was the poppies. When we drove through the field, she had felt an indescribable sense of peace wash over her, overwhelming her to the point of tears. The feeling was so overpowering, she said, that she thought she could even smell the poppies. I found the story incredible, primarily because my wife was a city girl who didn't normally have such experiences in nature.

And then I remembered St. Thérèse and how she promised she would visit people *in flowers*. To this day, we are convinced that the Little Flower had visited Julie, showering her with poppies and reflecting Christ's grace to her. Such a simple act of faithfulness, but it made all the difference. Julie's peace never left her that trip, and when we returned home, we learned that her father had made a full recovery. Since that day, St. Thérèse has remained our patron saint and her little way our model of faithfulness in the midst of a busy life of working and raising three children. Although I still struggle with road rage, and although I find it challenging to love and serve those who displease me in everything, I am encouraged by the prayers of St. Thérèse and by her simple but lovely flowers.

CHAPTER TWELVE

Desmond's Humanity

*We are different so that we can know our need
of one another, for no one is ultimately self-sufficient.
The completely self-sufficient person would be subhuman.*

—Desmond Tutu, *No Future Without Forgiveness*, 265

Our study of the saints reveals a central truth about the Church, namely, that its identity is marked not by a certain time, a certain place, or a certain ethnicity or race but by the singular confession that Christ is Lord. As such, the Church exists in all times, in all places, and among all people groups who have made this common confession. As different as Perpetua is from John, or as either is from Martin or Phoebe, or as any of these saints are from twenty-first-century Christians, we all are members of the same Church. This is the original meaning of the ancient attribute *catholic*, and it has been recognized as central to the definition of the Church since its earliest days. As Paul puts it, "There is no longer Jew or Greek, there is no longer slave or free, there is no longer male and female; for all of you are one in Christ Jesus" (Gal 3:28).

The Church's catholic nature stands against the way of the world, which, in all cultures through history, has made distinctions of ethnicity/race, sex, and socioeconomic status the basis of its hierarchically ordered societies. Thus, the world defines itself not by its common humanity or a common creed or even a common nationality (e.g., African Americans in the Jim Crow South or German Jews in 1930s Berlin) but rather by these arbitrary and ultimately irrelevant physical distinctions. Moreover, as the latter two examples demonstrate, with the distinctions always come value judgments so that it is never just "those others" are different from "us," but rather "we" are better than "those others." The Church views this manner of dividing humanity as sinful, not the product of God's good creation.[1] Thus, in its countercultural way of being, the Church witnesses to restored humanity as it was originally created to be.[2] Unfortunately, because the Church is made up of redeemed but sinful people, the sad truth is that, more often than not, the Church has itself fallen into these same wicked patterns or supported governments that so ordered their societies.

While examples from history abound, perhaps the most notorious, at least in my lifetime, was the apartheid (meaning "apartness") system that marked South Africa in the latter half of the twentieth century. Although there were always segregationist attitudes in the country, in 1948, the National Party came to power and passed government-enforced separation of the four ethnicities comprising South Africa—European, Colored (mixed heritage), Indian, and Black—with all of the political power and economic advantages going to the Europeans or whites, who comprised just 21 percent of the population.[3] Nonwhites were denied the right to vote, hold office, or receive a standard education and were often removed from their homes to make room for posh white living areas. Generations of Black South Africans, if they worked at all, were forced into servitude of the European class at significantly lower wages. South Africa under the apartheid system was, in other words, a society based purely on racial distinctions.[4]

The various Christian denominations in South Africa were critical of the system but initially had no sustained theological voice of resistance. Some scholars have suggested that practices of the Dutch Reformed Church of South Africa, with its four segregated congregations for people of different

---

1 As the creation narratives and first eleven chapters of Genesis symbolize. Women were created with men in the image of God (Gen 1:27), represented by Eve being created as a co-gardener with Adam (Gen 2:18). However, after their sin, Eve is cursed to have her husband "rule over" her (Gen 3:16), thus inaugurating unjust patriarchal systems that have marked nearly every human society. Likewise, humans were created as one community, but after the sin of Babel, they were scattered with different languages, which, very quickly, leads to violence (Gen 11:1–9).

2 This is the significance of Pentecost (Acts 2), where at the coming of the Spirit, everyone can understand the same language.

3 John Allen, *Rabble-Rouser for Peace: The Authorized Biography of Desmond Tutu* (New York: Free Press, 2006), 55.

4 See Allen, *Rabble-Rouser*, 55–60 where he recounts the initial restructuring of the society.

races, provided "a model for apartheid."[5] Because the National Party was anticommunist at a time when communism was perceived as the greatest threat to world peace, few Western countries wanted to confront a potential ally. Accordingly, the Anglican Church replaced one of its South African Bishops, who was deported in 1960 over his outspoken stance against apartheid, with a more docile one who preferred to stay out of politics.[6] As in many other similar situations through history, the Church seemed at best impotent against and at worst complicit with a human government that divided and judged people on the basis of skin tone. Our twelfth saint, Desmond Tutu, a Black South African, forged a different way in terms of both his fearless fight against apartheid and his gracious forgiveness of his oppressors in the wake of apartheid's fall. As such, his actions, informed by his deeply theological account of humanity, offer a model for twenty-first-century Christians still caught in the same racial mire.[7]

Desmond was born in 1931 in Klerksdorp to the principal of a Methodist school and a domestic servant, seventeen years before apartheid began. "We were shielded to some extent from the worst of the rigors of South Africa's racism, which predated apartheid as refined by the National Party government," he would later write.[8] His family had enough to survive, and he received

---

5 Allen, *Rabble-Rouser*, 56.

6 Allen, *Rabble-Rouser*, 75.

7 For biographical information regarding Desmond, I have consulted the Allen biography already cited. In regard to his spiritual development, I have found Michael Battle, *Desmond Tutu: A Spiritual Biography of South Africa's Confessor* (Louisville, KY: Westminster John Knox Press, 2021) very helpful. Both authors knew Desmond, the latter rather intimately, so in their accounts are included personal reflections that are helpful in gaining a picture of who the saint was. Desmond was a prolific speaker and writer, so I have consulted many of his writings, though most helpful is his account of his work of reconciliation after apartheid's fall, Desmond Tutu, *No Future Without Forgiveness* (New York: Double Day, 1999).

8 Tutu, *No Future*, 93. The refining of an already racist society under apartheid included such acts as the Western Areas Removal Scheme, which resulted in the displacement of numerous Black South Africans and the further shrinking of land allotted to the much larger Black population. Many Black neighborhoods were destroyed in the scheme, including Desmond's childhood village, the village where he was married, and the once-thriving Black town Sophiatown, to make room for more white settlements. Battle, *Desmond Tutu*, 21. There was also the pass law system, which required Black people to carry a pass restricting the freedoms of their movements and resulting in numerous arrests. Desmond describes the effect: "The system conspired to undermine your sense of worth . . . It is difficult to describe what it meant in daily and public humiliation, having to produce your pass or be part of a human crocodile file of those who had fallen foul of

a strong early education, setting the foundation for his later academic work in education and theology. Nevertheless, like all Black South Africans, he faced daily inequalities. Desmond reflects, "It was not usually the big things, the awful atrocities, that got at you. No, it was the daily pinpricks, the little discourtesies, the minute humiliations, having one's dignity trodden underfoot, not always with jackboots—though that happened too."[9] As a young boy, Desmond would see the clear difference between white areas and Black areas; he would watch young white people disrespect his father—a principal!—by calling him *boy* or making him wait to be served. The effect was a sort of malformation into a racialized world. He writes, "I even thought that the racist ordering of affairs was something divinely ordained. That is how things were and you had better accept it and not be too fussy."[10] So ordered was his world that Desmond always found it remarkable when white people would do the littlest things that indicated a recognition of his humanity. Many times through his life, he told the story of a white priest who would always take his hat off every morning in a respectful greeting to his mother. Such actions broke through the darkness, suggesting to the young South African another way of being.

Although Desmond was baptized in the Methodist Church, his family joined the Anglican Church a few years later. This change introduced Desmond to one of the most important spiritual influences in his life, namely Father Trevor Huddleston and the Anglican monastic community called the Community of the Resurrection (CR).[11] The monks of the CR were formed in the ascetic spirituality we have witnessed in previous chapters, including specified hours of daily prayer and Scripture readings; ordered, celibate life in community; and the like. Moreover, this deep spirituality manifested itself in the monks' outspoken stance and visible protests against the racial inequalities

---

the law and were now handcuffed together, a public spectacle, while the police waited to have a large enough quota to fill their troop carrier." Tutu, *No Future*, 95.

9 Tutu, *No Future*, 96.

10 Tutu, *No Future*, 93–94.

11 After King Henry VIII closed the monasteries in the sixteenth-century English Reformation, the Church of England was absent a monastic tradition. However, in the nineteenth century, an Anglican monastic community developed out of a concern that the Church of England had become disconnected from England's working-class people. Allen, *Rabble-Rouser*, 28. Thus, at the heart of this monastic community was a focus on justice for people on the margins, a characteristic that permeated the CR that came to South Africa at the beginning of the twentieth century.

of the country, a rarity among white religious communities. Father Huddleston stood in community with the oppressed Black people against unjust policies. Desmond came to see that these aspects—disciplined spirituality and active fight for justice—went hand in hand. "It was surprising at first to see a priest so heavily involved in political affairs," he later recalled, "but it became clear that he was doing this not in spite of the fact that he was a priest and a religious to boot, but precisely because he was these things . . . It was because of his encounter with God in the spiritual life that he was constrained to be a man for others."[12] Notably, Father Huddleston was the priest who greeted his mother every day, for unlike other white South Africans, his vision was not ordered by race.

Thus, the time Desmond spent with Father Huddleston as a child began a re-formation in him, grounded in monastic spirituality, which helped him to see the injustices of his society. Nevertheless, unlike many of the saints we have studied, he did not feel an early vocation to ministry or the religious life. Because of childhood illnesses—namely, polio in infancy, which left his right hand permanently weakened, and tuberculosis as a high-schooler, from which he almost died—he wanted to be a doctor. Despite acceptance into medical school, however, his family could not afford the tuition, an all too common reality indicative of the hardships facing Black South Africans in improving their stations. So in 1951, right at the beginning of apartheid, he entered a teacher's college. After graduation, he took a job teaching English and reconnected with an old friend, Leah, who was also a teacher. The two married in 1955 and would have three daughters and a son, whom they named Trevor. Desmond was a caring, effective, and much-loved teacher and could have likely been so for the remainder of his life. But, as we saw with Phoebe, his true vocation emerged from the ashes of tragedy.

In 1953, the National Party began to enforce the terrors of the apartheid system beginning with the Bantu Education Act, which essentially gutted the education of Black South Africans by reducing it to preparation for positions of service to white South Africans, "education for serfdom" as Desmond would later describe it.[13] The lack of access to liberal education, Desmond saw, would hamstring his people for generations, and he and Leah made the difficult decision that they could not be part of such an unjust system, even

---

12 Quoted in Battle, *Desmond Tutu*, 21–22.
13 Tutu, *No Future*, 102.

though this meant forfeiting living wages, not an easy thing to achieve for Black South Africans. It was this principled stand against an unjust system, more than any initial internal call, that led Desmond to ministry. "It wasn't for very highfalutin ideals that I became a priest," he would later say. "I couldn't go to medical school [so] the easiest option was to go to theological college."[14] We have seen God work his purposes in the lives of the saints through tragedy such as illness, or the loss of a child or a parent, or disillusionment with a career choice. In Desmond's life, God worked through widescale human injustice, from which, though God does not cause or intend, he providentially works good (Rom 8:28). Moreover, his story demonstrates that God's calling to ministry comes in a variety of ways; the only common factor required is our willingness to hear and respond in faithfulness. Despite the loss of a steady income and the hardship that more schooling would require of him and his family, Desmond responded in faithfulness with the full support of his wife. This turn began his dramatic rise in the Anglican Church all the way to the front lines of the fight against apartheid in ways he could never have done as a doctor or teacher.

Desmond was educated for the Anglican priesthood at St. Peter's College, a theological college run by the CR. There, he entered fully into the monastic life and its rhythms of daily prayer of the hours, its deep sense of brotherhood, and its focus on the Eucharist. The spiritual practices he learned in this community remained with him for the rest of his life and sustained him in many dark periods when, like his mentor Father Huddleston, he turned to the fight against injustice.[15] He also experienced a different kind of community there, one that saw Black and white people living and working together as equals. He recounts his amazement, for example, that Timothy Stanton, the vice president of the school "and a white man to boot, would join the black students in doing some of the menial tasks."[16] Desmond's formation at the school planted the seeds for what true Christian community could and should look like, a stark contrast to the "Christian" society of South Africa. At no time was this more evident than in 1960, his final year of college, when a group of Black South Africans protesting unjust apartheid laws was indiscriminately fired on by white police in Sharpsville, resulting in sixty-nine deaths and over

---

14 Quoted in Allen, *Rabble-Rouser*, 61.
15 As Battle has clearly shown. Battle, *Desmond Tutu*, especially chs. 6–9. This aspect of Desmond's work is often overlooked in other biographical accounts.
16 Quoted in Allen, *Rabble-Rouser*, 65.

180 injuries.[17] This atrocity, and the subsequent lack of accountability for the police, must have been a startling reminder that if he and his people were to survive, Desmond's spirituality could never be divorced from the political struggles of the real world.

Desmond excelled in his theological studies, such that he was recommended and admitted for further study at King's College in London to train as a theology professor. In this new setting, he continued to thrive, earning a bachelor of divinity in 1965 and a master of theology in 1966. Although London was not without its prejudices, it was a more equitable society, in which Desmond reveled. He writes, "It was almost intoxicating to be treated as what one knew oneself to be, a person created in the image of God, perhaps for the first time in my life when the color of my skin was really a total irrelevance making not one iota's difference in any assessment that my professors might seek to make of me."[18] He no longer had to defer to white people in lines, no longer had to enter through back doors, no longer had to show a pass everywhere he went. The most significant friendship he made was with a fellow South African student named Brian Oosthuysen, who happened to be white. If they were inside the boundaries of apartheid South Africa, they could have never enjoyed such a friendship, but outside that oppressive land, they were just two brothers, laughing together, eating together, struggling with courses together, playing practical jokes on each other. Such friendships fed Desmond's lifelong conviction that the humanity of the oppressors, no less than that of the oppressed, was damaged by the unjust apartheid system. As he would later write, "The humanity of the perpetrator of apartheid's atrocities was caught up and bound up in that of his victim whether he liked it or not. In the process of dehumanizing another, in inflicting untold harm and suffering, inexorably the perpetrator was being dehumanized as well."[19]

Following his academic success at King's College, Desmond desired and was encouraged by professors to pursue a doctorate, which likely would have landed him a relatively well-paid university post in a country where his humanity was recognized and he and his family could live unmolested by a

---

17 Allen, *Rabble-Rouser*, 70. This was only one of numerous such examples that occurred in apartheid's long reign.

18 Quoted in Battle, *Desmond Tutu*, 30.

19 Tutu, *No Future*, 103. This conviction derives from Desmond's view of humanity informed by the concept of *ubuntu*, which I will explore in greater detail later in this chapter.

hostile government. But despite his love of theological study and of London society, he chose the hard road of returning to South Africa to stand in solidarity with his people suffering in bondage. This decision, inconceivable to those who knew him in London, followed perfectly the logic of the gospel to which he had conformed himself through his habitual spiritual disciplines. For in returning to South Africa, he embodied the life of Jesus Christ, who, "though he was God, [did not] think of equality with God as something to cling to. Instead, he gave up his divine privileges; he took the humble position of a slave and was born as a human being" (Phil 2:6–7, NLT). Like Jesus, Desmond embraced the life of suffering, both physically and emotionally, in solidarity with and on behalf of others.

Over the next few decades, Desmond stood with his people in many capacities, first as a theology teacher to Black South Africans in several different universities, then as a priest, then a bishop, and finally as the archbishop of Cape Town, all before apartheid's dismantling.[20] That a Black man could experience such a rise in apartheid South Africa is a witness to Desmond's extraordinary gifts in leadership and in working with people. Of all the saints we have studied, in fact, Desmond emerges as the most dynamic. Those who knew him regularly described him as jovial, full of life and humor. "Tutu's effervescent personality," writes Allen, "became and remained one of his most striking characteristics, and his infectious laughter one of his principal gifts."[21] Pictures of the man usually catch him in a big smile or a belly laugh, while YouTube clips of his speeches and interviews convey a deep sense of humor and vitality. Knowing the circumstances under which he labored, such a disposition speaks to a deep, spiritual joy. Desmond's rise is also a testament to the countercultural witness of the Anglican Church. In the midst of a society based purely on race, the Anglican Church stayed true to

---

20 In these broad categories, Desmond performed many more specified offices. For example, in 1972, he returned to London, where he served as the associate director of the World Council of Churches' Theological Education Fund, a position that saw him advocating for the theological training of Black priests in the Anglican communion. He returned to South Africa in 1975 to serve as dean of Johannesburg, where he regularly preached sermons advancing theological arguments against apartheid. After becoming a bishop, first of the small town of Lesotho and then Johannesburg, he served for a time as the general secretary of the South African Council of Churches and president of the All Africa Conference of Churches. This summary of his positions comes from Battle, *Desmond Tutu*, 32. Allen's biography covers his activities in these various positions in exhaustive detail.

21 Allen, *Rabble-Rouser*, 95.

the Church's catholic identity described at the beginning of this chapter and already exemplified in the CR that formed Desmond's notion of what a new humanity could be.[22]

In all of these ministry and leadership positions, Desmond fought tirelessly against the injustices of apartheid. He marched with his people, was arrested with them, sat in jail with them. He organized economic boycotts against pressure from his superiors as high up as the prime minister, whom he regularly accosted with letters protesting unjust decisions and actions. He brought the injustices of apartheid to the attention of the world by meeting with leaders of other nations, even though he knew such actions would put him at odds with the National Party.[23] Such public enemies of the state were either killed or put in prison for life, as he knew well from what had happened to his friend Nelson Mandela, a Black South African who had languished in prison since 1962 for his efforts to overthrow the apartheid government.[24] Although Desmond escaped such fates, they were true realities he faced. Attempts were made on his life, and he was under constant surveillance from the South African government, had his passport revoked several times, and was the subject of vicious rumors meant to discredit his character.[25]

Desmond refused to be silenced or bow to the fear of repercussion. He was spurred on by his radical trust in the goodness and justice of God and his equally radical hope that apartheid, as a sinful governmental structure, would fall and the truth of the gospel that all humans were created in the

---

22 Even in the Anglican Church, however, things were not perfect as Black clergy received less compensation than their white counterparts in the same posts. Desmond was equally critical of such injustices in his church as he was of the South African government. Allen, *Rabble-Rouser*, 95–98. For example, he fought for the ordination of women and often gave women opportunities to serve alongside him. In later years, he became a leading advocate for LGBTQ+ persons, who had often been treated as inhuman by churches. Familiar with having his own humanity undervalued, Desmond always championed the oppressed in whatever capacity that oppression manifested.

23 For example, he met with several US Congress members and even presidents. For an example of such work, see Allen, *Rabble-Rouser*, ch. 11. These efforts helped to inspire international pressure against the apartheid regime.

24 Allen, *Rabble-Rouser*, 79. During his long stay in prison, Mandela became an icon for Black South Africans. Desmond met Mandela for the first time when he was in college. Although they did not see eye to eye on everything, they were united in their fight against apartheid and in their hopes for a reconciled South African nation after apartheid's fall. For more on this crucial relationship, particularly in the early days after apartheid's fall, see Battle, *Desmond Tutu*, 107–10.

25 For a description of an assassination attempt, see Allen, *Rabble-Rouser*, 294.

image of God and were therefore one in Christ would prevail to the glory of God. As he once responded to someone who questioned the hope he had, "The Christian faith is hopelessly optimistic because it's based on the faith of a guy who died on Friday and everybody said it was utterly and completely hopeless—ignominious defeat. And Sunday He rose."[26] This spiritual work in maintaining hope was just as important as the physical work of suffering with and advocating for his people, for he hoped for all those who had lost hope. Thus, he emerges as a type of Blandina, the martyr mentioned in the introduction. What was said of her describes Desmond's significance in these years—when his fellow Black South Africans "looked at him they saw through their brother the one who was crucified for them."[27]

Desmond's hope was finally realized in 1994.[28] Apartheid fell, and the country elected a new parliament and a new president, Nelson Mandela. Desmond's description of the moment is apocalyptic, indicating his belief that the new day had come, that his vision of a new humanity in South Africa could be realized: "The sky looked blue and more beautiful. I saw the people in a new light. They were beautiful, they were transfigured. I too was transfigured."[29] Nevertheless, the crucial question remained of what to do with the perpetrators of the injustices as well as all those who stood by and did nothing. In his classic book on his reconciling work after apartheid's fall, *No Future Without Forgiveness*, Desmond notes that historically, widescale injustices had been dealt with in two ways. The first was simply forgetting and moving on, while the second, typified by the Nuremberg trials that convicted members of the Nazi Party following Germany's defeat in the Second World War, was harsh judgment, imprisonment, and even executions of the oppressors. Desmond observed that neither approach would work in South Africa. Pretending something didn't happen would lead to festering resentment on the part of the oppressed and perhaps future outbreaks of violence, or it would lead to forgetting and, thus, the forfeiture of justice. However, mass punishments would not create reconciliation of the two races and the new humanity he

---

26 Quoted in Allen, *Rabble-Rouser*, 183.

27 Desmond was awarded the Nobel Peace prize for his efforts in 1984. His acceptance speech, which conveys his protest against apartheid, his theological vision of new humanity, and his humor and life, can be viewed here: https://www.nobelprize.org/prizes/peace/1984/tutu/acceptance-speech/.

28 The full story of apartheid's collapse goes beyond the scope of this chapter. For those interested, see Allen, *Rabble-Rouser*, chs. 13–14.

29 Tutu, *No Future*, 5.

envisioned. "While the Allies could pack up and go home after Nuremberg," he writes, "we in South Africa had to live with one another."[30]

Even while he was experiencing the teeth of injustice at the height of apartheid's reign, Desmond advocated for a different way, one of forgiveness and reconciliation. For example, in a 1989 speech to Jews at Yad Vashem, Jerusalem's Holocaust museum, he said,

> I think it's important to be made to remember that we can sink to these levels. It is important also to be reminded that we all stand in need of forgiveness. My feeling would be to say, as our Lord would say, that in the end the positive thing that could come out of the horrors of the Holocaust—and also what comes from the prophets, your prophets—is the spirit of forgiving, not forgetting, the spirit of saying (and your martyrs used to say this too), "God, this has happened to us; we pray for those who made it happen. *Forgive them*. Help us to forgive and help us so that we in our turn will not make others suffer."[31]

This merciful offer of forgiveness to one's oppressors again embodies the hard way of Jesus. As Desmond said in another setting, "From the paradigm that Jesus provided, as he was being crucified, he said 'Father, forgive them.' It wasn't as if he was talking about something that *might* happen. He was actually experiencing one of the most excruciating ways of being killed, and yet he had the capacity to live out a prayer that he taught Christians, that we can expect to be forgiven only insofar as we are ready to forgive."[32]

Although it was unpopular among many South African Black citizens who understandably would have preferred the Nuremburg way, the new parliament followed Desmond's way of forgiveness and reconciliation.[33] To that end, it established the Truth and Reconciliation Commission (TRC) and appointed Desmond as its chair. The work of the TRC was to hear a public accounting of the injustices perpetrated by the white race in return

---

30 Tutu, *No Future*, 21.

31 In Desmond Tutu, *God Is Not a Christian and Other Provocations* (San Francisco: HarperOne, 2011), 26, italics added.

32 In Tutu, *God Is Not a Christian*, 27.

33 Allen notes that the establishment of the Truth and Reconciliation Commission had little to do with Tutu or "with noble Christian ideals" but was the outcome of political movements designed to meet with the pressures of different groups. Allen, *Rabble-Rouser*, 344. Nevertheless, there can be no doubt that the form of post-apartheid work was exactly what Desmond had advocated for years and, more significantly, that without Desmond's prestige as its chair, it would have lacked the significant buy-in, particularly on the part of the oppressed.

for which the commission would offer pardon on behalf of the oppressed.[34] The theological term for this sentiment is *confession*. The act of confession is necessary for pardon because it recognizes the wrongness of the act or injustice committed and so refuses simply to forget it. It brings the sin to light instead of simply moving on. For Scripture tells us that if sin is not brought to light, it cannot be healed (1 John 1:9). In Desmond's words, "Unless we look the beast in the eye we find it has an uncanny habit of returning to hold us hostage."[35] Yet, if it is brought to light, then pardon comes, which allows for healing and, in a way that forgetting or punishment alone can never do, brings true reconciliation.

As chair of the commission, Desmond graciously and expertly guided the country through this difficult and unprecedented process. The commission regularly heard confessions for crimes and injustices ranging from the daily inconveniences created by the pass laws to massacres that killed dozens. It heard confessions ranging from average people to soldiers to leaders in the Dutch Reformed Church and the apartheid government. It allowed a space for Black South Africans to be heard, to share their stories so long pushed under the rug or assumed not to have happened. It told them their stories mattered. It even heard confessions from members of the Black community who had engaged in the same gross violations of human rights against whites in their struggle for liberation, for, as Tutu wrote, "a gross violation is a gross violation whoever commits it and for whatever motive."[36] It was difficult work, sustained only by their chair's unflagging commitment to Jesus Christ. Desmond insisted that meetings be opened and closed in prayer because he understood that the commission's work was theological:

> Theology helped us in the TRC to recognize that we inhabit a moral universe, that good and evil are real and that they matter. They are not just things of indifference. This is a moral universe, which means that, despite all the evidence that seems to be to the contrary, there is no way that evil and oppression and lies have the last word. For us who are Christians, the death and resurrection of Jesus Christ is proof positive that love is stronger than hate, that life is stronger

---

34 The commission restricted itself to a period of two, later expanded to three, years so that its work could be completed and the country could heal. It also restricted confessions to the time since 1960, even though, Desmond noted, they could have gone back to the year the Dutch arrived on African soil. These parameters demonstrate that the work of the TRC was not simply idealistic or theoretical but a practical means of achieving a true reconciliation. Tutu, *No Future*, 104–6.

35 Tutu, *No Future*, 28.

36 Tutu, *No Future*, 107.

than darkness, that laughter and joy, and compassion and gentleness and truth, all these are so much stronger than their ghastly counterparts.[37]

Desmond, thus, was not simply the chair of the TRC or some political figurehead; he was, in Michael Battle's description, "South Africa's confessor," and this work gave the people of South Africa a chance to heal and, as always happens following confession, a chance for a new beginning.[38]

Desmond's vision of the new humanity that could exist following confession guided his work both in protesting apartheid and in the TRC. It is rooted in the gospel vision and summarized in the African word *ubuntu*, which names the essence of what it means to be human. But for the African, unlike the westerner, this essence is not defined by a soul or by reason or by personal rights. Rather, what *ubuntu* names as the essence of being human is its relationship to others. He writes that *ubuntu* "is to say, 'My humanity is caught up, is inextricably bound up in yours.' We belong in a bundle of life. We say, 'A person is a person through other persons.' It is not, 'I think therefore I am.' It says rather: 'I am human because I belong, I participate, I share.'"[39] *Ubuntu* captures the vision of humanity in Scripture better than any Western individual notions. The description of humanity's creation, in Desmond's most often quoted Scripture verse, is specifically communal: "So God created humankind in his image, in the image of God he created them; *male and female* he created them" (Gen 1:27, italics added). And the God in whose image these humans are created is also communal. Nevertheless, the oneness of God, and thus the oneness of humanity created in God's image, is forged not from sameness but from *difference*. As Irenaeus showed us long ago, the Father is not the Son or the Spirit, the Son is not the Father or the Spirit, and the Spirit is not the Father or the Son, and yet all three divine persons are one God. So, too, humanity's oneness is not found in having the same race or sex or socioeconomic status; it is found only in Christ Jesus.

---

37 Tutu, *No Future*, 86.

38 Battle writes, "It is my contention that [Desmond], as South African confessor, played a vital role in shaping the social conscience of South Africa and its response to apartheid. This role was especially important in creating access for both black and white people to reinstate a country that represented everyone, not just white people." Battle, *Desmond Tutu*, 111. The commission held over twenty-five hundred amnesty hearings over its three-year life and granted over fifteen hundred amnesties. https://www.britannica.com/topic/Truth-and-Reconciliation-Commission-South-Africa. Though the work was not without its problems and has received its fair share of criticism, it is generally considered a success. See Allen's nuanced assessment in *Rabble-Rouser*, ch. 15.

39 Tutu, *No Future*, 31.

This is the theological reason Desmond believed post-apartheid South Africa could not simply reverse apartheid with Black people now receiving the upper hand, the ultimate result of a Nuremberg-type reckoning. Instead, he believed that humanity must become one in all its beautiful, God-created difference. The model for this is the restored community of the baptized centered on their crucified and risen Savior, a community whose scope and mission are nothing short of the inclusion of all humanity:

> There is a movement, not easily discernable, at the heart of things to reverse the awful centrifugal force of alienation, brokenness, division, hostility, and disharmony. God has set in motion a centripetal process, a movement toward the center, toward unity, harmony, goodness, peace, and justice, a process that removes barriers. Jesus says, "And when I am lifted up from the earth I shall draw everyone to myself" as he hangs from His cross with outflung arms, thrown out to clasp all, everyone and everything, in a cosmic embrace so that all, everyone, everything, belongs. None is an outsider, all are insiders, all belong. There are no aliens, all belong in the one family, God's family, the human family. There is no longer Jew nor Greek, male nor female, slave nor free—instead of separation and division, all distinctions make for a rich diversity to be celebrated for the sake of the unity that underlies them.[40]

Desmond's vision speaks right to the challenges facing the Church in many areas of the world, not least of which is the United States. The slavery that existed at America's roots and the Jim Crow South, only officially ended in the 1960s, were their own apartheid, and twenty-first-century US Christians live in the aftermath, absent of a public confession as offered by the TRC in South Africa. As a result, the consequences of those sins remain, the hurts still hurt, and the divisions are still present. Martin Luther King Jr. famously observed in the 1960s that eleven o'clock Sunday morning is the most segregated hour in America, and the same can be said today.[41] As a result, we are unwittingly formed into this impoverished vision of the kingdom. As I noted in the introduction, the diversity of the saints in the cloud of witnesses can help us change this vision both in terms of their prayers for us and in our recognition of their existence—in their beautiful differences, the saints are the human community as it was originally intended.

Desmond's vision can help us as well. Sometimes race issues seem so big that we are paralyzed into doing nothing. Let us remember, however,

---

40 Tutu, *No Future*, 265.

41 http://www.louisianaweekly.com/eleven-oclock-on-sundays-is-still-the-most-segregated-hour-in-america/.

Desmond's story, how in the face of a wickedly racist society, the simplest acts of kindness, the smallest recognition of his humanity, nurtured his hope that things could be different. We may not all be able to fix the structural problems that keep us segregated, but each of us can make change in our own communities. We can recognize the humanity in others who are different from us and in others with whom we disagree. We can invite our "enemies" to church, or we can make partnerships with churches of different races and nationalities. We can, to recall another saint we have studied, be faithful in the little things. For if every Christian would seek to be so faithful, the Church as a whole might better approach Desmond's beautiful vision for humanity.

Desmond died of cancer in 2021 at age ninety. He departed the world, his vision never fully realized.[42] But he never ceased working for its reality, holding out hope that, as he said, "it could be so different."[43] As many have commented in the days since his death, the world misses his voice. But in truth, the world still has his voice, if we would only be open to listen. For from his place in the cloud of witnesses, where he sits around the thrown in full unity with his God and with his brothers and sisters in all their glorious differences, he still works for our reconciliation through his prayers. And he still holds out hope for all those who feel they can hope no longer.

---

42 https://www.newyorker.com/news/daily-comment/mandelas-dream-for-south-africa-is-in-ruins/.

43 Tutu, Nobel Lecture, December 11, 1984. https://www.nobelprize.org/prizes/peace/1984/tutu/lecture/.

Conclusion

*Therefore, since we are surrounded by such a
great cloud of witnesses,
let us throw off everything that hinders and the sin that so
easily entangles.And let us run with perseverance the race
marked out for us, fixing our eyes on Jesus,
the pioneer and perfecter of faith. (Heb 12:1–2, NIV)*

Following the remarkable litany of holy people mentioned in chapter 11, the writer of Hebrews issues a charge to his readers, a charge to "run with perseverance the race marked out for us." Coming so soon after the list of saints, the implication is clear: we are to run the race in the manner they had, living our lives in the same holy manner on display in those lives, all of us with the same goal in mind: to reach "Jesus, the pioneer and perfecter of faith." As the scriptural reference to the saints *par excellence*, Hebrews 11–12 reveals, then, both the ultimate concern of the saints as a feature of theological study and the motivation for engaging the saints as a spiritual practice, namely, the pursuit of holiness.

The purpose of this book has been to give the same charge. In writing to Protestants, I have addressed a particular group of Christians who are well trained in the practice of "fixing our eyes on Jesus" in the pursuit of holiness but who historically have neither noticed those who surround us and cheer us on nor considered the ways in which this audience can aid us in our pursuit. In narrating the stories of twelve particular saints, I have argued that they do this in a myriad of ways. Most clearly, they help us to read Scripture better, they bridge the gap between our doctrinal convictions and the content of Scripture, and they model for us Christlike lives in different times, in different places, and in the midst of different challenges. The saints, to follow the metaphor, give us hope that the race can be finished well, and that hope helps us to keep running.

My guess is that readers who have made it to this conclusion are either in agreement with the argument or, perhaps with a healthy dose of skepticism, are intrigued enough by these stories to be open to learning more about the spiritual practice of engaging the saints. Either way, the question left to address is "What now?" Throughout this book, I have offered, under the three broad categories mentioned above, many examples of the ways the saints can teach us to live faithful and holy lives. Perpetua's efforts to make *Christian* her primary identity or Origen's allegorical reading or Macrina's ascetic practices, to name just a few. However, with the exception of some comments on praying to saints, I have not yet offered practical suggestions of implementing the practice of engaging the saints as a spiritual discipline. By way of conclusion, then, I offer three ways Protestants might begin this practice, that we might, to again follow the analogy, begin to take notice of those dead folks who surround us and cheer us on as we run.

READ MORE LIVES OF THE SAINTS

Because of the trajectory of development of Protestantism following the sixteenth-century Reformation, most Protestants simply have little to no knowledge about the lives of the saints who literally pervade Christian history from its first century to its twenty-first. What is worse, many Protestants have been formed in an understanding of Christian history that sees the years between the book of Acts (or, in some denominations, Constantine's embrace of Christianity) and Martin Luther (or, in some denominations, even later figures) as thoroughly corrupt and devoid of faithful Christians. This lack of knowledge presents a significant barrier to this practice; therefore, the first practical way of engaging the saints as a spiritual discipline is to read about the lives of the saints. This book has been a first step in that direction, but it is merely a primer. There are lovely books on offer to be read on each of the saints in this text, most of which go into much greater detail about their lives. For those interested, the bibliography offers suggestions. Moreover, as eclectic as the group of twelve saints in this book is, it is a mere snapshot of the numerous saints who populate the cloud of witnesses. Folks like Athanasius, Augustine, Marjery Kemp, Teresa of Ávila, John Wesley, and Thérèse's parents, all of whom I have mentioned in passing, are saints in their own right, and their stories also need to be known.

This way is a good place for Protestants to start the spiritual practice of engaging the saints because it requires no challenge to the ways we have practiced our faith in the past. It need not involve prayer or adulation or thinking of these people as anything other than faithful Christians of the past. Moreover, the goal of such reading is not education, which can be intimidating. The goal of such reading is, rather, enjoyment. This is the kind of reading that Alan Jacobs has called "reading at whim," that is, reading for the sheer pleasure of it, reading what you want to read.[1] Thus, the bar for this way is quite low. Read what interests you. Read widely. Read from all different geographical areas and traditions. Read from different eras. Read the lives of both male and female saints. And don't simply read books *about* the saints, but read their own autobiographies, books like Augustine's *Confessions* or Teresa of Ávila's *Life*, to mention only two classics.

Because the saints are living, they have the peculiar ability to be present to us in their stories, to come alive through their past words and actions. To put it another way, this kind of reading allows us to fall in love with the saints, to begin to see them as dear friends. I remember having this experience with St. Thérèse, a figure I knew nothing about when I first picked up her autobiography. However, the setting of my pilgrimage to Italy made me a particularly open reader. So the stories of her childhood were enjoyable to me and immediately drew me in. The stories of her coping with the death of her mother and her illness made me recall times of struggle in my own life, particularly those times when I have also felt a dryness in prayer. I resonated with her cries for answers. I rejoiced with her when she felt resolution and got her wish to enter the monastery. By the last chapters of her book, I felt like I knew her. I laughed with her when she described the sister who displeased her in every way. I was indignant for her when the older nun was difficult. I mourned for her when she spoke of her pain. I did not know it then, but I know it now—through reading her story, I had come to love her. And as I have argued in this book, that love for her strengthened my love for Jesus, the one whom she loved so well.

If you take this first way and read widely in the lives of the saints, you may begin, as I was, to be drawn to a particular saint through identifying with their background or struggles. Be open to this discovery, and this identification, for the saint might be speaking to you through their story.

---

1 Alan Jacobs, *The Pleasures of Reading in an Age of Distraction* (Oxford: Oxford University Press, 2011), 13ff.

You may even be developing what Catholics call a *patron saint,* that is, a saint to whom a person feels particularly close and who is praying specifically for that person. St. Thérèse is my patron saint because of the way she visited my wife so clearly and so graciously in her time of need. But I never would have seen her visitation if I had not already read her story and come to see her as a beloved friend.

CELEBRATE THE FEASTS OF SAINTS

The second practical way of engaging the saints as a spiritual discipline is to celebrate the feast days of certain saints. As I mentioned in a previous chapter, feast days of the saints fill out the Christian liturgical calendar marked by the more familiar holy days of Christmas and Easter, which most Protestants celebrate. (Certain Protestant denominations celebrate even more of these traditional feasts, including All Saints Day, Ash Wednesday, and the days of the Triduum.) Because Protestants already celebrate such feasts, this way represents another easy way for us to engage the saints. We are already used to investing the time of our year with theological meaning and using those days to celebrate the salvific acts of God in history. The saints' feast days simply give us more to celebrate!

This second way might give Protestants more pause than simply reading the lives of the saints because celebrating a saint's feast day seems at first to elevate the saint to a place of worship. But this is a misunderstanding of the purpose of the feast days. Indeed, celebrating the feast days of saints in no way entails worship of them or, again, anything that would challenge a Protestant's faith. Rather, these celebrations confirm to us that the God who worked mightily in the life of Christ, as celebrated at Christmas and Easter, continues to work mightily in the lives of Christians throughout history and is thus able to work in us.

Going back to the origins of the saints' feast days as the remembrance of the martyrs on the anniversaries of their death, the feast days of saints are typically the days they died, the days on which they passed into the cloud of witnesses. This gives us a good analogy to another practice common among Protestants, namely, the celebration of family members who have died. I have known many families who gather on the anniversary of a departed grandfather or grandmother, for example, to tell stories about them to children who might not have clear memories or might have never known them. These gatherings help us keep the memory of these beloved family members alive. The same is true of a saint's feast day. We eat and drink and tell the stories of the saint. We may decorate a room with things indicative of the saint's story, such as flowers for the feast of St. Thérèse or icons for the feast of St. John or crucifixes for the feast of St. Julian. (St. Martin does not have a feast day as such, but I can imagine some clever Protestants hanging up the 95 Theses in honor of his bold act.) We may do things on the feast day that the saint was known for, such as cleaning up trash or litter to honor St. Francis on his feast day or the practice of giving gifts on the feast of St. Nicholas. (St. Phoebe does not have a feast day as such, but I can imagine people honoring her by witnessing to their own experiences of sanctification on her celebration.) And if we use the celebrations of Christmas and Easter as models for these feast days, we'll remember that we are ultimately celebrating the work of God in the life of the saint.

Numerous websites exist that give the saint of the day (most days, in fact, celebrate numerous saints) as well as a bit of the saint's story.[2] Planning a party for friends on a day of a popular saint, such as St. Francis or St. Nicholas, might be a good place to start. Because everyone likes another reason to have a party. Or if you have already tried the first way and begun to develop a patron saint, you might look up their feast day and mark it on your calendar. On that day, you might plan to read particularly meaningful passages in their writings. If you are already practiced in daily Bible-reading, this reading should not replace that practice but supplement it. If you are not quite ready to pray to your patron saint, perhaps you can offer up prayers to God for the faithful life of the saint who has come to mean so much to you. However you choose to celebrate, you are engaging the saints and beginning to take notice of those who surround us.

PRAY WITH THE SAINTS

The final way I might suggest of engaging the saints is, admittedly, the most difficult for Protestants and, when approached in the wrong way, can challenge a Protestant's faith. I speak, of course, of praying with the saints. This practice is challenging to Protestants because we have been formed to believe we need no intermediaries to God. Indeed, this is one of the primary convictions that,

---

2 As an example, see https://www.catholic.org/saints/sofd.php.

historically, led to the Protestant Reformation.[3] Praying to a saint seems to be asking a fellow human for blessings instead of the Triune God. I have addressed these concerns in the chapter on Mary, but in the context of next steps, some points bear repeating.

Recall that when we pray to the saints, we are not asking for blessings from them, nor are we worshipping them as gods. We are speaking to fellow Christians, asking for their prayers to God on our behalf, much like we speak to those fellow Christians living on earth of whom we regularly ask for prayers. In the words of the best-known prayer to a saint, "Holy Mary, Mother of God, *pray for us sinners* now and in the hour of our death." While we can certainly pray directly to God at any point, we can also ask others— both the living and the dead—to pray with us and to pray for us. As with the suggestion of reading passages from a saint to supplement our reading of Scripture, our prayers to saints can supplement our prayers to God. And if we are honest, there are some times in our lives when we cannot pray to God for ourselves, times of extreme grief in loss or extreme shame in sin, for example. In these moments, as St. Desmond hoped for those Black South Africans who could not hope, the saints can pray for us when we cannot pray for ourselves.

This practice is new and will likely feel uncomfortable at first. It did for me. In fact, I had long been convinced in the reality of the saints and the benefits for my sanctification that come from engaging them as a spiritual practice through the first two ways before I actually began praying to the saints. When I finally decided to try it, I started in small ways; I tried by simply adding a sentence or two addressed to a saint in my normal prayer time. Though cognitively, that practice had seemed wrong to me, it did not feel wrong as I began to do it. So when I felt a little more comfortable with the practice, I tried what is a more traditional prayer practice for Catholics, namely, novenas.

A novena (from the Latin *novem*, meaning "nine") consists of nine days of prayers to saints preceding their feast days, asking for their intercession. Like the seasons of Advent and Lent, which precede Christmas and Easter,

---

3 Although, as we have seen by now, the belief that the Catholic Church required intermediaries is a misperception aided by corrupt practices of some Catholic leaders in the Middle Ages and continued today by Protestants who do not bother to learn about actual Catholic beliefs and practices. Saints from Julian of Norwich to Thérèse of Lisieux believed they needed no intermediaries.

respectively, novenas are a means of preparation for a feast through which our friendship with the saint deepens. They can be prayed in public settings with other Christians or in private. They can be spontaneous prayers that come from our hearts or traditional prayers written by others, which we read. Like all prayers, they are formative. Because they are addressed to a particular saint, the novena prayers can be formative in the manner of Christlike holiness embodied by that saint. A novena to St. Mary, for example, might form us to have greater obedience to the seemingly impossible calls of God, while a novena to St. Irenaeus might form our minds to be better thinkers against errant beliefs.

At the time of this writing, I have just completed the novena to St. Thérèse. I prayed it along with several other Christians, a few of whom are Protestants (!), though each in our own space. We decided to use the prayers provided by a website called praymorenovenas.com so that we would all be using the same words. The prayer from the first day of the novena is as follows:

In the name of the Father, and of the Son, and of the Holy Spirit. Amen.

Dearest Saint Thérèse of Lisieux, you said that you would spend your time in heaven doing good on earth.

Your trust in God was complete. Pray that He may increase my trust in His goodness and mercy as I ask for the following petitions:

(State your intentions.)

Pray for me that I, like you, may have great and innocent confidence in the loving promises of our God. Pray that I may live my life in union with God's plan for me and one day see the face of God, whom you loved so deeply.

Saint Thérèse, you were faithful to God even unto the moment of your death. Pray for me that I may be faithful to our loving God. May my life bring peace and love to the world through faithful endurance in love for God, our Savior.

Loving God, you blessed St. Thérèse with a capacity for a great love. Help me to believe in your unconditional love for each of your children, especially for me.

I love you, Lord. Help me to love you more!

Glory be to the Father, to the Son, and to the Holy Spirit. As it was in the beginning, is now, and ever shall be, world without end.

Amen.

In the name of the Father, and of the Son, and of the Holy Spirit. Amen.[4]

A few observations of this prayer are worth mentioning. First, while the prayer is addressed to St. Thérèse, notice that we are asking for her prayers to God on our behalf. As with the "Hail Mary," in this prayer, God remains the only one worthy of worship and the ultimate granter of our petitions. As she herself noted, St. Thérèse merely reflects God's grace to us. Second, the prayer to St. Thérèse does not replace any prayers directed at God, as if the mere act of asking for intercession from an intermediary would challenge the direct access we have to God through Christ. Indeed, within the novena itself are sentences directed toward God. This demonstrates that praying to God and asking for intercession from friends are complementary.

Third, the novena is specific to St. Thérèse's story. We are asking for her intercession that we might be gifted the kind of faith that she had, her "great and innocent confidence in the loving promises of our God" and her "capacity for a great love." As I prayed the novena, I thought often of St. Thérèse's little way of faithfulness. During the nine days, I found my eyes more open to the little things and the ways I could be faithful in them. A few times early in the novena, I shrugged the feeling off. But after about the third day, I realized what was happening, and I found myself responding and being more faithful in these little things. Once while entering a restaurant, I helped an elderly man with a cane get through the door, even though he had initially shrugged me off, a move that I most certainly would have heeded at other times. Another time, I stopped on my way to a meeting to talk with and encourage a custodian at my place of work because she was fearful of losing her job, even though this made me late for a meeting, an act of kindness I would not normally have done for fear of being late. Most out of character was the day I saw a turtle in the middle of a busy road and pulled my car over, got out, and helped it get to the other side safely. As I got back into my car, I chuckled as I gave a prayer of thanks to the Little Flower, who felt very close in that strange act.

I do not say these things to brag about myself. As I have noted, I don't think I would have done any of these things otherwise due to the inconvenience each of them caused me—and for the record, I have never once before helped

---

4 https://www.praymorenovenas.com/st-therese-novena. For those who prefer, this site also has an Instagram account that will send daily reminders.

a turtle get to safety. But praying the novena to St. Thérèse opened my eyes to all the possibilities of such faithfulness in a day, the vast majority of which I normally miss. I believe I was faithful in more of these little things because my prayers to St. Thérèse were making me more attentive to her manner of living, and in turn, her prayers to God for me were giving me the strength to pursue her little way. Put differently, the spiritual discipline of praying St. Thérèse's novena was helping me to become more like her. And in becoming more like St. Thérèse, I am ultimately becoming more like Christ.

Hopefully, for those readers who are interested, something in these practical suggestions provides a good place to start. In reality, because you have read this book, you have already started, for you have begun to see the dead who are still living among us. The truth is that the saints in the cloud of witnesses have always been active. To return to the great metaphor of Hebrews, they are always surrounding us, cheering us on, and encouraging us to finish the race as they did. We, as Protestants, have just too long been ignorant of them. In engaging them as a spiritual discipline, we simply become aware of them. In that awareness, their cheers become real to us, their faith "the assurance of things hoped for, the conviction of things not seen" (Heb 11:1). While much in our faith is invisible, the saints can be seen. They can be seen in their writings. They can be seen in their prayers, both the ones they wrote while on earth and the ones they pray on our behalf from the cloud of witnesses. They can even be seen in their visitation of us, if we would only open our eyes to them. Paradoxically, once our eyes are opened to the saints, they help us to fix our eyes on Jesus, the one to whom we are running.

So it is that the dead help us to live.

Bibliography

PRIMARY

Eusebius. *Church History*. Translated by Paul L. Maier. *Eusebius: The Church History*. Grand Rapids, MI: Kregel Publications, 1999.

Gregory of Nyssa. *Letters*. Translated by Anna Silvas. *Macrina the Younger, Philosopher of God*. Turnhout: Brepols, 2008.

———. *Life of Macrina*. Translated by Kevin Corrigan. *The Life of Saint Macrina*. Eugene, OR: Wipf and Stock Publishers, 2001.

Francis of Assisi. *The Admonitions*. Translated by Regis J. Armstrong and Ignatius C. Brady. *Francis and Clare: The Complete Works*. The Classics of Western Spirituality, edited by Richard J. Payne and John Farina, 25–36. Mahwah, NJ: Paulist Press, 1982.

———. *The Canticle to Brother Sun*. Translated by Regis J. Armstrong and Ignatius C. Brady. *Francis and Clare: The Complete Works*. The Classics of Western Spirituality, edited by Richard J. Payne and John Farina, 37–39. Mahwah, NJ: Paulist Press, 1982.

———. *The Earlier Rule*. Translated by Regis J. Armstrong and Ignatius C. Brady. *Francis and Clare: The Complete Works*. The Classics of Western Spirituality, edited by Richard J. Payne and John Farina, 107–36. Mahwah, NJ: Paulist Press, 1982.

———. *The Later Rule*. Translated by Regis J. Armstrong and Ignatius C. Brady. *Francis and Clare: The Complete Works*. The Classics of Western Spirituality, edited by Richard J. Payne and John Farina, 136–45. Mahwah, NJ: Paulist Press, 1982.

Ignatius of Antioch. *Epistle to the Romans*. Translated by Michael W. Holmes. *The Apostolic Fathers*, 166–76. Grand Rapids, MI: Baker Books, 1999.

Irenaeus. *Against Heresies*. Translated by Robert M. Grant. *Irenaeus of Lyons*. The Early Church Fathers. London: Routledge, 1997.

———. *Demonstration of the Apostolic Preaching*. Translated by John Behr. *St. Irenaeus of Lyons, On the Apostolic Preaching*. Crestwood, NY: St. Vladimir's Seminary Press, 1997.

John of Damascus. *On the Divine Images*. Translated by Andrew Louth. *St. John of Damascus, Three Treatises on the Divine Images*. Crestwood, NY: St. Vladimir's Seminary Press, 2003.

Julian of Norwich. *The Showings, Long Text*. Translated by Mirabai Starr. *The Showings of Julian of Norwich: A New Translation*. Charlottesville, VA: Hampton Roads Publishing Company, 2013.

Luther, Martin. "95 Theses." In *The Reforming Treatises of Martin Luther*, translated by C. A. Buchheim, A. T. W. Steinhauser, and R. S. Grignon, 21–28. Prague: e-artnow, 2019.

———. "To the Christian Nobility of the German Nation." In *The Reforming Treatises of Martin Luther*, translated by C. A. Buchheim, A. T. W. Steinhauser, and R. S. Grignon, 35–76. Prague: e-artnow, 2019.

Martyrdom of Polycarp. Translated by Michael W. Holmes. *The Apostolic Fathers*, 227–45. Grand Rapids, MI: Baker Books, 1999.

Origen. *Commentary on John*. Translated by Joseph W. Trigg. *Origen. The Early Church Fathers*, 103–78. London: Routledge, 1998.

———. *Commentary on Lamentations, Selected Fragments*. Translated by Joseph W. Trigg. *Origen. The Early Church Fathers*, 73–85. London: Routledge, 1998.

———. *Commentary on Psalms 1–25*. Translated by Joseph W. Trigg. *Origen. The Early Church Fathers*, 69–72. London: Routledge, 1998.

———. *On First Principles*. Translated by G. W. Butterworth. Repr. *Christian Classics*. Notre Dame, IN: Ave Maria Press, 2013.

Palmer, Phoebe. *The Way of Holiness: With Notes By the Way; Being a Narrative of Experience Resulting from a Determination to Be a Bible Christian*. Repr. London: Forgotten Books, 2012. First published 1843 by Piercy and Reed (New York).

The Passion of Perpetua and Felicity. Translated by Bryan M. Liftin. *Early Christian Martyr Stories: An Evangelical Introduction with New Translations*, 93–109. Grand Rapids, MI: Baker Academic, 2014.

Thérèse of Lisieux. *The Story of a Soul*. Translated and edited by Robert J. Edmonson, CJ. *St. Thérèse of Lisieux: The Story of a Soul, A New Translation*. Christian Classics. Brewster, MA: Paraclete Press, 2006.

Tutu, Desmond. *God Is Not a Christian and Other Provocations*. San Francisco: HarperOne, 2011.

———. *No Future Without Forgiveness*. New York: Double Day, 1999.

Wesley, John. "Journals." Vol. 1 of *The Works of John Wesley*. 3rd ed. Grand Rapids, MI: Baker Books, 2002.

———. "The Scripture Way of Salvation." Vol. 6 of *The Works of John Wesley*, 43–54. Grand Rapids, MI: Baker Books, 2002.

SECONDARY

Abraham, William J. *Canon and Criterion in Christian Theology: From the Fathers to Feminism*. Oxford: Oxford University Press, 1998.

Allen, John. *Rabble-Rouser for Peace: The Authorized Biography of Desmond Tutu*. New York: Free Press, 2006.

Ayres, Lewis. *Nicaea and Its Legacy: An Approach to Fourth-Century Trinitarian Theology*. Oxford: Oxford University Press, 2006.

Baker, Mark D., and Joel B. Green. *Recovering the Scandal of the Cross: Atonement in New Testament and Contemporary Contexts*. 2nd ed. Downers Grove, IL: IVP Academic, 2011.

Battle, Michael. *Desmond Tutu: A Spiritual Biography of South Africa's Confessor*. Louisville, KY: Westminster John Knox Press, 2021.

Barth, Markus. *Ephesians 4–6*. Anchor Bible Commentary, vol. 34A. Garden City, NY: Doubleday and Company, 1960.

Benedict XVI. *Jesus of Nazareth. The Infancy Narratives*. Translated by Philip J. Whitmore. New York, NY: Image, 2012.

Bonaventure. *The Life of Saint Francis*. Translated by Evert Cousins. *Bonaventure*. The Classics of Western Spirituality, edited by Richard J. Payne, 177–327. Mahwah, NJ: Paulist Press, 1978.

Bonhoeffer, Dietrich. *The Cost of Discipleship*. Translated by R. H. Fuller. New York: Touchstone, 1995. First published 1937 by Chr. Kaiser Verlag München.

Bronner, Leila Leah. *From Eve to Esther: Rabbinic Reconstructions of Biblical Women*. Louisville, KY: Westminster John Knox Press, 1994.

Brown, Peter. *The Body and Society: Men, Women, and Sexual Renunciation in Earliest Christianity*. 2nd ed. New York: Columbia University Press, 2008.

Brown, Raymond E. *The Birth of the Messiah: A Commentary on the Infancy Narratives in the Gospels of Matthew and Luke*. 2nd ed. New York: Doubleday, 1993.

Butterworth, G. W. "Translator's Introduction." In *On First Principles*, xxxiii–lxxvi. Translated by G. W. Butterworth. Repr. *Christian Classics*. Notre Dame, IN: Ave Maria Press, 2013.

Chase, Frederick H., Jr. "Introduction." In *Saint John of Damascus, Writings*. Fathers of the Church 37, edited by Hermigild Dressler et al., v–xxxviii. Repr. Washington, DC: The Catholic University of America Press, 1999.

Chesterton, G. K. *Saint Francis of Assisi*. New York: Image Books, 2001. First published 1924 by George H. Doran Company (New York).

Coakley, John W., and Andrea Sterk, eds. *Readings in World Christian History, Volume 1: Earliest Christianity to 1453*. Maryknoll, NY: Orbis Books, 2004.

Cohick, Lynn, and Amy Brown Hughes. *Christian Women in the Patristic World: Their Influence, Authority, and Legacy in the Second through Fifth Centuries*. Grand Rapids, MI: Baker Academic, 2017.

Colledge, Edmund, and James Walsh. "Introduction." In *Julian of Norwich: Showings*. The Classics of Western Spirituality, edited by Richard J. Payne, 17–119. New York: Paulist Press, 1978.

Chadwick, Owen. *The Reformation*. 4th ed. London: Penguin Books, 1990.

Davies, Norman. *Europe: A History*. Oxford: Oxford University Press, 1996.

De Lubac, Henri. "Introduction." In *On First Principles, xi–xxxii*. Translated by G. W. Butterworth. Repr. *Christian Classics*. Notre Dame, IN: Ave Maria Press, 2013.

Dove, Mary. *The First English Bible: The Text and Context of the Wycliffite Versions*. Cambridge Studies in Medieval History 66. Cambridge: Cambridge University Press, 2007.

Evans, C. A. "Messianism." In *Dictionary of New Testament Background*, edited by Daniel G. Reid, 698–707. Downers Grove, IL: InterVarsity Press, 2000.

Fitzgerald, Kyriaki Karidoyanes. "Mary the Theotokos and the Call to Holiness." In *Mary, Mother of God*, edited by Carl E. Braaten and Robert W. Jenson, 80–99. Grand Rapids, MI: Eerdmans, 2004.

Flannery, Austin, ed. *Vatican Council II: The Basic Sixteen Documents*. Northport, NY: Costello Publishing Company, 1996.

Fry, Roland M. "Language for God and Feminist Language: Problems and Principles." In *Speaking the Christian God: The Holy Trinity and the Challenge of Feminism*, edited by Alvin F. Kimel Jr., 17–43. Grand Rapids, MI: Eerdmans, 1992.

Frykholm, Amy. *Julian of Norwich*. Brewster, MA: Paraclete Press, 2010.

Gaventa, Beverly Roberts. *Mary: Glimpses of the Mother of Jesus*. Minneapolis: Fortress Press, 1999.

Gaucher, Guy. *The Story of a Life*. San Francisco: HarperSanFrancisco, 1987.

Heath, Elaine. *Naked Faith: The Mystical Theology of Phoebe Palmer.* Eugene, OR: Pickwick Publications, 2009.

Heffernan, Thomas J. *The Passion of Perpetua and Felicity.* Oxford: Oxford University Press, 2012.

Hurtado, Larry. *Lord Jesus Christ: Devotion to Jesus in Earliest Christianity.* Grand Rapids, MI: Eerdmans, 2003.

Jacobs, Alan. *The Book of Common Prayer: A Biography.* Princeton, NJ: Princeton University Press, 2013.

———. *The Pleasures of Reading in an Age of Distraction.* Oxford: Oxford University Press, 2011.

Jenson, Matt. *Theology in the Democracy of the Dead: A Dialogue with the Living Tradition.* Grand Rapids, MI: Baker Academic, 2019.

Jenson, Robert W. "A Space for God." In *Mary, Mother of God,* edited by Carl E. Braaten and Robert W. Jenson, 49–57. Grand Rapids, MI: Eerdmans, 2004.

Jensen, Robin M. *The Substance of Things Seen: Art, Faith, and the Christian Community.* Grand Rapids, MI: Eerdmans, 2004.

John Paul II. *"Rosarium Virginis Mariae,"* 2002. https://www.vatican.va/content/john-paul-ii/en/apost_letters/2002/documents/hf_jp-ii_apl_20021016_rosarium-virginis-mariae.html.

Lashier, Jackson. *Irenaeus on the Trinity.* Supplements to *Vigiliae Christianae* 127. Leiden: Brill, 2014.

Laveille, August Pierre. *The Life of St. Thérèse of Lisieux.* Translated by Rev. M. Fitzsimons, OMI. Notre Dame, IN: Christian Classics, 1929.

Leithart, Peter J. *Defending Constantine: The Twilight of an Empire and the Dawn of Christendom.* Downers Grove, IL: InterVarsity Press, 2010.

Lewis, C. S. *The Great Divorce.* Repr. San Francisco: HarperSanFrancisco, 2001. First published 1945 by Geoffrey Bless (London).

———. *The Magician's Nephew.* Book Six of *The Chronicles of Narnia.* New York: Collier Books, 1955. First published 1955 by Bodley Head (London).

Liftin, Bryan M. *Getting to Know the Church Fathers: An Evangelical Introduction.* Grand Rapids, MI: Baker Academic, 2016.

Louth, Andrew. *Greek East and Latin West: The Church AD 681–1071.* Vol. 3 of *The Church in History.* Crestwood, NY: St. Vladimir's Seminary Press, 2007.

Luomanen, Patri, and Antti Marjanen, eds. *A Companion to Second-Century Christian 'Heretics.'* Leiden: Brill, 2005.

Madigan, Kevin. *Medieval Christianity: A New History.* New Haven, CT: Yale University Press, 2015.

Marius, Richard. *Martin Luther: The Christian between God and Death.* Cambridge, MA: Belknap Press of Harvard University Press, 1999.

Marsh, Karen Wright. *Vintage Saints and Sinners: 25 Christians Who Transformed My Faith.* Downers Grove, IL: InterVarsity Press, 2017.

Martens, Peter W. *Origen and Scripture: The Contours of the Exegetical Life.* Oxford Early Christian Studies. Oxford: Oxford University Press, 2012.

Noll, Mark A. *America's God: From Jonathan Edwards to Abraham Lincoln.* Oxford: Oxford University Press, 2002.

———. *Turning Points: Decisive Moments in the History of Christianity.* 3rd ed. Grand Rapids, MI: Baker Academic, 2012.

Oberman, Heiko A. *Luther: Man between God the Devil.* Translated by Eileen Walliser-Schwarzbart. New Haven, CT: Yale University Press, 1989.

Osborn, Eric. *Irenaeus of Lyons*. Cambridge: Cambridge University Press, 2001.

Perry, Tim. *Mary for Evangelicals: Toward an Understanding of the Mother of Our Lord.* Downers Grove, IL: IVP Academic, 2006.

Prothero, Stephen. *God Is Not One: The Eight Rival Religions That Run the World.* New York: HarperOne, 2010.

Richey, Russel E., Kenneth E. Rowe, and Jean Miller Schmidt. Vol. 1 of *The Methodist Experience in America*. Nashville: Abingdon Press, 2010.

Robertson, John. *Enlightenment: A Very Short Introduction*. Oxford: Oxford University Press, 2015.

Rolf, Veronica Mary. *Julian's Gospel: Illuminating the Life and Revelations of Julian of Norwich*. Maryknoll, NY: Orbis Books, 2013.

Salisbury, Joyce. *Perpetua's Passion: The Death and Memory of a Young Roman Woman.* New York: Routledge, 1997.

Schmidt, Joseph F. *Everything Is Grace: The Life and Way of Thérèse of Lisieux*. Frederick, MD: The Word Among Us Press, 2007.

Selderhuis, Herman. *Martin Luther: A Spiritual Biography*. Wheaton, IL: Crossway, 2017.

Silvas, Anna. *Macrina the Younger, Philosopher of God*. Turnhout: Brepols, 2008.

Six-Means, Horace. "Saints and Teachers: Canons of Persons." In *Canonical Theism: A Proposal for Theology and the Church*, edited by William J. Abraham, Jason E. Vickers, and Natalie E. Van Kirk, 97–118. Grand Rapids, MI: Eerdmans, 2008.

Soskice, Janet Martin. *The Kindness of God: Metaphor, Gender, and Religious Language.* Oxford: Oxford University Press, 2007.

Taylor, Charles. *A Secular Age*. Cambridge, MA: Belknap Press of Harvard University, 2007.

Tennent, Timothy C. *Theology in the Context of World Christianity: How the Global Church Is Influencing How We Think About and Discuss Theology*. Grand Rapids, MI: Zondervan, 2007.

Thompson, Augustine, OP. *Francis of Assisi: A New Biography*. Ithaca, NY: Cornell University Press, 2012.

Trigg, Joseph, "Introduction." In *Origen, the Early Church Fathers*, 1–66. London: Routledge, 1998.

Watson, Kevin M. *Perfect Love: Recovering Entire Sanctification—the Lost Power of the Methodist Movement*. Franklin, TN: Seedbed, 2021.

Wheatley, Richard, ed. *Life and Letters of Mrs. Phoebe Palmer*. New York: W. C. Palmer, Jr., 1876.

White, Charles Edward. *The Beauty of Holiness: Phoebe Palmer as Theologian, Revivalist, Feminist, and Humanitarian*. Repr. Eugene, OR: Wipf and Stock, 1986.

Wilken, Robert Louis. *The First Thousand Years: A Global History of Christianity*. New Haven, CT: Yale University Press, 2012.

———. *The Spirit of Early Christian Thought: Seeking the Face of God*. New Haven, CT: Yale University Press, 2003.

Wills, Gary. *The Rosary: Prayer Comes Round*. New York: Penguin Books, 2005.

Index of Subjects and Names

Even Protestants should venerate the saints

Protestant Christians should venerate the saints. This shocking claim lies at the heart of *Great Cloud of Witnesses*, in which Jackson Lashier presents the practice's biblical foundations and highlights the Christian belief in the resurrection of the dead. Each chapter tells the story of a different saint from varying places, times, and traditions, both to connect readers to the saints as spiritual companions and to relate more practical lessons from the saints' lives. Readers will encounter creative ways of reading Scripture, learn important doctrines, and experience ways of living like a monk, even while having a job and a family.

The book openly addresses common objections: Are the saints divine? Does our devotion to the saints take away from our devotion to Christ? Are the saints without sin? Who decides who gets to be a saint? Protestant readers will gain a greater appreciation of the saints and the spiritual practice of saint veneration, as well as the motivation to engage it for themselves.

Praise for *Great Cloud of Witnesses*

"Is there a biblical case for living out our Christian life in communion with the holy dead? The traditional Protestant answer is a resounding 'No.' Lashier helpfully shows us that this answer needs deeper reflection, and enlists a great cloud of witnesses to help us see why this is so."

—**Justus H. Hunter**, United Theological Seminary

"Protestants typically have an uneasy relationship with the tradition of the saints. In this wonderful book, Lashier addresses concerns that deter Protestants from revering the saints of old, challenges us to rethink our often-misinformed conceptions about them, and highlights lessons from their lives so that we too may run well the race marked out for us."

—**Anthony Briggman**, Candler School of Theology, Emory University

"A quiet revolution is underway in Christian theology. East and West, Protestant and Catholic, theologians are working to renew Christianity by retrieving long-neglected beliefs and practices. In *Great Cloud of Witnesses*, Lashier makes a case for the saints that is both convincing and inspiring."

—**Jason E. Vickers**, Baylor University

Jackson Lashier is associate professor of religion at Southwestern College. He is the author of *Irenaeus on the Trinity* (2014) and writes theology for church renewal, particularly in the United Methodist Church, of which he is a longtime member.

Historical Theology   US$29.00

ISBN 978-1-5064-8965-0
52900

9 781506 489650

fortress press
scholarship that matters
fortresspress.com